英文类型影片赏析

主 编 郭 蕾
副主编 胡龙春

图书在版编目(CIP)数据

英文类型影片赏析/郭蕾主编. —北京：北京大学出版社，2013.5
ISBN 978-7-301-22438-0

Ⅰ. ①英… Ⅱ. ①郭… Ⅲ. ①英语－阅读教学－高等学校－教材②电影－赏析－世界 Ⅳ. ①H319.4：J

中国版本图书馆 CIP 数据核字(2013)第 079487 号

书　　　名：	英文类型影片赏析
著作责任者：	郭　蕾　主　编　胡龙春　副主编
责任编辑：	李　颖
标准书号：	ISBN 978-7-301-22438-0/H·3290
出版发行：	北京大学出版社
地　　　址：	北京市海淀区成府路 205 号　100871
网　　　址：	http://www.pup.cn　新浪官方微博：@北京大学出版社
电子信箱：	zbing@pup.pku.edu.cn
电　　　话：	邮购部 62752015　发行部 62750672　编辑部 62754382　出版部 62754962
印　刷　者：	北京虎彩文化传播有限公司
经　销　者：	新华书店
	787 毫米×1092 毫米　16 开本　10.5 印张　400 千字
	2013 年 5 月第 1 版　2020 年 4 月第 3 次印刷
定　　　价：	29.00 元

未经许可，不得以任何方式复制或抄袭本书之部分或全部内容。
版权所有，侵权必究
举报电话：010-62752024　电子信箱：fd@pup.pku.edu.cn

前 言

观看英文影片近年来已经成为大学生学习英文，了解英美国家社会文化的一个重要手段。然而目前很多大学生欣赏英文影片仅满足于视觉享受和情节观赏，忽略了影片本身所体现的社会文化价值以及影片对白中的语言价值。编者连续多年在大学开设"英文电影赏析"课程，期间一直探索如何才能更充分地发掘英文影片的教学价值。鉴于此，编者基于课堂教学实际和大学生学习规律，经过搜集和整理素材，完成了该教材的编写。希望本教材既为学生提供观影指导，又能在一定程度上提高学生的英文水平和促进学生对英美国家社会文化的了解。

本教材以英美影片类型为章节进行介绍和分析，共分为十个单元，基本包罗了主要的英文影片类型。每个单元又分为五个部分：第一部分是该影片类型的中文介绍，力求对该类型影片的主要特点和发展趋势作一个宏观性的介绍。其中还包括对所选取的三部代表性影片的简要介绍。第二部分是该类型影片的英文介绍，主要从某一个侧面对该类型影片进行介绍。为保证语言质量，内容均出自原版教材或书籍。文章后设计了四道阅读理解题目，并对文章中生词、难句以及与电影有关的词条进行了解释和翻译。第三部分是该类型影片中一部经典影片的影评，影评多选自英文电影期刊或权威网站。生词和难句均有中文翻译，并配以相应阅读理解题目。第四部分是围绕该部影片内容和对白设计的练习题目，包括根据对白回答问题，对白听力填空，经典对白翻译，以及影片内容讨论等。第五部分是该类型的另外两部经典影片的内容梗概和英汉对照经典台词。每单元所有问题均配有参考答案。

教材特色：1. 根据影片类型安排章节，并编写中文介绍，增进读者对类型影片的兴趣和了解。2. 发挥英文影评的教学价值。本教材对影评中所包含的电影类型、电影评论、电影文化等专业知识进行了梳理并提供了尽可能详细的注释，同时设计了相应的阅读理解题目供读者考查对英文影评的理解程度。3. 本教材选择的影片既有经典影片，也有根据当代大学生特点搜罗了的时代性较强的影片。4. 所有练习均配有参考答案，便于读者进行自主学习。

本教材既可作为高等院校人文专业通识类课程或公共选修课程教材，也可作为面向对英文电影有兴趣，或希望通过英文影片提高英语综合水平的读者的参考读物。

本书由郭蕾策划并主编，副主编胡龙春，参编黎燕雨。另外，陈乐、李彦娜、赵莹、潘晓婷、郭志赞、陈树博等参与了本书的部分工作。在本教材的编写过程中得到了很多老师、朋友和同学的热情帮助和建议，在此深表感谢。特别感谢上海外国语大学博士生导师俞东明老师的鼓励和帮助，让编者保持着对英语影视教学的热情。感谢上海海事大学王云松老师所提供的宝贵建议。感谢上海海事大学将本教材列为校规划教材，并提供相应的指导和支持。感谢英国Portsmouth University 和美国Las Vegas University图书馆在编者们

访学期间所提供的文献查考帮助。感谢北京大学出版社以及出版社责编李颖所提供的大力帮助。感谢丈夫和孩子在教材编撰过程中的理解和支持。本书的编写过程中参考了国内外著作以及网络相关内容，由于选材较广，在主要参考书目处如有疏漏还望谅解，并在此向相关作者谨表谢忱。由于编者水平有限，书中不足在所难免，恳请使用本教材的教师和同学批评指正。

郭 蕾

上海海事大学

2013年3月

目　录

Unit 1　Hero Movies 英雄影片 1
　Part 1　Chinese Summary 1
　Part 2　Text 1 2
　Part 3　Text 2 5
　Part 4　Exercises 10
　Part 5　More Hero Movies 13

Unit 2　Women Movies 女性影片 17
　Part 1　Chinese Summary 17
　Part 2　Text 1 18
　Part 3　Text 2 24
　Part 4　Exercises 27
　Part 5　More Women Movies 29

Unit 3　Holocaust Movies 大屠杀影片 33
　Part 1　Chinese Summary 33
　Part 2　Text 1 34
　Part 3　Text 2 39
　Part 4　Exercises 43
　Part 5　More Holocaust Movies 46

Unit 4　Animations 动画影片 50
　Part 1　Chinese Summary 50
　Part 2　Text 1 51
　Part 3　Text 2 54
　Part 4　Exercises 57
　Part 5　More Animations 60

Unit 5　Science Fiction Movies 科幻影片 66
　Part 1　Chinese Summary 66
　Part 2　Text 1 67
　Part 3　Text 2 70
　Part 4　Exercises 73
　Part 5　More Science Fiction Movies 76

Unit 6　Romance Movies 爱情影片 81
　Part 1　Chinese Summary 81

Part 2　Text 1 ·· 82
   Part 3　Text 2 ·· 86
   Part 4　Exercises ·· 90
   Part 5　More Romance Movies ·· 93

Unit 7　Fantasy Movies 奇幻影片 ·· 97
   Part 1　Chinese Summary ··· 97
   Part 2　Text 1 ·· 99
   Part 3　Text 2 ··· 102
   Part 4　Exercises ·· 106
   Part 5　More Fantasy Movies ··· 110

Unit 8　Social Dramas 社会问题影片 ···································· 114
   Part 1　Chinese Summary ··· 114
   Part 2　Text 1 ··· 115
   Part 3　Text 2 ··· 117
   Part 4　Exercises ·· 121
   Part 5　More Social Dramas ·· 123

Unit 9　Thrillers 悬疑影片 ··· 128
   Part 1　Chinese Summary ··· 128
   Part 2　Text 1 ··· 130
   Part 3　Text 2 ··· 134
   Part 4　Exercises ·· 138
   Part 5　More Thrillers ·· 140

Unit 10　Teen Movies 青春影片 ·· 145
   Part 1　Chinese Summary ··· 145
   Part 2　Text 1 ··· 146
   Part 3　Text 2 ··· 149
   Part 4　Exercises ·· 153
   Part 5　More Teen Movies ·· 155

Bibliography 主要参考文献 ··· 160

Hero Movies 英雄影片

Part 1 Chinese Summary

好莱坞的英雄影片

美国是个崇拜超级英雄的国家。在美国的文化中，英雄是不可缺少的一个文化因素。为了满足观众无意识中对英雄的期待和崇拜心理，美国电影总是不断重演着英雄的故事。不论是地球危机，生化灾难，外星人入侵，恐怖分子作乱，还是民主、自由受到威胁，总是有一位或几位美国孤胆英雄挺身而出，不惧死亡，化险为夷，拯救人类。电影中的超级英雄（superhero），是幻想中的英雄角色，早期多为漫画所塑造，据统计，美国的漫画英雄人物从20世纪30年代起，总共出现了七千多名的虚拟英雄。后来在电视和电影中都有了原创的超级英雄。他们拥有超越普通人的特殊能力，做出一些不同寻常的壮举和英勇的行为，保护人民，与恶势力搏斗。

和欧洲国家相比，美国的英雄文化和这个国家一样年轻。作为移民国家，它的英雄不免带有旧大陆英雄文化的影子。但这个年轻国家自成立的第一天起就不断开疆拓土，国力急剧膨胀，它所塑造的英雄普遍具有一种相似的特质：个人主义、进攻性和绝对的自信。美国人崇拜个人主义，因此更倾向于个人英雄主义。也就是一个民族所有的优良品质都集中在一个人身上，所以他们在观影过程中总能在主人公身上或多或少的找到自己的影子。影片主人公与邪恶势力作斗争的过程中所体现出来的人格魅力会时不时地激发美国人强烈的民族自豪感。好莱坞善于通过各种类型的影片来表现美国人的英雄情结：西部片通过对傲立于西部荒野的牛仔形象的塑造，形成了绵延不绝的美国历史和英雄的神话。《独立日》*Independence Day*（1996）和《黑客帝国》*The Matrix*（1999）等科幻片里那种千篇一律的美国英雄拯救人类于危难的主题叙述，更是对美国的大国意识形态和沙文主义的神话隐喻。强盗片、黑帮片中渲染的是对个人主义和法律秩序的双重承认所导致的美国式的英雄主义。这些影片的主题是美国的个人价值、个人英雄主义、美国全能信仰的一次次展示。美国大国文本的存在无一不在表明好莱坞的确营造了一个富有民族主义色彩的"美国神话"的梦幻世界。

"9·11"事件之后的美国是挫败、敏感的，表现在电影上或许更为直观一些。英雄题材影片不再强调英雄的不可战胜（《黑鹰坠落》*Black Hawk Down*, 2001），而是更加重视刻画英雄的内心挣扎和恐惧（《四片羽毛》*The Four Feathers*, 2002）。通过美国电影可以看到美国人民在自省、在反思，继而开拓进取。影片中对的英雄的诠释也以同情、博爱、宽容作为对英雄人物新的定义。

《蝙蝠侠：黑暗骑士》*The Dark Knight*（2008）是2008年DC漫画公司的巅峰之作。该片蕴含了商业片里少有的严肃和深邃的思考。《蝙蝠侠：黑暗骑士》被很多影评人誉为"最好的漫画电影"。《黑暗骑士》里的蝙蝠侠是个丧失了神秘感，同时也丢掉了"敬畏"的英雄。影片的一大突破就是反英雄、反类型。导演诺兰借小丑之口，提出了一个漫画英雄都绕不过去的悖论：一旦他们凌驾于司法之上，超脱了道德的约束，那和反派们还有多大的区别？观众看到了一个十分不完美的漫画英雄，他不再有神秘感，他不能提供太多的惊喜，所作所为仅仅是个编外的"反恐尖兵"。

《勇敢的心》*Braveheart*（1995）是一部反映人性、思考人生的英雄主义影片。影片中塑造的民族英雄华莱士更让我们相信英雄是属于现实中的，有血有肉有感情的英雄。他并不是天生英雄，如果他的家园没有被占领，如果他的新婚妻子没有被残害，或许他一辈子都是一个普通人。但是在爱人被残忍杀害后，他心中的怒火终于爆发，带领苏格兰人揭竿而起，成为了民族英雄。影片为观众全方位呈现了英雄成长的历程，满足了人们对英雄梦的期待。

《肖申克的救赎》*The Shawshank Redemption*（1994）表现了美国社会孕育强大的个人英雄的能力。影片展示了英雄的强大和梦想的力量。主人公安迪，没有人不承认他是一个真正的英雄。他被人陷害杀妻，被判终身监禁，从一个前途光明的银行行长一夜之间沦为阶下囚。更可怕的是，他将在形同炼狱的肖申克监狱中度过余生。事实上，在他策划越狱到完成自身救赎的这几十年里，他并不是没有对希望、对生活绝望过。但是，令人敬佩的是，他还是忍耐了下来，并一天一天地完成了对自己和对别人的救赎。

Part 2 Text 1

Heroes in America

All cultures have heroes. Based on myth, heroes represent the best we can be. Our heroes save us from danger, protect us from evil, even risk their own lives for **justice**. The intent of heroes is to be moral and just, not to be antisocial. Through the hero's journey, the person is **transformed** and reborn. Usually the hero is the one who shows great courage, **valor**, bravery and sacrifice in the face of danger or injustice, and who is admired for his/her noble qualities and achievements.

Hero worship is a fundamental component of American culture. Compared with the heroes in ancient mythology, superheroes in superhero movies are representing the modern hero model. While superhero movies emerged in America in the 1940s, the first superhero was born in the comic medium in 1938 and introduced a superhero comics fever afterward.

The **countervailing** force of the hero is the shadow[1], representing a life-giving but potentially **destructive** part of human nature. Threatening events bring forth the self-protective functions of the shadow. The main battle of good vs. evil, however, is not just an external, outward struggle against evil forces, but an internal struggle within oneself. More specifically, part of the evolution of the hero that is equally **germane** to the evolution of moral development is choosing a path of forgiveness and compassion over a darker path of anger, hatred, revenge, and retribution[2]. These movie characters best demonstrate the "heroic" nature.

Batman, a character who was **haunted** by his past and who struggled with his inner **demons**, was perceived to be heroic when he was **compassionate** and when he used **restraint** rather than **vengeance** in his **interactions** with **villains**.

Males typically **identify with** male characters, and females are more likely to identify with female characters, though females will sometimes identify with male superheros.

It is commonly believed that heroes are in control of their lives, the head should be used before the sword, and that good always **triumphs over** evil. **Aggression** was generally unrelated to perceptions of heroic status, and when it was, the relationship was negative.

We believe that the **template** developed about heroes and villains by youth are a complex weaving of cultural influences, both real and embedded in cultural stories presented via media. Most cultures cultivate and reinforce heroic templates through their stories and teachings. US students view a heavy **dose** of heroic films that convey particular beliefs about heroes, beliefs that are reinforced and cultivated by literature and traditions of society. Many Western films, such as *Batman Forever*, have the hero walk away from killing for revenge. Others show the moral **downfall** of a character who follows the path of revenge, as in Star Wars where the innocent child Anakin Skywalker will become the evil Darth Vader[3].

After-reading questions

1. Which of the following does NOT represent the features of the hero?
   A. To protect the people from being hurt by the evil force.
   B. To display his heroic intention, which is not necessarily moral and just.
   C. To be admired by the people for his quality and achievements.
   D. To show his great qualities such as braveness, courage and willingness to sacrifice in front of the danger.
2. According to the article, what is the real struggle between good and evil?
   A. It is an external, outward struggle against evil forces.
   B. It is an internal struggle within oneself.
   C. It is an introvert reflection upon the outside world.
   D. It is an outward character struggle between the hero and the shadow.

3. According to the article, which sources are believed to develop the template of the heroes?

   A. Literature.

   B. Media.

   C. Tradition of the society.

   D. All of the above.

4. Which of the following heroic qualities does the Movie **Batman Forever** want to emphasize?

   A. Braveness.

   B. Self-sacrifice.

   C. Compassion.

   D. Strong will to revenge.

Words and expressions

1. **justice** *n.* the fair treatment of people 公平；公正
2. **transform** *v.* to completely change the appearance or character of sth, especially so that it is better 使改变外观（或性质）；使改观
3. **valor** *n.* great courage, especially in war （尤其指战争中的）英勇或勇气
4. **countervailing** *adj.* having an equal but opposite effect 抗衡的，抵消的
5. **destructive** *adj.* causing destruction or damage 引起破坏（或毁灭的），破坏（或毁灭性的）
6. **germane** *adj.* (of ideas, remarks, etc.) connected with sth in an important or appropriate way 与……有密切关系；贴切；恰当
7. **haunt** *v.* to continue to cause problems for sb for a long time 长期不断的缠扰 (某人) be haunted by 受（某种经历或情绪的）困扰
8. **demon** *n.* an evil spirit 恶魔 the inner demon 内心的魔鬼
9. **compassionate** *adj.* feeling or showing sympathy for people who are suffering 有同情心的；表示怜悯的
10. **restraint** *n.* the quality of behaving calmly and with control 克制；抑制；约束
11. **vengeance** *n.* the act of punishing or harming sb in return for what they have done to you, your family or friends 报复；报仇；复仇
12. **interaction** *n.* communication with sb, especially while you work, play or spend time with them 交流；沟通 interaction with sb 和某人的接触
13. **villain** *n.* the main bad character in a story, play, etc. （小说、戏剧等中）的主要反面人物
14. **identify with sb** to feel that you can understand and share the feelings of sb else 与某人产生共鸣；谅解；同情
15. **triumph over** to defeat sb/sth; to be successful 打败；战胜；成功
16. **aggression** *n.* feelings of anger and hatred that may result in threatening or

violent behavior 好斗情绪；攻击性

17. **template** *n.* a thing that is used as a model for producing other similar examples 样板；模框；标准
18. **dose** *n.* an amount of sth 一份；一次；一点 a heavy dose of 大量的
19. **downfall** *n.* the loss of a person's money, power, social position, etc.; the thing that causes this 衰落，衰败，垮台；衰落（或衰败、垮台）的原因

Notes

1. **shadow**, is the antagonist who creates conflict in the story by opposing the Hero
   影子指在故事中成为英雄主人公反面的反派主人公。
   注：出自Vogler's seven character archetypes: 沃格勒的七个角色原型。其中角色原型分别为：Hero英雄，Mentor导师，Threshold Guardian关卡守门人，Herald信使，Shapeshifter变化者，Shadow影子和Trickster小丑。

2. More specifically, part of the evolution of the hero that is equally germane to the evolution of moral development is choosing a path of forgiveness and compassion over a darker path of anger, hatred, revenge, and retribution.
   译文：特别是英雄概念的变革与人们在道德意识上的改变是分不开的。比起通过愤怒、怨恨、复仇和报复等这些阴暗手段，人们更倾向于选择谅解和同情的方式（来解决问题）。

3. Many Western films, such as *Batman Forever*, have the hero walk away from killing for revenge. Others show the moral downfall of a character who follows the path of revenge, as in *Star Wars* where the innocent child Anakin Skywalker becomes the evil Darth Vader.
   译文：很多诸如《永远的蝙蝠侠》这类西方英雄类题材电影，主人公最后没有为了复仇而杀死反派。相反的例子则是一些角色因陷入了仇恨中性格由善转恶。比如在《星球大战前传》中那个善良的男孩安纳金后来却变成了邪恶的达斯·维达。
   注：《星球大战》是美国导演／制作人乔治·卢卡斯所制作拍摄的一系列科幻电影。首先问世的是《星球大战》三部曲，自1999年开始，卢卡斯制作拍摄的《星球大战前传》三部曲也相继问世。至此，《星球大战》最终成为完整的六部系列影片。

Part 3 Text 2

The Dark Knight[1]

The differences between the old and new Batman films have as much to do with the portrayal (描绘，描述) of The Joker as with Batman himself. For his earlier movie, Burton[2] gave Nicholson[2]'s Joker the explanation of his disfigurement pioneered in Alan Moore[3] and Brian Bolland's 1988 graphic novel (漫画小说) *Batman*[3]: *The Killing*

Joker[3], in which the arch-villain falls into a chemical plant after a botched(搞砸的)heist (抢劫). By contrast, and characteristic of Nolan's entire approach to the Batman story, Heath Ledger[4]'s incarnation (化身) mocks (嘲弄) a series of victims throughout the film with bogus (假的，伪造的) explanations of "how I got my scars." By the end, one feels that he did it to himself to scare people, but we'll never know, and in this case his clownish greasepaint (化妆油彩), mottled (斑驳的) and half worn-away by sweat in the heat of battle is at least as frightening as his actual disfigurement (毁容).

Much has been made of Ledger's final performance as The Joker, and deservedly so. In the opening scene, he masterminds (策划，操纵) a mob bank robbery using a variety of accomplices (同谋，共犯)who conveniently dispatch (分派，派遣) each other during the commission of the crime in a cascading (连锁式, 级联式) practical joke comprised of mass murder. Near the end of the film, he sleds down a mountain of cash and then burns it. What The Joker wants has been the question of the contemporary Batman story. The Joker's first appearance involves a terrible pun (双关语) on Nietzsche[6] (尼采): "What doesn't kill you makes you stranger." By the end of the film he is theorizing on the death of humanity, claiming that "I'm not a monster, I'm just ahead of the curve (引领潮流的, 有前瞻性的)." "I just do things, " he says. "Guns are too quick—you can't savor all the little emotions." A few of his favorite things? "Dynamite, gunpowder, and gasoline—you know what they have in common?" "They're cheap." The Joker emphasizes his desire to have a relationship with Batman, asking aptly, "What would I do without you?" The suggestion that The Joker wants to impress Batman, that he is a little in love with him is as compelling (引起兴趣的) an explanation as any.

Although he is caught, The Joker has weirdly triumphed by the end of The Dark Knight. Rachel Dawes (Maggie Gyllenhaal), Batman's childhood sweetheart, has been murdered; Harvey Dent (Aaron Elkhart), Gorham's district attorney and "White Knight," lies dead, disfigured, and disgraced (使名誉扫地的); and Batman is fleeing Gotham, a failure being hunted down by the city he's saved from mere anarchy (无政府状态，混乱).The Joker's key failure involves a compelling and memorable sequence in which he conducts a sociological "experiment," attempting to get two boatloads of passengers on two Staten Island Ferries to blow each other up. Both boats are wired with explosives, but one boat can save itself by detonating (引爆) the other. Common decency (正义，正直) prevails against the odds and fellow feeling (同情心，共同的利害观念) overcomes terror, one of few optimistic points in the entire movie.

The Joker, an anarchist hell-bent (拼命的，固执的) on destruction, is constantly prodding (刺激) Batman, pushing him to cross the line between hero and villain. Even the topical question of warrantless (未经授权的，不正当的) surveillance (监视，监督) is taken up when Batman invents a method for finding The Joker using a sonar map of every square inch of the city—"spying on thirty million people." in dealing with men who simply "want to watch the world burn". In one sequence, the film stretches PG-13 [7] violence to the limit when Batman brutalizes The Joker, who's "got no rules," explicitly comments on the worthlessness of "all the little rules" of civil society. (Meanwhile, a mobster complains that "criminals in this town used to believe in things.")

After their torture session, The Joker, completely unfazed, reveals that Batman will have to choose between the lives of his oldest friend, Rachel, and Dent, Gotham's potential savior. In the end, although The Joker is captured, it seems cold comfort in a film where the love interest is blown up. Dent is transformed into the monster Two Face, and Batman exits the film accused of the murders Dent has committed after going berserk (狂暴的), so that the city can retain its heroic picture of the D.A. "I'm not a hero," Batman keeps repeating throughout the movie, while Dent's self-fulfilling prophecy (预言) parroted by Batman near the end, is that "You either die a hero or live long enough to see yourself become the villain." This notion seems acquiescent (默许的, 默认的) to The Joker's victory, in moral terms. Alfred (Michael Caine) offers a different interpretation, however, when he suggests that Batman can be "More than a hero" by accepting the hatred of the world for a crime he didn't commit. Is this the triumph of the martyr (烈士、殉道者), a prelude (序幕，前奏) to later redemption (救赎，弥补)?

After reading questions

1. The first paragraph tells us the different portraits of the Joker in two films: *Batman*: *The Killing Joker* (1988) and *The Dark Knight* (2008). The former one gives a clear explanation on the disfigurement of the Joker, while in the latter film
   A. The joker tells his victims clearly how he got his scar.
   B. Some scenarios give an explanation on how the joker got his scar.
   C. By giving different versions of what happened to him, the joker might just want to terrify people.
   D. The joker falls into a chemical plant in a robbery.
2. The joker is a mad criminal but intriguing as well. He wants to reveal the dark side of the human nature by creating endless chaos in Gotham. In the second paragraph, we are exploring the possible intentions of the joker by looking at some of his remarks. Which of the following is the reason being highlighted in the paragraph?
   A. What he did is just to provoke people to act in immoral ways.

B. He likes to explore the hidden dark feelings of people by depriving their lives slowly.

C. The Joker is in love with Batman, so he wants to impress Batman with his evil conduct.

D. The accident which the joker survived but disfigured him has distorted his character.

3. In the fight against the joker, Batman doesn't win. In paragraph 3, "a social experiment" was carried out by the Joker. According to the paragraph, what makes it different from other crimes committed by the Joker?

A. The intention of the "experiment" is to test people's human nature.

B. Most of the crimes are successfully committed according to the joker's plan, but this time he failed because Batman saved people on the ferries.

C. People in the experiment revealed the dark side of the human nature.

D. The joker failed this time because he underestimated the righteousness and compassion existing in citizens of Gotham.

4. Heroic actions sometimes conflict with the social rules and laws. According to paragraph 4, the superhero Batman had violated the rules at least twice: one is he brutally beat the joker when he was in custody. What is the other time Batman violated the rules?

A. He watches over the joker secretively.

B. He killed the joker brutally.

C. He invents a sonar map.

D. He uses high-tech to watch over other innocent citizens.

5. Batman flees from Gotham by taking blame of the crimes committed by Dent, the deceased white knight, for Batman wants to retain the glorious image of Dent among people. According to the paragraph, which could interpret Batman's thought except:

A. Tired of being a hero he wants to be a villain.

B. The world is evil; righteousness will fade away as time goes by.

C. He sacrifices his own fame so as to retain conscience among people.

D. Gotham needs its own hero instead of a vigilante (义警).

Notes

1. ***The Dark Knight* (2008)** was released by Warner Brothers and directed by Christopher Nolan. It won two Oscar awards in the year of 2009: Best Achievements in Sound Editing and Best Performance by an Actor in a Supporting Role.

《蝙蝠侠：黑暗骑士》是由克里斯托弗诺兰导演，华纳公司于2008年发行的作品。

于2009年获得了奥斯卡最佳音效奖以及最佳男配角奖。

2. ***Batman* (1989)** was directed by Tim Burton. In this version of Batman, the Joker was played by famous actor Jack Nicholson.

1989年，蒂姆·波顿执导的《蝙蝠侠》具有哥特电影的浓郁气息。迈克尔·基顿的儒雅，金·贝辛格的感性，还有杰克·尼克尔森的癫狂，造就了这部黑暗巨作。

3. ***Batman: The Killing Joker*** is an influential on-shot superhero graphic novel written by Alan Moore, drawn by Brian Bolland, and published by DC Comics in 1988.

《蝙蝠侠：致命小丑》是一部具有影响力的超级英雄漫画小说。Alan Moore 编写，BrianBolland绘制，并由ＤＣ漫画公司于1988年出品。

4. **Heath Ledger**, An Australia actor, who was well known for his versatile performance as the leading role in Brokeback Mountain (2005), Ennis Del Mar. The joker in *The Dark Knight* (2008) is his most marvelous performance, from which he won Academy Award for Best Supporting Actor in the year 2009. But he was found dead on 22 January 2008 (aged 28), resulting from the abuse of prescription medications.

《蝙蝠侠：黑暗骑士》祭出了蝙蝠侠一生的死敌———小丑希斯·莱杰生命里最绚烂的演出，而我们只能在他辞世之后才能欣赏领略，这也让这部电影带上了一层无法表述的悲伤气息。

5. **arch-villain**, or arch-enemy, arch-foe, is the principal enemy of a character in a work of fiction, often described as the hero's worst enemy. 大反派。

6. **Friedrich Nietzsche**, (1844—1900) German philosopher. He wrote critical texts on religion, morality, contemporary culture, philosophy and science. Nietzsche's influence remains substantial within and beyond philosophy, notably in existentialism and postmodernism. "That which does not kill us makes us stronger." is one of the most famous quote from Nietzsche. The Joker makes use of this quote by changing it as "What doesn't kill you makes you stranger."

弗里德里希·威廉·尼采：1844—1900，德国哲学家，他的著作对于宗教、道德、现代文化、哲学以及科学等领域提出了广泛的批判和讨论。尼采对于后代哲学的发展影响极大，尤其是在存在主义与后现代主义上。"没有杀死我们的（磨难）会让我们更坚强"是尼采重要的名言之一。

7. **PG-13**, it is a notion from MPAA system (the Motion Picture Association of America's film-rating system). The system is to rate a film's thematic and content suitability for certain audiences in terms of issues such as sex, violence, substance abuse, profanity, impudence or other types of mature content. A particular issued rating is called a certification. The ratings include G, PG, PG-13, R and NC-17.

   G: General audiences. All ages admitted. There is no content that would be objectionable to most parents.

PG: Parental Guidance suggested. Some material may not be suitable for children under 10.

PG-13: Parents strongly cautioned that some content may be inappropriate for children under 13.

R: Restricted. Under 17 requires accompanying parent or legal guardian.

NC-17: No one 17 and under admitted.

美国电影协会分级制度。其中PG-13是特别辅导级，13岁以下儿童尤其要有父母陪同观看。一些内容对儿童很不适宜。

Part 4 Exercises

I. Answer questions after listening to the dialogues taken from the film.

1. By narrating an experience in Burma, Alfred emphasizes the common points of the criminals like the Joker and the bandit in Burma. What are the reasons for them to commit crimes?
2. According to Wayne, who is the real hero of Gotham?
3. Alfred told Wayne how they finally caught the bandit in Burma. What does the result imply?

Script

Scenario 1: *After the Joker has killed some important judges and police commissioners, he just gets away with this.*

Wayne sits at his video screens—they all play the Joker's video with different IMAGE TREATMENTS and SOUND TUNINGS. Wayne turns to Alfred. Indicates the screens.

WAYNE: Targeting me won't get their money back. I knew the mob wouldn't go down without a fight, but this is different. They've crossed a line.

ALFRED: You crossed it first, sir. You've hammered them, squeezed them to the point of desperation. And now, in their desperation they've turned to a man they don't fully understand.

WAYNE: Criminals aren't complicated, Alfred. We just have to figure out what he's after.

ALFRED: Respectfully, Master Wayne, perhaps this is a man you don't fully understand, either.

ALFRED: I was in Burma. A long time ago, my friends and I were working for the local government. They were trying to buy the loyalty of tribal leaders, bribing them with precious stones. But their caravans were being raided in a forest north of Rangoon by a bandit. We were asked to take care of the problem, so we started looking for the stones. But after six months, we couldn't find anyone who had traded with him.

WAYNE: What were you missing?

ALFRED: One day I found a child playing with a ruby as big as a tangerine. (*shrugs*) The bandit had been throwing the stones away.

WAYNE: So why was he stealing them?

ALFRED: Because he thought it was good sport. Because some men aren't looking for anything logical, like money... they can't be bought, bullied, reasoned or negotiated with. (*grave*) Some men just want to watch the world burn.

Scenario2: *Rachel and Dent were both kidnapped by the Joker; batman can only save one and must sacrifice the other. He rescued Dent but left Rachel, his childhood sweetheart, to die.*

ALFRED: I prepared a little breakfast. Nothing.

ALFRED: Very well.

WAYNE: Alfred?

ALFRED: Yes, Master Wayne?

WAYNE: Did I bring this on us? On her? I thought I would inspire good, not madness—

ALFRED: You have inspired good. But you spat in the face of Gotham's criminals—didn't you think there might be casualties? Things are always going to have to get worse before they got better.

WAYNE: But Rachel, Alfred...

ALFRED: Rachel believed in what you stood for. What we stand for.

ALFRED: Gotham needs you.

ALFRED: Which is why for now, they'll have to make do with you.

WAYNE: She was going to wait for me. Dent doesn't know. He can never know...*Alfred glances at the envelope. Takes it off the tray.*

WAYNE: What's that?

ALFRED: It can wait. *Alfred puts the envelope in his pocket.*

WAYNE: That bandit, in the forest in Burma... Did you catch him? (*Alfred nods*) How?

ALFRED: (*uneasy*) We burned the forest down.

II. Fill the blanks with the missing words or phrases after listening to the lines taken from the film.

DENT: But that's not why we're demanding he turn himself in. We're doing it because we're 1)_____. We've been happy to let Batman clean up our streets for us until now—

HECKLER: Things are worse than ever!

DENT: Yes. They are. But the night is darkest just before the 2)_____.

DENT: And I promise you, the dawn is coming. (*the crowd quiets*) One day, the Batman will have to answer for the laws he's 3)_____ — but to us, not to this madman.

COP HECKLER NO MORE DEAD COPS!!

REPORTER WHERE IS THE BATMAN?

DENT So be it. Take the Batman into 4)_____.

DENT I am the Batman.

RACHEL Why is he letting Harvey do this, Alfred?

ALFRED I don't know. He went down to the 5)_____

RACHEL And just 6)_____?!

ALFRED Perhaps both Bruce and Mr. Dent believe that Batman stands for something more important than 7)_____, Miss Dawes, even if everyone hates him for it.

ALFRED That's the 8)_____ he's making—to not be a hero. To be something more.

RACHEL Well, you're right about one thing—letting Harvey 9)_____ is not heroic.

RACHEL You know Bruce best, Alfred... 10)_____.

ALFRED How will I know?

RACHEL It's not sealed.

RACHEL Goodbye, Alfred.

ALFRED Goodbye, Rachel.

III. Complete the following memorable lines by translating the Chinese into English.

1. I believe that (没有杀死你的事)_____ simply makes you stranger (stronger).

2. Their morals, their code... it's a bad joke. Dropped at the first sign of trouble. (他们只是在世界允许的范围内保持良善)_____. You'll see— I'll show you... when the chips are down (关键时刻), these civilized people...they'll eat each other.

3. You thought we could be decent men in an indecent world. You thought we could lead by example. (你以为规则可以弯曲而不被打破)_____... you were wrong. The world is cruel. And the only morality in a cruel world is chance. Unbiased. Unprejudiced.

4. ...he's the hero Gotham deserves... but not the one it needs right now. So we'll hunt him, because he can take it. Because he's not our hero... (他是一个沉默的守护者, 一个警惕的保卫者)_____... a dark knight.

IV. Oral practices—answer the following questions.

1. What is the motivation of the merciless Joker when he carries out mass-killing?

2. Why does Batman finally take the blame for Harvey's killings?

Part 5 More Hero Movies

Plot Summary of *Braveheart*

William Wallace is a Scottish riser who leads an uprising against the cruel English ruler Edward I. His father and brother lost their lives in trying to free Scotland when he was young. Once he loses his loved wife, William Wallace begins his long quest to make Scotland free once and for all, along with the assistance of Robert Bruce.

The movie begins in the small town of Elderslie, Scotland. William's father and brother are called to a meeting a few miles from their home where they were all hanged. At the funeral, William meets his uncle Argyle who taught him a lot, "First, learn to use this (Argyle taps William's head), then I'll teach you to use this (the sword)." And then he takes him away to live with him. After young William grew up, he goes back to his hometown and falls in love with a girl, named Murron. In order to avoid being insulted by the Lords, William marries Murron in secret. Lords kills Murron to arrest William. This enrages Wallace and then he builds himself a fine army. In the battle of Stirling, Wallace finds a good idea to fight against the heavy cavalry of England from the ground. They decide to make hundreds of spears which are twice as long as a man. These are used in the battle to kill the entire heavy cavalry at the last minute. Eventually they reach York, the most important military city. At the battle of Falkirk, Williams loses the war because of his betrayal by two Scottish nobles. Captured, he refuses to bow down as a loyal subject of king Edward I, Longshanks, who wishes to inherit the crown of Scotland for himself. In his last moments, Williams is tortured to death shouting "freedom." William's body is torn to pieces. And his head is placed on top of London Bridge and his arms and legs are sent to the four corners of Britain as a warning to the citizens. After Wallace's death, Robert Bruce leads the whole army, winning the battle of Bannockburn for Scotland's freedom.

Memorable lines in the film

Settings: William Wallace came to the front to pep the soldiers fighting bravely against the Englishmen. Encouraged by his braveness, the Scottish won the battle—the battle of Sterling.

Wallace: Fight, and you may die. Run, and you'll live at least a while. And dying in your beds many years from now. Would you be willing to trade? All the days from this day to that, for one chance, just one chance, to come back here and tell our enemies that they may take our lives, but they'll never take our FREEDOM!

战斗，你可能会死；逃跑，至少能苟且偷生。年复一年，直到寿终正寝。你们！愿不愿意用这么多苟活的日子去换一个机会，仅有的一个机会！那就是回到战场，告诉敌人，他们也许能夺走我们的生命，但是，他们永远夺不走我们的自由！

Plot Summary of *The Shawshank Redemption*

Having been wrongly convicted of murdering both his wife and her lover, Andy Dufresne is sentenced to life sentence, and is sent to the terrible Shawshank Prison. During his first night, the barbaric treatment by prison guards, most notably, the chief guard Byron Hadley, leads to the death of a fellow new inmate. About a month later, Andy becomes familiar with Ellis Redding, also known as Red, and his friends. A friendship begins after Red, "the man who knows how to get things," procures a rock hammer for Andy, an object he wishes to own in order to pursue a hobby in rock collecting.

Over the first few years of his imprisonment, Andy works in the prison laundry service, and is dogged by threats and harassment, and instances of rape by a group of sadistic homosexuals known as the "Sisters." Andy's former life as a banker and his knowledge of accounting and income taxes comes to the attention of a guard during

an outdoor work on the ceiling, and after assisting the chief guard with an inheritance sum, Andy is moved to work with Brooks Hatlen in the library, where he shortly sets up an office to deal with finance related queries brought to him by various guards. His activities become so popular that everybody is very familiar about this finance help. While working within the library, Andy begins to try a lot to improve the library. When Andy is brutally raped again, the prison guards punished the "sister" and it becomes clear that they are now protecting Andy from the mistreatment. Andy's victimizations come to a close.

Warden Samuel Norton soon makes use of

Andy's ability and deduces a Program to put prison inmates to work for local contracts in construction, road-building, and other labour projects. Andy is corruptly employed to hide the embezzled funds for Norton, and he does this by "creating" an alternate fraudulent identity through which all the paperwork is completed. In the same year, the prison library is extended and Andy begins educating other prisoners to pass high school diplomas. A young prisoner named Tommy who knows the truth of Andy's innocence enters Shawshank in 1965. Fearing the loss of great help from Andy about the criminal funds, Norton kills Tommy and sends Andy to solitary confinement. Two months later, Andy has a chat with Red and manages to give him instruction for his future life, and all of his other friends are concerned that he may commit suicide. The following morning, he is missing from his cell and an investigation is launched.

Following the events that led to his departure, it becomes clear that Andy escaped from the prison having tunneled through the walls with the rock hammer he got from Red shortly after his arrival. Having recorded the corruption within the prison, he sends his notes to a local newspaper, and makes away with Warden's fortunes, identifying himself as the man with the bank accounts, who was really non-existent. Refusing to be arrested, Norton kills himself in his office. When Red is finally released from prison, he follows the instructions that Andy gave him, which eventually leads to the happy reunion of Red and Andy on the coast of Mexico.

Memorable lines in the film

Settings: *In an outdoor work of preparing a ceiling, Andy risks his life to offer help to guardian Hadley in dealing with his tax application; then all his coworkers were granted a good rest and bottles of cold beer.*

Red: We sat and drank with the sun on our shoulders and felt like free men. Here, we could have been tarring the roof of one of our own houses. We were the lords of all creation. As for Andy-he spent that break hunkered in the shade, a strange little smile on his face, watching us drink his beer.

我们坐在太阳下，感觉就像自由人，见鬼，我好像就是在修自己家的屋顶。我们是造物主，而安迪——他在这间歇中蹲在绿荫下，一个奇特的微笑挂在脸上，看着我们喝他的啤酒。

Settings: *Andy broadcast a musical record in Shawshank's broadcast station, which is not permitted and rarely happened before. The beautiful music flew into the heart of every prisoner.*

Red: I have no idea to this day what those two Italian ladies were singing about. Truth is, I don't want to know. Some things are best left unsaid. I'd like to think they were singing about something so beautiful, it can't be expressed in words, and it makes your heart ache because of it. I tell you, those voices soared higher and farther than anybody in a gray place dares to dream. It was like some beautiful bird flapped into our drab little cage and made those walls dissolve away, and for the briefest of moments, every last man in Shawshank felt free.

　　到今天我还不知道那两个意大利女人在唱些什么,其实,我也不想知道。有些东西还是留着不说为妙。我想她们该是在唱一些非常美妙动人的故事,美妙得难以用语言来表达,美妙得让你心痛。告诉你吧,这些声音直插云霄,飞得比任何一个人敢想的梦还要遥远。就像一些鸟儿来到我们褐色的牢笼,让那些墙壁消失得无影无踪。就在那一刹那,肖申克监狱的每一个人感受到了自由。

UNIT 2

Women Movies 女性影片

Part 1 Chinese Summary

好莱坞的女性影片

西蒙·德·波娃（Simon de Beauvoir）将萨特（Jean-Paul Sartre）的存在主义哲学中的主体的透明状态（the subject's transcendence）重新诠释，并在《第二性》中谈到，在人类社会的历史和文化长河中，男人是作为绝对的主体（the Subject）存在的，人就是指男人；而女人是作为男人的对立面和附属体存在，是男人的"客体"和"他者"（the Other）波娃认为：女性之所以为女性，不是天生的，而是后天形成的，是在以男性为中心的文化中被建构的"他者"，是男性主体的客体，充当着男性中心社会赋予她们的规定性角色。女性通常被建构为依从、被动、流浪、封闭、孤独、忠贞或物质狂和非理智性等固定形象模式。

女性主义电影理论者根据波娃的"他者"理论提出：以男权为主宰的社会文化秩序统治着好莱坞的主流意识形态，好莱坞电影中的女性常被塑造成固有的女性模式，因为女性在电影中长久以来是作为"他者"被观看的。她们抑或被套用在某种固定的形象模式中，如美丽的女神，性感的情妇，忠贞的家庭妇女……抑或在影片中承担"奖品"的角色，反衬或支持男性英雄实现计划，并在最后让英雄"抱得美人归"。

女性意识在电影领域的觉醒从20世纪60年代至今一直渗透于好莱坞的电影制作、影视文学评论、影视批评等各个领域，这在相当程度上改变了男性意识统治好莱坞的局面。影视作品中的女性形象逐渐从背景走向前景，女性角色更日趋呈现出复杂、立体、独立的人格特点。越来越多的银幕女性形象具有独立的人格精神，虽然绝大多数女性荧幕形象仍未实现向"本我"的转变，但至少已经部分摆脱了男性视角下完全是"被观看"、"被窥视"、"被瓜分"的形象。

随着女性观众与日俱增，经典好莱坞时期诞生了大量的浪漫剧情片以取悦广大的女性观众，一些以夸张过分的情感打动女性的类型影片也随之诞生，如哭片（weepies）、少女电影（chick flicks）等。然而在许多以女性为主角的好莱坞电影当中，一些创作者只是为了商业的考虑而选择了这一类女性题材影片，其展现的更多的是"戏剧中的女性"。其所表现的情节和女性的情感特点大多大同小异。往往这类影片还会贯穿男权的意识形态：当女主人公遭遇事业和爱情的冲突时，爱情往往成为女性的理想选择；婚姻与家庭才是女性的终极目标。相对于这些商业女性题材影片，也有一些影片创作者会着力刻画"生活中的女性",伴随自然、朴实的生活情节发展对女性心理进行细致入微的刻画,从而反映女性更深层次的心理和社会诉求。

《末路狂花》Thelma & Louse(1991)将女性话题用公路片(road picture)和搭档类型片(buddy film)的形式进行表现。在商业上能够吸引对这两种影片类型较为热衷的观影者。然而,虽然表面上看该影片类型更接近男性化——影片的主要叙事地点都发生在美国的公路上,并且两位主人公也是以搭档形式出现、攻克一个个难关,与警察斗智斗勇——然而其实质却是表现美国20世纪80年代女性的社会地位以及其自身身份觉醒的一部女性题材影片。

《克莱默夫妇》Kramer vs Kramer(1979)是一部家庭伦理片,在同时期电影作品中,这部作品表现出对女性问题少有的深刻与成熟的思考。影片以普通人的日常生活为着眼点,在平凡中展现人物性格的复杂性。但是影片中的女性中即便在戏中不是反面人物, 至少也是麻烦制造者。并且影片的重点都着力于刻画男性面临女性思潮所带来的社会、家庭变化时产生的不安与痛苦。在对这部影片的评论中,相当多的论者对女主人公的批评相当严苛或刻薄,对男主人公却多持同情和偏袒的态度,这也一定程度上反映了男性中心批评的价值观念。

《蒙娜丽莎的微笑》Mona Lisa's Smile(2003)故事发生在20世纪50年代的美国,一群出身于上流社会的优秀女学生就读于维护正统的Wellesley女子学院,欣然接受着社会赋予她们相夫教子的传统角色,而一位"离经叛道"的艺术史教师Katherine Watson的到来却打破了这种平静。

Part 2 Text 1

Women in Hollywood

During the **heyday** of the big Hollywood studio era[1]— especially the 1930s through the 1950s—the status of women within the industry was **dismal**. There were no women in the upper **echelons** of management. Out of the thousands of movies produced by the studios, only a handful were directed by women, and virtually none were produced by them. The unions also **discriminated** against females, allowing very few of them to enter their ranks.

True, there were some women in the areas of screenwriting, editing and costuming, but only in the field of acting did women enjoy a degree of **prominence**, After all, it was simply not economically feasible to exclude women from in front of the camera. To this day, most of the powerful women in Hollywood have come from the acting ranks.

Even female stars were treated like second-class citizens during the big studio era. Rarely did the leading lady get top billing over the male lead. Females usually had shorter careers because they were thought to be too old for leading roles once they were past forty. Male stars like Cary Grant, Gary Cooper, and John Wayne were still playing leads in their sixties[2].

Within the movies themselves, women were usually socially constructed as "the other" or "the outsider" in a male-dominated world, as feminist critic Annette Kuhn has pointed out. Women didn't get to tell their own stories because the images were controlled by men. Generally, women were treated as sex objects—valued primarily for their good looks and sex appeal. Their main function was to support their men, seldom to lead a fulfilling life of their own. Marriage and a family were their most frequent goals, rarely a meaningful career.

In the majority of studio-produced films, female characters were marginalized, seldom at the center of the action. The heroine's function was to cheer **from the sidelines**, to wait passively until the hero claimed her for his reward. Certain characteristics were regarded as **intrinsically "masculine"**: intellect, ambition, sexually confidence, independence, professionalism—all of these traits were generally presented as inappropriate and unseemly in women.

Certain Hollywood genres were more hospitable to women—love stories, domestic family dramas, **screwball** and romantic comedies, musicals, and women's pictures—usually domestic **melodramas** emphasizing a female star and focusing on "typical" female concerns such as getting (or holding on to) a man, raising children, or balancing a career with marriage. Marriage was almost invariably presented as the wiser choice when a woman was confronted with a conflict between her career and her man. Women who chose otherwise usually suffered for their folly—like the heroine of Mildred Pierce[3]. It was in such genres as these that some of the studio era's greatest actresses flourished—Bette Davis, Katharine Hepburn, Claudette Colbert, Barbara Stanwyck, Carole Lombard, Marlene Dietrich, and Greta Garbo, to name a few[4].

Today there are about two dozen women directors working in the mainstream Hollywood film industry, and their presence has made a difference: The range of female roles has broadened considerably since the 1960s.

Feminist filmmakers—both male and female—are attempting to overcome prejudice through their movies by providing fresh perspectives. "What do women want?" Freud[5] once asked in **exasperation**. Film critic Molly Haskell has answered succinctly: "We want nothing less, on or off the screen, than the wide variety and dazzling diversity of male options[6]".

After-reading questions

1. Which of the following phenomenon demonstrates the discrimination against females in Hollywood?

   A. There were some women in the areas of screenwriting, editing and costuming.

   B. The top management positions of Hollywood were mostly occupied by males.

C. There were few feminist film critics at that time.

D. There were a great many female stars during the big studio era.

2. According to the article, why are the female movie stars inferior in the status compared with their male counterparts?

A. They were paid less than the male actors.

B. They were from the inferior social class.

C. Their art lives were much shorter than the male stars.

D. They didn't organize an effective union.

3. Which of the following best demonstrates the reason why those famous actresses like Bette Davis, Katharine Hepburn, etc, were very popular in the studio era?

A. They were all beautiful.

B. They all showed the characteristics that most wamen of those times possessed.

C. They reinforced the values related to women that society had then.

D. They are wise in their choices between career and marriage.

4. Today, as more women directors appeared in Hollywood film industry, what changes might be brought about by this phenomenon?

A. More women films will be produced.

B. Women in the films will be displayed in a more profound way.

C. The discrimination and prejudice against women will be greatly reduced.

D. More films will discuss about the question: What do women want?

Words and expressions

1. **heyday** *n.* the period of a person's or thing's greatest success, popularity, activity, or vigor （人或物）最成功（受欢迎、活跃或有活力）的时期

2. **dismal** *adj.* depressing; dreary 压抑的, 沉闷的

3. **echelon** *n.* a level or rank in an organization, a profession, or society（组织、职业或社会的）等级；阶层

4. **discriminate** *v.* make an unjust or prejudicial distinction in the treatment of different categories of people or things, especially on the grounds of race, sex, or age（尤指根据种族、性别或年龄）区别对待

5. **prominence** *n.* the state of being important or famous 重要性；卓越, 显著, 著名

6. **from the sideline** from a position where one is observing a situation but is unable or unwilling to be directly involved in it 当旁观者, 当局外人

7. **intrinsic** *adj.* belonging naturally; essential 固有的, 内在的, 本质的

8. **masculine** *adj.* having qualities or appearance traditionally associated with men 具有男子气质的

9. **screwball** *n.* a style of fast-moving comedy film involving eccentric characters or

ridiculous situations（情节离奇、人物荒诞）动作迅速的戏剧电影
10. **melodrama** *n.* a sensational dramatic piece with exaggerated characters and exciting events intended to appeal to the emotions 传奇剧，情节剧，煽情剧作
11. **exasperation** *n.* the state of being intensely irritated; infuriated 激怒，气恼

Notes

1. the big studio era

The studio system was a means of film production and distribution dominant in Hollywood. The period stretching from the introduction of sound to the court ruling and the beginning of the studio breakups, 1927/29—1948/49, is commonly known as the Golden age of Hollywood. During the Golden Age, eight companies constituted the so-called major studios that promulgated the Hollywood studio system.

好莱坞的电影制片厂制度（大约从20世纪30年代到60年代）。其特点是大量生产和大量发行电影。其中包含五大三小八家电影制片企业。五大分别为米高梅（MGM）、派拉蒙（Paramount）、20世纪福克斯（20th Century—Fox）、华纳兄弟（Warner Brothers）和雷电华（RKO）。三小分别为：环球（Universal）、哥伦比亚（Columbia）和联美（United Artists）。

2. Male stars like Cary Grant, Gary Cooper, and John Wayne were still playing leads in their sixties.

译文：男性影星如加里·格兰特，加里·库柏，约翰·韦恩在他们六十多岁的时候还饰演主角。

Gary Grant（1904.1—1986.11）
其主演希区柯克一系列电影是他最为世人所熟悉的。如《深闺疑云》、《寂寞芳心》等。五六十年代的格兰特身上仍然几乎看不出岁月的痕迹，这期间他和希区柯克合作的《捉贼记》和《西北偏北》都成为影史上的经典。

Gary Cooper（1901.5—1961.5）
是有史以来获奥斯卡奖最多的一位男演员。他主演的《约克军曹》和《正午》是两部最受欢迎的影片，他塑造的约克军曹的形象成为美国军人的楷模。

John Wayne（1907.5—1979.6）

以演出西部片和战争片中的硬汉而闻名。韦恩是那个年代所有美国人的化身：诚实、有个性、英雄主义。其作品《关山飞渡》蜚声世界影坛，一生共拍片250部，影响甚大。

3. Mildred Pierce

《幻世浮生》1945，故事发生在美国经济大萧条时期，女主人公Mildred Pierce与失业的丈夫分了手，靠一份女服务员的工作维持生计。她一方面想维持自己的社会地位，另一方面又渴望独立和自由。在为生活奔忙的同时，她还要想尽一切办法赢得女儿的爱与尊重。

4. It was in such genres as these that some of the studio era's greatest actresses flourished—Bette Davis, Katharine Hepburn, Claudette Colbert, Barbara Stanwyck, Carole Lombard, Marlene Dietrich, and Greta Garbo, to name a few.

译文：正是在这样类型的影片中，一些女星在制片厂时代受到了广泛的欢迎。比如：贝蒂·戴维斯，凯瑟琳·赫本，克劳德特·科尔伯特，芭芭拉·斯坦威克，卡洛·隆巴德，玛琳·黛德，丽葛丽泰·嘉宝。

Bette Davis（1908.4—1989.10）

"华纳影后"，银幕上从不选择单一的角色，不断地挑战自己的演技高度。

Katharine Hepburn（1907.5—2003.6）

好莱坞常青树。曾主演《清晨的荣誉/牵牛花》《费城故事》和《金色池塘》出演过40余部影片，12次获奥斯卡奖提名，并四度摘取"最佳女演员"的桂冠。

Claudette Colbert（1903.9—1996.7）

曾出演《一夜风流》《埃及艳后》（1939）《棕榈滩的故事》等影片。荣获第七届奥斯卡最佳女演员奖。

Barbara Stanwyck（1907.7—1990.1）
曾在《双重赔偿》中饰演过蛇蝎美人"黑寡妇"。

Carole Lombard（1908.10—1942.1）
以饰演标准的金发女郎起步，在改名为卡洛尔·隆巴德后渐渐走红。1932出演《20世纪号快车》而名扬天下。此后，卡洛尔成为好莱坞头号喜剧明星。1938年与克拉克·盖博结婚。1942因飞机失事而丧生。

Marlene Dietrich（1901.12—1992.5）
德国女演员，20年代中期，演艺事业开始走红，1930年《蓝天使》大获成功，成为国际知名的影星。同年跟派拉蒙签约，并在由斯登堡导演的多部影片中出任主角，与葛丽泰·嘉宝分庭抗礼，一度成为片酬最高的明星。

Greta Garbo（1905.9—1990.4）
嘉宝出生于瑞典，曾饰演《安娜·卡列尼娜》、《瑞典女王》、《茶花女》等。她那神秘的气质、独特的性格和非凡的演技象征着美、忧伤与孤独。被誉为好莱坞的女神。晚年离群索居。

5. Freud

西格蒙德·弗洛伊德（Sigmund Freud, 1856.5.6—1939.9.23）, was an Austrian neurologist who became known as the founding father of psychoanalysis.
犹太人，奥地利精神病医生及精神分析学家。精神分析学派的创始人。他认为被压抑的欲望绝大部分是属于性的，性的扰乱是精神病的根本原因。著有《梦的释义》、《精神分析引论》等。好莱坞很多影片都受到弗洛伊德精神分析学理论的投影的影响。美国的电影导演们巧妙地用心理分析方法表现出一般美国人的心理动向，使影片具有深刻的社会性，产生了广泛的感染力。

6. We want nothing less, on or off the screen, than the wide variety and dazzling diversity of male options.
译文：无论在银幕内还是银幕外，我们（女性）只希望能够拥有和男人一样多样和丰富的选择范围。

Thelma & Louise[1]

Feminism was one of many liberation movements that rose to prominence in America and Europe during the 1960s. Virtually every powerful woman in the Hollywood film industry today has been influenced by the movement. Thelma & Louise explores the intimate bond between two best friends whose weekend getaway (非正式，假期) unexpectedly takes them on an adventure across America. The movie explores such themes as marriage, work, independence, female bonding, and male chauvinism (大男子主义), often from a humorous perspective. Interestingly, the movie's structure is indebted to two traditionally male genres—the buddy film[2] and the road picture[3].

It starts out larkishly (闹着玩的) enough. Thelma (Geena Davis) needs a respite (缓解) from her traditionally male, that is to say, endlessly oinking (猪叫声，无聊喊叫), husband, and Louise (Susan Sarandon) is tired of waiting for her musician boyfriend to return from his one-night gigs (演唱会) in Ramada Inn cocktail lounges. A weekend at a friend's mountain cabin sounds just right. Thelma and Louise go on the run for killing a drunken man who tried to rape Thelma in a bar parking lot; regardless of whether this despicable (卑劣的，可鄙的) lout (笨拙的人) deserved to die. What's shocking is that he's portrayed as the typical late-20th-century guy. From Thelma's buffoonish (丑角) husband Darryl (Christopher McDonald) to hunky thief J.D. (Brad Pitt) and Louise's greaser[4] boyfriend Jimmy (Michael Madsen), every man in the film is either an untrustworthy smooth operator, a slick romantic with latent violent tendencies, or an abusive monster with a passion for brutality or domination, and it's this kind of clear cut black-and-white world which Scott and screenwriter Callie Khouri's[5] ladies revolt against (反抗)[6].

Thelma and Louise's crime spree (狂欢) is a symbolic rejection of the oppressed victim status men have forced women to accept, and, as a result of Davis and Sarandon's commanding performances, is frequently an exhilarating (令人愉快的) ride. Yet because the only way these outlaw martyrs (殉道者) can reclaim their freedom is to nobly strike back against a society characterized by male-propagated (传播，宣传) sexism and objectification—in one of many instances of overkill, a truck driver, simply gesturing obscenely (下流的) to the women—Thelma and Louise's feminist call to arms winds up sounding woefully (可悲的) simple-minded[7].

But the title clearly announces the film's most significant innovation. Thelma & Louise is the first important movie to put two women in a car and send them careering down open western roads with the cops in wheel-spinning pursuit. And it is the first movie to use sexism as the motivating force for their misdeeds. The uncomprehending world may see them as the dangerous perpetrators (犯罪者，作恶者) of a colorful crime spree. We, however, are encouraged to understand them not as public enemies but as public victims. It's an unfeeling society that is really responsible for their wicked deeds.

After reading questions

1. According to paragraph 1, which of the following statements about Thelma & Louise is not true?

    A. *Thelma & Louise* depicts two women's adventure across America.

    B. *Thelma & Louise* is a combination of genres of both buddy film and road film.

    C. *Thelma & Louise* is a humorous comedy movie.

    D. *Thelma & Louise* reflects the influence of the woman liberation movements.

2. In paragraph 2, the main male characters in the movie are described. Most of them are.

    A. irresponsible

    B. untrustworthy or abusive

    C. violent

    D. despicable

3. Why do some critics assume that Thelma and Louise call to arms end as woefully simple-minded?

    A. because in the male-propagated world, they should have made their strike in a noble way

    B. because they overkill

    C. because they committed the crime in a spree way

    D. because they are the outlaw martyrs

4. What is NOT the significance of Thelma & Louise?

    A. It's the first road picture with women as the main characters.

    B. It's the first movie using sexism as the motivation for misdeeds.

    C. It causes us to sympathize with them as victims of the male chauvinism.

    D. It's the first movie women acting as criminals.

Notes

1. ***Thelma & Louise*** (1991) 该片被认为是向男权社会发出抗争的女性主义电影代表作。生活在沉闷与琐碎家务中的家庭主妇赛尔玛（Susan Sarandon）与在某间咖啡厅做女侍应生的闺中密友路易丝（Geena Davis）对平凡的生活与工作产生厌倦后，结伴一起外出旅游散心。路上，在某家酒吧外的停车厂，赛尔玛险遭无名男子强暴，幸好路易丝及时赶到，拔枪将该男子射杀。两位女性在一路上遭遇各种男性，在与他们的交往和对抗中，塞尔玛和路易丝的个性在成长，她们的友谊也在不断加深。

2. ***the buddy film*** The buddy film is a film genre in which two people of the same sex (historically men) and contrasting personalities are paired. The buddy film is commonplace in American cinema. It endured through the 20th century with different pairings and different themes. 搭档类型片（一种电影类型）。早期的伙伴电影主角常为男性。

3. ***the road picture*** or A road movie is a film genre in which the main character or characters leave home to travel from place to place. They usually leave home to escape their current lives. 公路电影（一种电影类型）。

4. **greaser**: a working class youth subculture that originated in the 1950s among young northeastern and southern United States street gangs. [美俚] 不务正业的人 特指墨裔男性或拉丁裔男性

5. ***Callie Khouri***: American screen writer and film director, In 1992 she won the Academy Award for Best Screenplay written directly for the Screen for the film, Thelma & Louise. 卡莉·克里，在1992年凭借影片末路狂花荣获奥斯卡最佳编剧奖

6. From Thelma's buffoonish husband Darryl to hunky thief J.D. and Louise's greaser boyfriend Jimmy, every man in the film is either an untrustworthy smooth operator, a slick romantic with latent violent tendencies, or an abusive monster with a passion for brutality or domination, and it's this kind of clear cut black-and-white world which screenwriter Callie Khouri's ladies revolt against.

译文：从赛尔玛小丑式的丈夫达利到东欧小偷J.D.，再到路易丝的不务正业的男友吉米，片中的男性角色或者是不值得信任的钻营者，或者是有潜在暴力倾向的爱慕者，亦或是残暴专横的魔鬼、暴力狂。这黑白分明的世界正是剧作家卡莉笔下的女性所反抗的。

7. Yet because the only way these outlaw martyrs can reclaim their freedom is to nobly strike back against a society characterized by male-propagated sexism and objectification—in one of many instances of overkill, a truck driver, simply gesturing obscenely to the women—Thelma and Louise's feminist call to arms winds up sounding woefully simple-minded.

译文：然而这两个逍遥法外的烈女只能够以体面地方式反击男性话语权下的男性至上论和女性物化论。正因如此，末路狂花中的女权主义者在诉诸武力时就显得可悲而又简单。尤其是影片中有反抗过度的例子：那个只因向她们做了不雅动作而被报复的卡车司机。

Unit 2 Women Movies 女性影片

Part 4 Exercises

I. Answer questions after listening to the dialogues taken from the film.

1. What can you conclude about the characters of Thelma and Louise when you listen to the conversation?
2. Why didn't Louise regret not turning to the police in the first place when they shot Harlan?

Script

Scenario 1: *Louise and Thelma decided to have two-day's-getaway. They are arranging the appointment on the phone.*

THELMA: Hello?

LOUISE: How you doing, housewife? Packed? We're out of here tonight.

THELMA: I still have to ask Darryl if I can go.

LOUISE: You mean you haven't asked him yet? Thelma, for Chris sake. Is he your husband or your father? It is just two days, for God's sake. Don't be a child. Tell him you're going with me. Say I'm having a nervous breakdown.

THELMA: That don't carry much weight. He already thinks you're crazy. Are you at work?

LOUISE: No, I'm at the Playboy Mansion. — Call you back. (later...)

THELMA: What time are you picking me up?

LOUISE: I'll be there around two or three.

THELMA: Okay. Say, what kind of stuff do I bring?

LOUISE: I don't know. Warm stuff, I guess. The mountains get cold at night. I'll bring everything.

THELMA: Okay. I will too, then.

LOUISE: Steal Darryl's fishing stuff.

THELMA: don't know how to fish.

LOUISE: Neither do I, but Darryl does it. How hard can it be? See you in a bit.

THELMA: Okay. All right, bye.

Scenario 2: *After all of the experience on the trip. Changes and growth have taken place in Thelma: she is more mature and self-determined. In recalling the bad accident which triggered the flight, she shows no regrets in not surrendering to the police.*

LOUISE: Should've gone to the police in the beginning. Why didn't I?

THELMA: You said why before.

LOUISE: What'd I say?

THELMA: That nobody would believe us. You know that jerk was really hurting me, and if you hadn't come along when you had he would've hurt me even worse. And probably nothing would've been done with him because I was dancing with him all night and everybody saw it and they'd figure I had it coming. My life would've been ruined a whole lot more than it is now, now I'm having fun. I'll tell you something else, I'm not the least bit sorry that creep is dead, I'm just sorry it was you who did it and not me.

II. **Fill the blanks with the missing words or phrases after listening to the lines taken from the film.**

1. **LOUISE:** [*to a truck driver*] Where do you get off 1)_____ that way with women you don't even know, huh? How'd you feel if someone did that to 2)_____?

2. **STATE TROOPER:** [*Sobbing*] Please! I have a wife and kids.
   THELMA: Oh really, well, 3)_____. You be 4)_____, 5)_____ your wife. My husband wasn't sweet to me. Look how I 6)_____.

3. **LOUISE:** [*Talking about her husband Darryl*] He says he's still 7)_____. He 8)_____ on being infantile.
   THELMA: She thinks he's a pig.
   LOUISE: I KNOW he's a pig.

III. **Complete the following memorable lines by translating the Chinese into English.**

1. Thelma: I feel really awake. I don't recall ever feeling this awake. You know?. You feel like that? _____ (一切都看上去不一样了) You feel like you got something to live for now?

2. Thelma: Thank you, now everybody just stay down on the floor until I leave, _____(谢谢大家配合) and have a good day.

3. Where do you get off_____ (如此对待你甚至都不认识的女性), huh? How'd you feel if someone did that to your mother or your sister or your wife?

4. If she calls, just be gentle, you know? _____ (就好像你很高兴接到她的电话). Like you miss her. Women love that shit.

IV. **Oral practices—answer the following questions.**

1. Which movie type does *Thelma & Louise* most appropriately belong to?

2. Do you agree with Thelma & Louise's method of revenge against the society characterized by male-propagated sexism?

Part 5 More Women Movies

Plot Summary of *Kramer vs Kramer*

Ted Kramer (Dustin Hoffman) is a workaholic advertising executive who has just been assigned a new and very important account. Ted arrives home and shares the good news with his wife Joanna (Meryl Streep) only to find that she is leaving him. Saying that she needs to find herself, she leaves Ted to raise their son Billy (Justin Henry) by himself. Ted and Billy initially resent one another as Ted no longer has time to carry his increased workload and Billy misses his mother's love and attention. After months of unrest, Ted and Billy learn to cope and gradually bond as father and son.

Ted befriends his neighbor Margaret (Jane Alexander), who had initially counseled Joanna to leave Ted if she was that unhappy. Margaret is a fellow single parent, and she and Ted become kindred spirits. One day, as the two sit in the park watching their children play, Billy falls off the jungle gym, severely cutting his face. Ted sprints several blocks through oncoming traffic carrying Billy to the hospital, where he comforts his son during treatment.

Fifteen months after she walked out, Joanna returns to New York to claim Billy, and a custody battle ensues. During the custody hearing, both Ted and Joanna are unprepared for the brutal character assassinations that their lawyers unleash on the other. Margaret is forced to testify that she had advised an unhappy Joanna to leave Ted, though she also attempts to tell Joanna on the stand that her husband has profoundly changed. Eventually, the damaging facts that Ted was fired because of his conflicting parental responsibilities, forcing him to take a lower-paid job, come out in court, as do the details of Billy's accident.

The court awards custody to Joanna, a decision mostly based on the assumption that a child is best raised by his mother. Ted discusses appealing the case, but his lawyer warns that Billy himself would have to take the stand in the resulting trial. Ted cannot bear the thought of submitting his child to such an ordeal and decides not to contest custody.

On the morning that Billy is to move in with Joanna, Ted and Billy make breakfast together, mirroring the meal that Ted tried to cook the first morning after Joanna left. They share a tender hug knowing that this is their last daily breakfast together. Joanna calls on the intercom, asking Ted to come down to the lobby. She tells Ted how much she loves and wants Billy, but she knows his true home is with Ted. She will therefore not take him. As she enters the elevator to go and talk to Billy, she asks her ex-husband

"How do I look?" The movie ends with the elevator doors closing on the emotional Joanna, right after Ted answers, "You look terrific."

Memorable lines in the film

Settings: *Joanna and Ted are confronting each other in the court fighting for the custody of their son, Billy.*

Joanna: Yes. I tried to talk to Ted—my ex-husband about it, but he wouldn't listen. He refuses to discuss it in any serious way. I remember one time he said I probably couldn't get a job that would pay enough to hire a baby-sitter for Billy. I left my child—I know there is no excuse for that. But since then, I have gotten help. I have worked hard to become a whole human being. I don't think I should be punished for that. I don't think my son should be punished for that.

我曾尝试过与我的前夫Ted讨论过此事（指Joanna谋职一事），但是他不听。他从来不认真和我讨论此事。记得有一次他说也许我挣的钱还不够请一个看孩子的人。是的，我离开了孩子，我知道这是不可原谅的。但自从离开以后，我得到了一些帮助，我努力工作以期成为一个完整的（社会）人，我不应该为我付出的努力而受惩罚，我的儿子也不应该为此受惩罚。

Ted: The only thing that's supposed to matter here is what's best for Billy... When Joanna said why shouldn't a woman have the same ambitions as a man, I suppose she's right. But by the same token (同理) what law is it that says a woman is a better parent simply by virtue of (因为) her sex? I guess I've had to think a lot about whatever it is that makes somebody a good parent: constancy, patience, understanding... love. Where is it written that a man has any less of those qualities than a woman?

我觉得在这里重要的是讨论怎么选择对Billy最好。Joanna期待女人能和男人一样拥有事业心，我认为她是对的。但是同理，哪条法律说女人就比男人更适合做家长？我觉得我们应该重点放在讨论拥有什么条件才能成为好家长：它需要一贯性，耐心，理解和爱。哪里说过男人不如女人拥有这些素质？

Plot Summary of *Mona Lisa's Smile*

Mona Lisa's Smile is a gender-switching rehash (改编) of Dead Poets Society. Roberts plays Katherine Watson, an art history instructor newly hired at the all-girls Wellesley College in 1953. There, Watson, a forward-thinking feminist and California "bohemian (波希米亚人，放逐者)," is dismayed (灰心的) to find that her students' academic and professional ambitions take a backseat (居次要的) to etiquette lessons and the all-important snaring (诱惑、陷阱) of a husband. On the first day of class, Katherine is disconcerted (不安的) to find out that her students have all read and apparently memorized the textbook. And they're snooty (傲慢的，目中无人的) about it, besides. So Katherine has to redo her syllabus just to be able to teach them something they don't already know. Watson zeroes in on a foursome of friends: Joan (Stiles), wavering between the opposing tracks of law school and housewifery; Constance (Goodwin), a sweet but "plain" girl convinced of her unworthiness; the boozy, sexually brazen (厚颜无耻的) Giselle (Gyllenhaal); and her most formidable challenge is Betty, a ferocious Kirsten Dunst, who has her entire life planned. She's going to marry her boyfriend, then graduate, then have babies

and be enormously happy forever. Betty sizes up Katherine, who is unmarried, as a "subversive," which was the third-worst thing anyone could be called in the early 1950s (after "Communist" and "fellow traveler") (以上词汇来自于20世纪50年代麦卡锡冷战思维下对共产主义的攻击：编者按) Betty wrote editorials in the college paper decrying Watson's "radicalism." Watson's radical, see, because she teaches Picasso and Pollock (波拉克，美国抽象主义画家)and requires her students to think outside the textbook and to question what art really is.

Memorable lines in the film

Settings: *Betty has composed scathing pieces in the school's paper about Katharine's subversive, forward-thinking teaching methods. After reading the article, Katharine enters the classroom angrily.*

Katharine: Quiet! Today you just listen. What will the future scholars see when they study us? A portrait of women today? There you are, ladies. The perfect likeness of a Wellesley graduate. Magna cum laude, doing exactly what she was trained to do. Slide. A Rhodes scholar. I wonder if she recites Chaucer while she presses her husband's shirts. Slide. Now, you physics majors can calculate the mass and volume of every meat loaf you make. Slide. A girdle to set you free. What does that mean? What does that mean? What does it mean? I give up. You win. The smartest women in the country. I didn't realize that by demanding excellence, I would be challenging...What did it say? What did it say? "The roles you were born to fill." Is that right? The roles you were born to fill? It's my mistake. Class dismissed.

安静！今天你们只需听讲。未来的学者会怎样看待今天的我们？今天女性的风范？你们是以优等成绩毕业的卫斯理女性们，做的却是被训练而做的事。下一张。罗氏奖学金获得者。我想当她给老公熨衬衫的时候是否会背诵乔叟的诗。下一张。好，你们现在所学的物理学知识可以帮助你们精确地测量每块肉饼的分量。下一张。让女人解放的塑身衣！什么意思！到底是什么意思！我放弃，你赢了。祖国最有才智的女性们，我没料到我对你们要求卓越反倒会被攻击。（校报上）怎么说的？"你们生来要担当的使命"是不是？是我错了，下课。

Settings: *Betty wrote another editorial to express her gratitude and appreciation for her art*

teacher Katherine.

Betty: My teacher Katherine Watson, lived by her own definition, and would not compromise that, not even for Wellesley. I dedicate this, my last editorial to an extraordinary woman, who lived by example, and compelled us all to see the world through new eyes. By the time you read this, she'll be sailing to Europe, where I know she'll find new walls to break down, and new ideas to replace them with. I've heard her called a quitter for leaving, an aimless wanderer. But not all who wander are aimless, especially not those who seek truth beyond tradition, beyond definition, beyond the image.

我的老师凯瑟琳·沃森，坚信自己的原则，她不会为任何人哪怕是卫斯理而放弃她的准则。我把最后一篇社评献给这位卓越的女性。她为人师表，并激励我们用新的眼光来看待世界。当您们读这篇文章时她已经启航前往欧洲了，我知道在那儿她会找到新的需要破除的传统，新的思想去替换旧观念。有人称她是逃跑者，漫无目的的漫游者。然而并非所有漫游者都是漫无目地的。尤其是她这种为追寻真理而勇于超越传统、突破定势和想象的人。

UNIT 3

Holocaust Movies 大屠杀影片

Part 1 Chinese Summary

大屠杀影片

首先，大屠杀（holocaust）与历史上的屠杀（massacre）不同。在西方话语中，massacre 和Holocaust 都有"屠杀"之意，都与数量较大的死亡事件有关。massacre 的含义比较宽泛，Holocaust 有着强烈的话语规定性：当"屠杀事件"（massacre）指发生在二战期间纳粹德国对犹太人的集体灭绝行为时，才被判定是"大屠杀"（Holocaust），即希伯莱语"Shoah"。大屠杀是独裁政治、种族歧视、道德失序、民族仇恨、野蛮战争、理性的倒塌、良知的泯灭等种种"恶因素"的混合体，而屠杀仅仅是其表象。这场惊骇的人间惨剧带来了深刻的话语资源。

然而，20世纪后半叶的大屠杀叙事始终在拒绝言说和过度言说之间徘徊。一方面，大屠杀这一历史事件所特有的个体内在创伤性一度在很大程度上剥夺了公众妄加言说的资格，同时也令那些享有言说特权的亲历者（受害者或施暴者）因为身份的耻辱而三缄其口。另一方面，后现代语境则为大屠杀叙事提供了更大的自由阐释空间，历史真实与虚构之间界限的模糊化不仅为篡改史实的大屠杀否定论创造了契机，更使大屠杀得以超越犹太种族经历之特殊性的局限，成为人类苦难与救赎的一个普适性隐喻。

展现大屠杀不仅是为了集体修复种族灭绝的记忆，更是为了避免人们重复自我毁灭的盲目性。大屠杀话语在电影史上的建立可用三部影片划分为三个时期：以《夜与雾》*Night and Fog*（1956）为代表的启示时期（revelation），以《浩劫》为代表的反思时期（reflexion）和以《辛德勒的名单》为代表的表现时期(representation)。

好莱坞大屠杀题材影视作品通常都改编自较为成功的文学或戏剧作品。如早期的《安妮日记》*The Diary of Anne Frank* (1959)，《巴西来的孩子》*The Boys from Brazil* (1978)，《苏菲的选择》*Sophie's Choice*（1982）等。大屠杀话语在西方电影中不断复制和增生，并且格外受到奥斯卡奖青睐。从为人们所熟知的《辛德勒的名单》*Schindler's List*（1993）、到《美丽人生》*Life Is Beautiful*（意大利，1997）再到后期的《朗读者》*The Reader*（2008），也许正是由于这些好莱坞获奖影片才使得主流电影受众更为直接而深入的了解了二战期间对犹太种族的屠杀史实。这些影片引发了很多道德和美学上的争论：相当多的批评者认为好莱坞将这一人类历史上的灾难变成了对大众的娱乐；也有人认为大屠杀影片的叙事方式已经变得符号化和程式化了，只要包含铁丝网、火车车厢、烟肉、条纹囚衣等影像，大屠杀题材就能够不断地被复制甚至被编造。

为了避免粉饰罪恶，更为了避免让这场浩劫变得娱乐化，一些影片的叙事结构放弃了传统现实主义的做法，采用时光倒流或者彻底逆序的蒙太奇手法，阻断叙事的时间顺序，迫使观者运用自己的判断力和理性思维能力来重构事件的发展，籍此引领观者一起对这场浩劫进行反思。比如《苏菲的选择》Sophie's Choice（1982），《夜与雾》Night and Fog (1956),和《典当商》The Pawnbroker（1964）等。

今天，对大屠杀的电影表述已全面展开，并且向着纵深的方向发展。反映大屠杀的影片已经成为了一种电影类型受到了人们的广泛关注。其中既有《辛德勒名单》这样通过直接的现实手法展现大屠杀残酷性的，也出现了诸如《命运无常》Fate Less (2006)和《朗读者》The Reader (2008)这样的非主流大屠杀叙事影片。不得不提的是一部以黑色幽默的喜剧形式来表现大屠杀题材的影片《美丽人生》。用讽刺幽默手段反映大屠杀这一深刻创伤题材并不是对历史的亵渎，相反，灾难中对希望的追求恰恰反映了人类精神的坚韧和顽强，这也与犹太文化中所崇尚的"苦乐交织"的人生理念不谋而合。类似的讽刺幽默类型影片还有《坏女孩》The Nasty Girl（1990），《根哥斯科恩》Genghis Cohn（1996），《囚车使向圣地》Train of Life (法国，1998)等。

《辛德勒的名单》Schindler's List（1993）是由斯皮尔伯格导演，根据托马斯·科奈里（Thomas Keneally）1982年出版的同名纪实小说改编而成。《辛德勒的名单》把大屠杀话语带入到了"表现时期"，解除了大屠杀作为"不可再现的历史"的禁忌。而由《辛德勒的名单》所打造的大屠杀人物类型："幸存者"和"拯救者"分别代表了受害者崇拜（culture of victim hood）的美国后现代身份政治和扬善抑恶的"美国梦"传统视角。后者淡化大屠杀所暴露的人性凶残的一面，却强化其救赎所带来的灵魂净化和道德升华。

《钢琴师》The Pianist（2002）是一部真实反映纳粹在二战期间在犹太人聚居区所进行的惨绝人寰的屠杀。影片根据波兰钢琴家瓦拉迪斯罗·斯皮曼（Wladyslaw Szpilman）的自传体小说《死亡城市》改编。他最好的一次钢琴演奏，不是在战后的波兰电台，不是在灯火辉煌的音乐厅，甚至也不是他在避难所那次惊心动魄的空弹，而是在废墟般的空城华沙，为那个纳粹军官的弹奏。

《美丽人生》Life Is Beautiful（1997）这是一部让人们在苦难的大屠杀中看到希望的童话故事。喜剧题材并没有使大屠杀的严肃性被亵渎，反而更彰显了人性的坚韧和伟大。主人公Guido留给观众的不仅是他的乐观，更有他对家人深深的爱。

Part 2 Text 1

Film and the Holocaust

Immediately following the war, and for decades afterward, survivors rarely spoke about their experiences in the Holocaust, partly because they knew the world was not prepared to listen. Now, however, the **Shoah Foundation**[1]'s completed videotaping of more than fifty-one thousand survivors in fifty-seven countries corresponds to two phenomena: younger generations—especially in Germany—wanting to know more about the Holocaust, and the aging survivors feel the urgency to speak before it's too late.

It never occurred to me that, by the year 2001, films about the Nazi era and its Jewish victims would be so numerous as to constitute a **veritable** genre including consistent Oscar winners—nor did I foresee how this genre would be part of a wider cultural embracing of the Shoah.

Almost all American movies dealing with the Holocaust are adapted from another medium—successful plays (*The Diary of Anne Frank*), **cabaret** or novel (*Exodus, Ship of Fools, The Boys from Brazil, Sophie's Choice*). It seems, therefore, that Hollywood will take a chance on films about the Holocaust only after the material has proven its commercial potential in another medium. And even then, the films merely touch upon the historical horror rather than grasp it. The American cinema often uses Nazi images to evoke instant terror or tears, whereas many European films use the cinematic medium as an instrument to probe responsibility. Perhaps the commercial **imperatives** of Hollywood and the networks tend to **preempt** the possibilities for truthful representation. And films about the Holocaust have provided images—of smoke, of **barbed** wire, of sealed train cars, of skeletal bodies—that now function as **synecdoches**, the visual part representing the unimaginable whole.[2]

Popular movies like *Schindler's List* and *Life Is Beautiful* proved controversial among critics, they played a considerable role in creating awareness of the Holocaust among mainstream film audiences who had known little about it beforehand. While there is always the danger of commercialization—horror neatly packaged and leading to numbness or inappropriate happy ends— this seems to me a lesser evil than having the memory of the Shoah disappear from cultural attention.

Films that depict a character's memory of a horrific past—and that character's **enslavement** by it—can have more consistency and integrity than a movie that **purports** to show the past in an objective way[3]. A fictional reconstruction of a concentration camp is not quite as "truthful" as one person's subjective memory of it, for the latter acknowledges the **partiality** of the **recollection**. Most effective films move us by alternating the present—marked by indifference to the Holocaust—with the past. This is a cinema of **flashback**[4]: a filmic device that permits the visible, **palpable** past to surface into the present. Editing in this cinema is not merely continuity, or the smooth **linear transition** from one shot to the next; the rhythms and **juxtapositions** of the cutting can create varied effects upon the viewer, from heightened **suspense** to an awareness of contraries[5]. The montage[6] of such films as *Sophie's Choice, Night and Fog*, and *The Pawnbroker* expresses the degree to which the relatively calm present is informed by the turbulent Holocaust.

Radu Mihaileanu[7] (the director of *Train of Life*) once said that he felt that the story

of the Shoah should not be kept in telling solely in the context of tears and horror. He wanted to tell the tragedy through the most Jewish language there is—the tradition of bittersweet comedy. It was a desire to go beyond the Shoah—not to deny or forget the dead, but to re-create their lives in a new and vivid way. Comedy is the genre that celebrates the soci. Traditionally, comedies end with a marriage, confirming the power of society to reproduce itself. Tragedy is the domain of the individual, traditionally ending with the death of the hero who can't conform to the demands of the community. A number of recent films have succeeded in creating fertile discomfort through the use of dark humor, from Michael Verhoeven's *The Nasty Girl and My Mother's Courage* to such controversial "comedies" as Genghis Cohn. Others, such as *Train of Life*, *Life Is Beautiful* use humor as a **balm and buffer**, with comic heroes whose **ruses** are **tantamount** to resistance. The extraordinary international popularity of *Life Is Beautiful* means that audiences—which might otherwise not have been aware of the Nazi **persecution** of Italian Jewry—embraced an appealing Jewish hero who inspires respect rather than merely pity.

After-reading questions

1. Why has the Shoah Foundation produced videotaping of Shoah survivors recently?
    A. Because they knew the world was not prepared to listen.
    B. Because German younger generations want to know something about the Holocaust.
    C. Because the survivors rarely spoke about their experiences in Holocaust.
    D. The survivors are too aged to speak about their experience.
2. Why, according to the author, are almost all American movies dealing with the Holocaust adapted from successful plays or novels?
    A. Because the producers have to first find evidence of the Holocaust movies' commercial potential.
    B. Because plays and novels are the closest medium to movies.
    C. Because the films find it's hard to portray the Holocaust.
    D. Because the American film producers want to evoke instant terror or tears in the Holocaust movies.
3. Which of the following statements belongs to the controversy among critics on movies like *Schindler's List* and *Life Is Beautiful*?
    A. Commercial movies present the horror of the holocaust in an amusing way.
    B. Before them the mainstream film audiences rarely know anything about the Holocaust.
    C. They have over-entertained the Holocaust and tend to make the mass feel

numb about it.

D. All of the above.

4. Which of the following ways of depicting will have more consistency and integrity in Holocaust movies?

A. a fictional reconstruction of a concentration camp

B. showing the past holocaust in an objective way

C. the depicting of a character's personal memory of the Holocaust

D. the character's indifference to the Holocaust

5. Which of the following is NOT the traditional difference between comedy and tragedy?

A. Comedy usually ends with a marriage.

B. The comedy hero usually conform to the power of society.

C. Tragedy usually ends with the death of the hero.

D. The tragedy hero can't conform to the demands of the community.

Words and expressions

1. **veritable** *adj.* [attrib.] used as an intensifier, often to qualify a metaphor [用作强调词，常用于修饰隐喻] 真正的；确实的

2. **cabaret** *n.* a series of acts at a night club 夜总会歌舞剧

3. **imperative** *n.* some duty that is essential and urgent 必须，必要，紧迫之事

4. **preempt** *v.* take the place of or have precedence over 取得优先

5. **barb** *n.* a sharp projection near the end of an arrow, fish-hook, or similar object, which is angled away from the main point so as to make extraction difficult（箭头、鱼钩等）倒钩

6. **synecdoche** *n.* a figure of speech in which a part is made to represent the whole or vice versa 提喻法（一种修辞方法，以局部代表全部和以全部指部分）

7. **enslavement** *n.* the act of causing (someone) to lose their freedom of choice or action 奴役

8. **purport** *v.* appear to be or do something, especially falsely 看起来，显得

9. **partiality** *n.* a particular liking or fondness for something 偏爱，癖好，特别喜爱

10. **recollection** *n.* the action or faculty of remembering or recollecting something 回忆，记忆，记忆力

11. **palpable** *adj.* (especially of a feeling or atmosphere) so intense as to be almost touched or felt（尤指感情、气氛强烈到）能感觉到的，能触摸得到的

12. **linear** *adj.* arranged in or extending along a straight or nearly straight line 摆成直线的，沿直线的，线形的，线性的

13. **transition** *n.* the process of a period of changing from one state or condition to another 过渡，转变，变革

14. **suspense** *n.* a quality in a work of fiction that arouses excited expectation or uncertainty about what may happen（小说中的）悬念
15. **balm** *n.* a fragrant ointment or preparation used to heal or soothe the skin 用于治疗（或舒爽皮肤的）香油膏
16. **buffer** *n.* a person or thing that prevents incompatible or antagonistic people or things from coming into contact with or harming each other 起缓冲作用的人（或物）
17. **ruse** *n.* an action intended to deceive someone; a trick 诡计；计策
18. **tantamount** *adj.* equivalent in seriousness to; virtually the same as 相当于的
19. **persecution** *n.* being subject to hostility and ill-treatment, especially because of their race or political or religious beliefs.（尤指由于种族、政治或宗教信仰的）迫害，残害，虐待

Notes

1. **Shoah Foundation**: In 1994, Steven Spielberg founded the Survivors of the Shoah Visual History Foundation (original title), a nonprofit organization established to record testimonies in video format of survivors and other witnesses of the Holocaust. 大屠杀基金会。由导演斯皮尔伯格在1994年建立。旨在建立由见证过大屠杀历史的人们口述的影像资料。

2. And films about the Holocaust have provided images of smoke, of barbed wire, of sealed train cars, of skeletal bodies—that now function as synecdoches, the visual part representing the unimaginable whole.
译文：大屠杀题材电影提供了一些影像，如烟雾、带倒钩的铁丝网、密封的火车车厢以及骨瘦如柴的尸体等。这些影像成为一种以局部代替整体的提喻手法，代替不可想象的全部历史。

3. Films that depict a character's memory of a horrific past—and that character's enslavement by it—can have more consistency and integrity than a movie that purports to show the past in an objective way.
译文：影片如果描述可怕的曾对角色产生永久性伤害的回忆，要比用所谓客观手法表现历史更具有延续性和完整性。

4. **flashback:** In movies and television, several camera techniques and special effects have evolved to alert the viewer that the action shown is from the past; for example, the edges of the picture may be deliberately blurred. 在影视作品中倒叙会采用一些特殊的画面或声音处理来提示观众正在对过去事件进行叙述。比如使用画面边缘模糊处理等特技。

5. Editing in this cinema is not merely continuity, or the smooth linear transition from one shot to the next; the rhythms and juxtapositions of the cutting can create varied effects upon the viewer, from heightened suspense to an awareness

of contraries.

译文：这种影片的剪辑并非为了实现让影片连贯或是让场景之间直线切换；不同的叙事节奏以及剪辑产生的场景叠加会给观众带来不同的观影效果；或者是悬念迭起，或者是冲突意识。

6. **Montage** is a technique in film editing in which a series of short shots are edited into a sequence to condense space, time, and information. 蒙太奇，一种电影的基本结构手段和叙事方式。通过电影剪辑把不同画面镜头按照新的顺序编辑排列，从而将空间时间和信息进行浓缩。

7. **Radu Mihaileanu** is a Jewish Romanian-born French film director and screenwriter.

Schindler's List[1]

Schindler's List is a story of moral polarities (两极)—between the demented (发狂的), omnipotent (集权的) Nazi commandant Goeth (Ralph Fiennes) and the vulnerable (易受伤害的), self-effacing (隐忍的) Jewish accountant Stern (Ben Kingsley). In between is Schindler, linked to both by an opportunity he can manipulate, but later by an awareness that both men mirror disparate (不同的) aspects of his own soul. After previous Holocaust films that centered on Jewish victims and Nazi perpetrators (作恶者), there had to be an audience surrogate (代理) beyond the oppressed survivor or the criminal one with whom a viewer would indeed want to identify.

The film's peaceful and timeless religious opening is immediately juxtaposed with the wartime chaos of a train where Jews were to be herded into the ghetto[2]. A hand lights a Sabbath (安息日，主日) candle, in color, as we hear the prayer in Hebrew (希伯来文). This image of continuity provides the frame of *Schindler's List*—survival, ritual, celebration. The candle burns, suggesting the passage of time, and the smoke end becomes the smoke from a train: the film turns into black-and-white. Color—connected to continuity—is then suppressed until the war is over. It will recur briefly at three privileged moments of the narrative: Schindler witnesses the brutal liquidation (清洗) of the a camp from a hill top and sees a little Jewish girl whose red coat is the only dot of color in a black-and-white image. She managed to hide in an abandoned ghetto apartment. But a few sequences later, her red coat will be visible atop a pile of corpses. If she represents the glimmer of hope that might still exist in childhood innocence, it disappears amid the war's horrors. Toward the end, only after Schindler suggests to a rabbi[3] in his factory that he prepare for the Sabbath, does color return for a moment in the lighting of candles.

Schindler's List now bids fair (有希望) to become the Holocaust's master narrative. In this context, it has been questioned whether public comprehension of Shoah should be culled from a commercial entertainment about the conversion of a womanizing petty Nazi entrepreneur into a righteous man—and one who only rescued a paltry number of Jews[4]. *Schindler's List* invites us to identify less with the victimized Jews (a given in most Holocaust films) than with an almost inexplicable heroism.

The divergent cultural conditions and mentalites of four major nations affected each's reception of *Schindler's List*. The film's enthusiastic American welcome was the culmination (顶点，高潮) of mounting (凭吊) interest in the Holocaust over the past two decades. Increased visits to European Holocaust locales and involvement with their preservation has been paralleled by the extensive construction of "virtual" Holocaust sites in United States memorials and museums.

Schindler's List's substantial German success was ascribed to (归因于) its fortuitous (偶然的) arrival at a time when the country was particularly preoccupied with mourning and atonement (赎罪) for the ruinous (毁灭性的) Nazi past. Schindler's status as "good German" offered heady (兴奋的) possibilities for identification.

In France, the left had already rated *Shoah*[5] as the most authoritative film text on the subject to date (迄今为止). In the prevailing artistic and political context, *Schindler's List* was often savaged as the vacuous (空洞的) endeavor (努力，尽力) of a Hollywood lightweight (无足轻重)to create facile (易做到的) closure (结论) where none could (or should) exist.

Surprisingly enough, *Schindler's List* also met with abundant disapproval in Israel. Vindication (证明) of the survivors, together with renewed interest in pre-war European Jewish life engendered (产生) intense feelings of Hebraic proprietorship (所有权) of the Holocaust: Israel had come to believe that it owned *Shoah*. From this perspective it was inevitable that *Schindler's List* should be rated a kitsch-ridden (充斥着粗劣作品的) bathetic (假装感伤的) catastrophe, its director deemed a crass interloper (闯入者) who was bent on (下决心) hijacking (劫持) the Holocaust to the United States—for Israel, a perennial (常在的，四季不断的) source of sustenance and suspicion—and to his own immense gain. It seems that Spielberg [6]needs the Holocaust, but the Holocaust does not need Spielberg.

After reading questions

1. In paragraph 1, it implies that *Schindler's List* is different from previous Holocaust films in that:

A. Other Holocaust films are produced by European countries while *Schindler's List* is produced by America.

B. Other holocaust films mainly describe the stories of either the victims or the Nazi killers of Holocaust while *Schindler's List* centered beyond their stories.

C. Other Holocaust films tend to polarize the moral characters while *Schindler's List* centered on a character neither too evil nor too benevolent.

D. the characteristics of the people in other Holocaust films are comparatively simpler than that of *Schindler's List*.

2. The most significant visual effect of *Schindler's List* is its switch from color to black-and-white. Which of the following statements is TRUE of the three privileged moments of the narrative?

   A. The three privileged moments are all presented in color.
   B. The three moments are all related to religions.
   C. The three moments are all about a little Jewish girl.
   D. A hand lights a Sabbath candle is in one of the three moments.

3. According to the author, why did *Schindler's List* receive enthusiastic welcome in America?

   A. Because Americans have possessed mourning interest in the Holocaust for almost twenty years.
   B. Because an increased number of Americans go to visit Holocaust locales.
   C. Because some "virtual" Holocaust sites were constructed in America.
   D. Because Americans have been involved with the preservation of the Holocaust evidence.

4. Which of the following statements is true according to the last three paragraphs?

   A. Germans dislike *Schindler's List* because it portrays the ruinous Nazi past.
   B. Some Frenchmen believe that Shoah, a classic Holocaust movie produced by France, is better than *Schindler's List*.
   C. Israel shows abundant disapproval against *Schindler's List* because they take it as a vindication of the survivors.
   D. In France, the left had rated *Schindler's List* as a kitsch-ridden bathetic catastrophe.

Notes

1. **Schindler's List** is a 1993 epic drama film directed and co-produced by Steven Spielberg. The film tells the story of Oskar Schindler, a German businessman who saved the lives of more than a thousand mostly Polish-Jewish refugees during the Holocaust by employing them in his factories. 《辛德勒的名单》，第66届奥斯卡最佳影片，根据澳大利亚小说家托马斯·科内雅雷斯所著的《辛德勒

名单》改编而成，真实的再现了德国企业家奥斯卡·辛德勒在第二次世界大战期间保护1200名犹太人免遭法西斯杀害的，真实的历史事件。

2. *ghetto:* the term was originally referred to a cluster of homes and buildings often outside Italian city walls, to describe the area where Jews, trades people or agricultural workers were compelled to live. During World War II, ghettos in occupied Europe were established by the Nazis to confine Jews into tightly packed areas of the cities of Eastern Europe, turning them into concentration camps and death camps in the Holocaust. 历史上是指在意大利城外建立的由犹太人、商人或农业人口聚居地区域。又被称为隔都。在二战语境下，欧洲被占领地区的隔都成为犹太人被法西斯暴政所管制的地区，这里生活资源极度匮乏，条件极为恶劣。很多隔都甚至成为另一形式的犹太人集中营和死亡营。

3. *rabbi* is a teacher of Torah. This title derives from the Hebrewword, meaning "My Master."
   犹太人所称的拉比，指师长或对犹太教学识渊博的人的尊称。

4. In this context, it has been questioned whether public comprehension of Shoah should be culled from a commercial entertainment about the conversion of a womanizing petty Nazi entrepreneur into a righteous man—and one who only rescued a *paltry* number of Jews.
   译文：在这种背景下，有人质疑公众对于大屠杀的理解会不会被商业娱乐所简化？影片描述了一个小气的好女色的纳粹商人转化为正直的人，而他仅仅拯救了很少一部分犹太人。

5. Shoah is a 1985 French documentary film directed by Claude Lanzmann about the Holocaust (also known as the Shoah). The film primarily consists of interviews and visits to key Holocaust sites.
   《浩劫》是一部长达九个半小时，以二战期间纳粹对犹太人大屠杀为背景的纪录片。是法国导演克劳德·朗兹曼花费11年，寻访当年事件发生地以及大屠杀亲历者拍摄而成的。全片充满了主人公痛苦的细节回忆和类似证人指证犯罪现场一样的故地重游，但朗兹曼的最终目的不是指控和问责，它更像一场对受难者的凝重丧礼，也像为了让幸存者解脱沉痛而进行的精神治疗。

6. Steven Spielberg is an American film director, screenwriter, produce and studio entrepreneur. In a career of more than four decades, Spielberg's films have covered many themes and genres. He is honored as "Movie Brads", together with Francis Ford Coppola, Martin Scorsese and George Lucas, who have led the trend of Post-classical Hollywood Films.
   史蒂芬·斯皮尔伯格，美国著名电影导演、编剧、制片和企业家。曾导演多种题材和类型影片。与弗朗西斯·福特·科波拉，马丁·斯克塞斯和乔治·卢卡斯并称为好莱坞的"电影小子"，引领后经典好莱坞时代的电影风向。

Unit 3 Holocaust Movies 大屠杀影片

Part 4 Exercises

I. Answer questions after listening to the dialogues taken from the film.

1. According to the talk between Mrs. and Mr. Schindler, what attitude does Schindler have on war?
2. Why is Schindler so angry with Stern?
3. What do Schindler and Stern think about Goethe?

Script

Scenario 1: *Schindler and his wife are sitting at the table, looking at each other and laughing. Schindler picks up a glass of wine and drinks it.*

MRS. SCHINDLER: It's not a charade (伪装；充场面), all this?

SCHINDLER: A charade? How could it be a charade? [*Schindler puts the drink down.*]

MRS. SCHINDLER: The clothes, the car, the apartment...

SCHINDLER: Wait a minute. [*Schindler supports his chin by his hand, still looking at his wife.*] Take a guess how many people are on my payroll?

MRS. SCHINDLER: Oskar.

SCHINDLER: My father, at the height of his success, had 50. I've got 350. 350 workers on the factory floor, with one purpose.

MRS. SCHINDLER: To make pots and pans?

SCHINDLER: To make money. For me. [*Mrs. Schindler turns round and feels bit boredom*]. Does anyone ask about me?

MRS. SCHINDLER: Back home? Everybody. All the time.

SCHINDLER: Eh-hum. They won't soon forget the name Schindler here, I can tell you that. "Oskar Schindler?" They'll say, "Everybody remembers him. He did something extraordinary. He did something no one else did. He came here with nothing...a suitcase...and built a bankrupt company into a major manufactory. And left with a steamer trunk, two steamer trunks full of money...all the riches of the world."

MRS. SCHINDLER: [*Mrs. Schindler reaches out a hand to fondle Schindler's face.*] It's comforting to see that nothing is changed. [*Schindler holds Mrs. Schindler's hand.*]

SCHINDLER: You are wrong, Emily. There is no way I could have known this before but there was always something missing. In every business I tried, I can see now, it wasn't me that failed. Something was missing. Even if I'd known what it was, there's nothing I could have done about it because you can't create this thing. And it makes all the difference in the world between success and failure.

MRS. SCHINDLER: Luck?

SCHINDLER: [*Schindler kisses the hand he is holding.*] War.

Scenario 2: *A Jewish girl asks Schindler to help her parents to get away from the camp. However, Schindler refuses her request angrily* [*Schindler dashes through the door of Stern's office. He walks to Stern.*]

SCHINDLER: People die. It's a fact of life. He wants to kill everybody? Great! What am I supposed to do about it? Bring everybody over? [*Schindler walks away from Stern.*] Is that what you think? Send them over to Schindler. Send them all. His place is a heaven. Didn't you know? It's not a factory. It's not an enterprise of any kind. It's a heaven for rabbis and orphans and people with no skills, whatsoever! You think I don't know what you're doing? You are so quiet all the time. I know! I know! [*Schindler walks to and fro in the office.*]

STERN: Are you losing money?

SCHINDLER: No, I'm not losing money. That's not the point.

STERN: What other point is...

SCHINDLER: It's dangerous! [*Schindler approaches the desk and put his hand on it.*] It's dangerous to me, personally! You have to understand. Goethe (电影中的纳粹军官，掌管所在地的犹太人) is under enormous pressure. You have to think of it in his situation. [*Schindler pulls a chair and sits down, facing Stern.*] He's got this whole place to run. He's responsible for everything goes on here, all these people. He's got a lot of things to worry about. And he's got the war which brings out the worst in people. Never the good, always the bad. Always the bad. But in normal circumstances he wouldn't be like this. He'd be all right. There'd just be the good aspects of which...hum hum...he's a wonderful crook (骗子；恶棍). A man who loves good food, good wine, the ladies, making money...

STERN: And killing.

SCHINDLER: [*Schindler stands up and then walks across Stern.*] He can't enjoy it.

STERN: Bejski (一个犹太人) told me the other day, somebody escaped from a work detail outside the wire. Goethe lined up everybody from the missing man's barracks (营房). He shot the man to the left of Bejski,

Unit 3 Holocaust Movies 大屠杀影片

the man to the right of him. He walked down the line shooting every other man with a pistol (手枪). Twenty-five.

SCHINDLER: What do you want me to do about it? [*Schindler opens his arms.*]

STERN: Nothing. Nothing. We're just talking. [*Shrugs*].

II. Fill the blanks with the missing words or phrases after listening to the lines taken from the film.

1. [*Schindler, the Gestapo clerk and one of the arresting officers cross the foyer.*]

GESTAPO CLERK: I'd advise you not to get too (1)_____. (2)_____, law prevails. No matter whom your friends are.

[*Schindler ignores the man completely. Reaching the front doors, the clerk turns over the D.E.F. records to their owner and offers his hand. Schindler lets it hang there.*]

SCHINDLER: You expect me to walk home, or what?

GESTAPO CLERK: [tightly] (3)_____ for Mr. Schindler.

2. **HUJAR:** She says the foundation was poured wrong, she's got to (4)_____. I told her it's a barracks, not a fucking hotel, fucking Jew engineer.

[*Goethe watches the woman moving around the shell of the building, pointing, directing, Telling the workers to take it all down. He goes to take a closer look. She comes over.*]

ENGINEER: The entire foundation has to be dug up and repoured. If it isn't, the things will (5)_____ before it's even completed.

[*Goethe considers the foundation as if he knew about such things. He nods pensively. Then turns to Hujar.*]

GOETH: [*calmly*] Shoot her.

3. **GOETHE:** You know, I look at you. I watch you, and you're never drunk. Oh, that's... that's real control. Control is power. That's power. Is that why they fear us? We have the fucking power to kill, that's why they fear us. They fear us because we have (6)_____. A man (7)_____, he should know better. We have him killed, and feel good about it. Or we kill him ourselves and we feel even better.

SCHINDLER: That's not power, though. That's justice. It's different than power. Power is when we have every (8)_____ to kill, and we don't.

GOETHE: You think that's power?

SCHINDLER: That's what the emperors had. A man stole something; he's (9)_____ before the emperor. He throws himself down on the ground, he begs for mercy. He knows he's going to die. And the emperor... pardons him. This (10)_____ man, he lets him go.

GOETHE: I think you are drunk.

SCHINDLER: That's power, Amon.

III. Complete the following memorable lines by translating the Chinese into English.

1. Once the war ends, forget it, but for now, it's great, _____ (你可以赚一大笔钱). Don't you think?

2. I want to thank you, sir, _____ (因为你给了我工作的机会).

3. Forget you got to build it all, getting the fucking permits _____ (那足以让你疯狂). Then the engineers show up. They stand around and they argue about drainage?

4. They trundled their belongings into the city. They settled. They took hold. They prospered in business, science, education, the arts. _____ (他们空手而来，他们无本发财).

IV. Oral practices—answer the following question.

1. What's the effect of the black and white frames in the movie in your opinion?

2. Why doesn't Goethe admit his love for Helen?

Part 5 More Holocaust Movies

Plot Summary of *The Pianist*

In September 1939, Wladyslaw Szpilman, a Polish-Jewish pianist, has his radio station rocked from German bombing with Nazi Germany's invasion of Poland and the subsequent outbreak of World War II. Hoping for a quick victory, Szpilman rejoices with family at home when learning that Britain and France have declared war on Germany, but the German army defeats Poland and captures Warsaw. Living conditions for the Jews deteriorate, as they are allowed a limited amount of money and later must wear armbands with the Star of David. By November 1940, they are forced into horrid and humiliating conditions in the Warsaw Ghetto, where Szpilman's family—including his father and mother —witness how the SS raid an opposite apartment and kill everyone there. Soon the family are rounded up for deportation to Treblinka extermination camp, but Szpilman is saved by a friend in the Jewish Ghetto Police.

Szpilman becomes a slave labourer working on the "Aryan" side, where he survives a random mass execution. Szpilman learns of a coming Jewish revolt and helps by smuggling weapons into the ghetto, narrowly avoiding a suspicious guard. He then manages to escape and goes into hiding with help from a non-Jewish friend Andrzej Bogucki and his wife Janina. In April 1943, Szpilman observes the rise and fall of the Warsaw Ghetto Uprising from his window near the ghetto wall. A year goes by and Szpilman is forced to flee after a neighbor discovers him. In a second hiding place provided to him, he is shown into a room with a piano but forced to keep quiet, and suffers jaundice.

In August 1944, Polish resistance mounts the Warsaw Uprising, attacking a German building across the street from Szpilman's hideout. A tank shells his apartment and he is forced to flee and hide elsewhere as fighting rages around. Over the course of the next months the city is destroyed and emptied of the population and Szpilman, entirely alone, searches desperately for shelter and supplies among the ruins. Eventually, he is discovered by the Wehrmacht officer Wilm Hosenfeld, who learns that Szpilman is a pianist and asks him to play on the grand piano nearby. The decrepit Szpilman plays Ballade in G minor, which moves Hosenfeld, who then allows Szpilman to hide in the attic of an empty house and regularly brings him food. As the Germans are forced to retreat due to the advance of the Red Army in January 1945, Hosenfeld meets Szpilman for the last time and promises to listen to him on Polish Radio. He gives Szpilman his greatcoat to keep warm and leaves, which is almost fatal for Szpilman when he is shot at by Polish troops liberating Warsaw, who apprehend him and realize he is Polish.

Elsewhere, former inmates of a Nazi concentration camp pass a Soviet prisoner-of-war camp for captured German soldiers and hurl abuse at them. Hosenfeld, now a prisoner, asks one of them, the violinist Zygmunt Lednicki, if he knows Szpilman, which the violinist confirms. Lednicki visits Szpilman and takes him to the site, but the POW enclosure has vanished. Later, Szpilman performs Chopin's Grand Polonaise brillante to a large and prestigious audience.

The epilogue states that Szpilman died at the age of 88 in 2000, while Hosenfeld died in Soviet captivity in 1952.

Memorable lines in the film

Settings: Szpilman met a German Captain in his shelter. He provided Szpilman with some food and clothes.

Wladyslaw Szpilman: I don't know how to thank you.

Captain Wilm Hosenfeld: Thank God, not me. He wants us to survive. Well, that's what we have to believe.

我不知该如何感谢你。

感谢上帝，不要感谢我，感谢上帝，他让我们活下来。这是我们应该抱有的信念。

Plot Summary of *Life Is Beautiful*

In the 1930s Italy, Guido Orefice (Benigni) is a funny and charismatic young man looking for work in a city. He falls in love with a local school teacher, Dora (portrayed by Benigni's actual wife Nicoletta Braschi), who is to be engaged to a rich but arrogant civil servant. Guido engineers further meetings with her, seizing on coincidental incidents to declare his affection for her, and finally wins her over. He steals her from her engagement party on a horse, humiliating her fiancé and mother. Soon they are married and have a son, Giosuè (Giorgio Cantarini).

Through the first part, the movie depicts the changing political climate in Italy: Guido frequently imitates Nazi party members, skewering their racist logic and pseudoscientific reasoning (at one point, jumping onto a table to demonstrate his "perfect Aryan bellybutton"). However, the growing racist wave is also evident: the horse Guido steals Dora away on has been painted green and covered in antisemitic insults.

In 1945, after Dora and her mother (Marisa Paredes) are reconciled, Guido, his Uncle Eliseo and Giosuè are seized on Giosuè's birthday, forced onto a train and taken to a concentration camp. Despite being a non-Jew, Dora demands to be on the same train to join her family. In the camp, Guido hides their true situation from his son, convincing him that the camp is a complicated game in which Giosuè must perform the tasks Guido gives him, earning him points; the first team to reach one thousand points will win a tank. He tells him that if he cries, complains that he wants his mother, or says that he is hungry, he will lose points, while quiet boys who hide from the camp guards earn extra points.

Guido uses this game to explain features of the concentration camp that would otherwise be scary for a young child: the guards are mean only because they want the tank for themselves; the dwindling numbers of children (who are being killed by the camp guards) are only hiding in order to score more points than Giosuè so they can win the game. He puts off Giosuè's requests to end the game and return home by convincing him that they are in the lead for the tank, and need only wait a short while before they can return home with their tank. Despite being surrounded by the misery, sickness and death at the camp, Giosuè does not question this fiction because of his father's convincing performance and his own innocence.

Guido maintains this story right until the end when, in the chaos of shutting down the camp as the Americans approach, he tells his son to stay in a sweatbox until everybody has left, this being the final competition before the tank is his. Guido tries to find Dora, but is caught and executed by a Nazi soldier. As he is marched off to be executed, he maintains the fiction of the game by deliberately marching in an exaggerated goose-step.

The next morning, Giosuè emerges from the sweatbox as the camp is occupied by an American armored division. They let him ride in the tank until, later that day, he sees Dora in the crowd of people streaming out of the camp. In the film, Giosuè is four and a half years old; however, both the beginning and ending of the film are narrated by an older Giosuè recalling his father's story of sacrifice for his family.

Memorable lines in the film

Settings: *The hatred against Jews was spreading, and the windows of some shops were painted with some insulting words against Jews.*

Giosuè：No dogs or Jews?

Guido：Some store owners just don't like certain things. what don't you like?

Giosuè：Spiders.

Guido：And I don't like Visigoths. Tomorrow we'll put up a sign in the store window saying, No spiders or Visigoths.

狗和犹太人不得入内？有些店主特别不喜欢某种东西。你不喜欢什么？蜘蛛。我不喜欢西哥特人，明天我们就在书店玻璃上写蜘蛛和西哥特人不许入内。

Settings: *Guido and his son Giosuè were driven to aboard a train which takes them to a concentration camp.*

Guido: [*being shipped to a concentration camp*] You've never ridden on a train, have you? They're fantastic! Everybody stands up, close together, and there are no seats!

Giosuè: There aren't any seats?

Guido: Seats? On a train? It's obvious you've never ridden one before! No, everybody's packed in, standing up. Look at this line to get on! Hey, we've got tickets, save room for us!

你从没坐过火车吧！火车很好玩，每个人都挤挤挨挨地站着，还没有座位！没有座位么？在火车上有座位？看来你是没乘过火车。每个人都挤进来，站着。沿着这条线上车，看我们有票，让一让！

UNIT 4

Animations 动画影片

Part 1 Chinese Summary

好莱坞的动画影片

美式动画电影以迪斯尼公司为龙头老大，还包括华纳、梦工厂、福克斯、哥伦比亚等公司，经过几十年的运作，形成了一套成熟的制作发行模式。总体而言，美国动画的商业性、娱乐性总是第一位的，讲求老少咸宜，技术总是大于思想。美国动画片的叙事策略是：动用全人类的财富，在世界各地挖掘素材，寻找"原型"，并且大胆地加以改造，融入自己的主流意识。"原型"所代表的往往是一种普遍的人生经验和历史经验，这种经验有的具有文化差异，更多的却是跨国界、跨时代、跨文化的。用原型来叙事的好处在于一个形象能发出千万人的声音，唤起大众的认同感。美国动画片在这些"原型"的基础上大胆地加以现代性的改造，巧妙地融入美国的现代思想和理念。诸如钟爱自由、重视个体价值、表现人间亲情、重视环境保护，以及人与自然共生共荣等是相当美国化的，但在最广泛的程度上又能得到世界观众的普遍认可。在这种观念的主导下，美国动画电影主题上总是较为浅显的，表达的是友谊、爱情、正义战胜邪恶、个人英雄主义、冒险、寻宝等与人类生存困境关系不很密切的主题。在叙事上一般都是采用单线结构，故事的发生、发展、高潮和结局总是非常明确的。在人物形象的刻画上一般以正邪分明、脸谱化的扁平人物为多，具有个人英雄主义和冒险精神的美国化了的非凡人物总是影片永恒的主角。在文化方面极力彰显美国熔炉文化的海纳百川，有容乃大的雄心和气魄，广泛采用世界各国特别是欧洲、阿拉伯和中国的童话、神化、民间传说和名著故事进行改编，用美国人的价值观对故事进行重新改装。尽管这些具有非凡影响的动画片在故事原产地的人看来已经被改造的荒诞不经，但是在后现代社会改写和重构经典的大的语境下，却在世界范围内取得了商业上的巨大成功。美国动画作为工业化生产线上出来的模式化的产品，大多数已经很难看到导演的个性，如同在大商场里琳琅满目但非常雷同的商品一样，他们只有一个共同的标签——"美国造"。

《辛普森一家大电影》*The Simpsons Movie*（2007）在《辛普森一家大电影》中，美国人的乐观主义不再简单表现为温和与轻松的普通幽默，而是更多地呈现为从残忍、痛苦中寻求乐趣的病态的、荒诞的幽默，即黑色幽默。其中暗示价值观念的贬值或丧失，并表达对社会问题的看法。该影片创下惊人票房，正是因为它迎合了美国人对充满黑暗、丑恶和不公正的社会现实感到忧虑和失望，却又要在幽默与讽刺中获得某种精神慰藉的复杂心理。

《超人总动员》The Incredibles（2004）从某种意义上说超人总动员是对美国中产阶级家庭的戏仿。处于中年危机困惑萎靡的父亲和强势能干的母亲的强烈对比，使得该片从上映伊始便锁定其主要受众为成年人。皮克斯（一家专门制作电脑动画的公司）的动画角色在面对难题和挑战的时候，不再像传统动画角色那样依赖仙女或魔法等外在的神奇力量去解决问题，而是转向开发自己的智慧、提升自己的技能，来谋求最后的胜利。这反映出皮克斯动画电影进取而务实、脚踏实地的人生观，并且使其部分影片具有了励志的审美内涵。

《机器人瓦力》Wall-E（2008）公元2805年，人类文明高度发展，却因污染和生活垃圾大量增加使得地球不再适于人类居住。机器人WALL-E负责对地球垃圾进行清理。该片秉承了皮克斯动画片的一贯套路：主人公是被孩子或社会抛弃抑或边缘化的角色，如玩具总动员中的Barn以及本片的机器人Wall-E等。别具一格的是，影片的情节推进几乎都是靠机器人之间的动作和表情进行的，语言似乎成了影片的附属品。这也凸现了皮克斯公司具备的精准而又颇具创意的动画表现力。由非生命物体占据动画片主角的经典作品就是皮克斯公司于1987年制作的首部动画短片《顽皮的跳灯》Luxo Jr.（1987）。如今，这盏台灯已经成为皮克斯的片头标志。

Animated Films

Animation, in the first instance, might seem to be **self-evident** texts made purely to entertain, and not to carry significant meaning about art and society. Further, as a film language and film art, animation is a more sophisticated and flexible medium than **live-action film**[1], and thus offers a greater opportunity for film-makers to be more imaginative and less **conservative**. The animated film enables the film-maker(s) to be more expressive and thus more **subversive** than is readily acknowledged. Almost **consciously**, animators, in being aware that they, and their works, are **marginalized** and/or **consigned to** innocent, inappropriate or accidental audiences, use this apparently unguarded space to create film with surface pleasures and hidden depths. **In Blackboard Jungle**[2], the cartoon carries with it the idea that appearance and identity is a relative and constantly changing thing—a key element in all cartoons, while *Sullivan's Travels*[3] uses the very **anarchy** and comic extremism of the cartoon to subvert the idea of representing the reality of the Depression in a film.

Disney animators believe that they do move beyond traditional modes of realist representation in their work, and maintain a **hyper-realism** which is neither a completely accurate version of the real world nor a **radical vindication** of the animated form. This may be defined as second-order realism, where every object and environment, though recognizably 'real', precise in its construction, and logical in the **execution** of its own laws, becomes essentially over-determined, moving into a realism which is simultaneously realistic but beyond the **orthodoxies** of realism. It may be argued, therefore, that the mode of realism in animation could be understood as **over-illusionism**. On the other hand, Disney's increasingly industrialized organization was an ironic **counterpoint** to **the folk sensibility** and **rural nostalgia** of its narrative content[4].

The dominance of the Disney brand enabled its competitors, the **Fleischer Brothers**[5], Warner Bros, MGM, and **UPA**[6], to differentiate their product through subversive techniques like **caricature**, irony, and satire.

After-reading questions

1. Which of the following characteristics belongs to the animators?
    A. Conservative.
    B. Serious.
    C. Expressive.
    D. Innocent.
2. Why it is said that animation enjoys an apparently unguarded space to create arts?
    A. Because no one is going to examine them.
    B. Because no one is going to attack them for their creativity.
    C. Because no one is supervising the animators as long as they are politically right.
    D. Because this belongs to the marginal areas.
3. Why were the two films *Blackboard Jungle* and *Sullivan's Travels* mentioned?
    A. To illustrate the point that cartoons have pleasant surface but hidden depth.
    B. To introduce two movies that have make a good use of cartoons for better illumination.
    C. To give two examples that use cartoons to reach the effect of hyper-realism.
    D. To prove that cartoons are indispensable factors for imaginative works.
4. Which of the following best describes the definition of hyper-realism?
    A: A completely accurate version of the real world.
    B. A radical vindication of the animated form.
    C. Every object and environment that are recognized as real.
    D. A realism which is simultaneously realistic but beyond the orthodoxies of realism.

Words and expressions

1. **self-evident** *adj.* obvious, needing no proof or explanation 不证自明的；不言而喻的
2. **conservative** *adj.* unwilling to accept changes and new ideas 保守的
3. **consciously** *adv.* deliberately 故意地

4. **marginalized** *adj.* being relegated to a lower or outer edge, as of specific groups of people 被排斥的，被忽视的，被边缘化的

5. **be consigned to** be intentionally put to an unpleasant situation or place 被弃置（于某地或某种境地）

6. **anarchy** *n.* the state that nobody seems to be paying any attention to rules or laws 无政府状态

7. **hyper-realism** 超现实主义。超现实主义电影于1920年兴起于法国，主要是将意象做特异、不合逻辑的安排，以表现潜意识的种种状态。

8. **radical** *adj.* very important or great in degree 重大的

9. **vindication** *n.* an action, decision or idea that is proved to be correct 证明正确

10. **execution** *n.* the action of carrying out a plan 执行

11. **orthodoxy** *n.* an accepted view about something 正统观念

12. **over-illusionism** *n.* 过度错觉艺术形式

13. **counterpoint** *n.* the differences when compared 对立之物

14. **folk sensibility** 民间情感

15. **rural nostalgia** 乡村怀旧

16. **caricature** *n.* a drawing or description of persons that exaggerates their appearance or behavior in a humorous or critical way 漫画

● **Notes**

1. live-action film 真人电影，实景电影，与卡通电影相对应

2. the cartoon in Blackboard Jungle.
   Blackboard Jungle（1955）美国第一部反映校园暴力的影片，影片中有一小段配有摇滚音乐的卡通短片，据称是由Fleischer Studio所创作。

3. *Sullivan's Travels*（1941）美国喜剧片。讲述一位喜剧导演为了拍摄社会问题剧而化妆成乞丐深入民间的故事。其中一个片断是黑人在社区教堂中观看卡通片。

4. On the other hand, Disney's increasingly industrialized organization was an ironic counterpoint to the folk sensibility and rural nostalgia of its narrative content.
   译文：另一方面，迪斯尼动画在组织管理上的日趋工业化与其动画片在叙事中所体现的民间和怀旧情怀形成讽刺性对照。

5. Fleischer Brothers, or Fleischer Studios, Unlike other studios, whose most famous characters were anthropomorphic animals, the Fleischers' were humans, like superman and Popeye the Sailor. Fleischer的动画片角色不像其他动画片公司，是具有人或神性的动物。Fleischer动画片的主角大多数是人类。诸如超人和大力水手。

6. UPA (United Productions of America) UPA had a significant impact on animation style, content, and technique, and its innovations were recognized and

adopted by the other major animation studios and independent filmmakers all over the world. UPA pioneered the technique of limited animation, and though this style of animation came to be widely abused during the 1960s and 1970s as a cost-cutting measure, it was originally intended as a stylistic alternative to the growing trend (particularly at Disney) of recreating cinematic realism in animated films. UPA为世界上其他主要动画工作室及独立影片制作公司所广泛认可。UPA在动画风格、内容及技术方面具有深远影响。UPA在有限动画技术上成为先驱，该技术在20世纪六七十年代为削减制作成本而被广泛应用。这种手法与以迪斯尼为代表的风靡一时的再现电影现实性的风格形成对照。

Part 3 Text 2

The Simpsons Movie[1]

What *The Simpsons* most fundamentally suggest about is the political life in the United States. The show broaches (提出) the question of politics through the question of the family, and this in itself is a political statement. By dealing centrally with the family, *The Simpsons* takes up real human issues everybody can recognize and thus ends up in many respects less "cartoonish" than other animations. Its cartoon characters are more human, more fully rounded, than the supposedly real human beings in many situation comedies. Above all, the show has created a believable human community: Springfield, USA. *The Simpsons* shows the family as part of a larger community and in effect affirms (肯定，断言) the kind of community that can sustain the family. That is at one and the same time the secret of the show's popularity with the American public and the most interesting political statement it has to make.

The Simpsons was by no means unique in its reaffirmation (重申，再断言) of the value of the nuclear family[2]. Several other shows took the same path in the past decade, reflecting larger social and political trends in society, in particular the reassertion of family values that has by now been adopted as a program by both political parties in the United States. *The Simpsons* is in many respects the most interesting example of this return to the nuclear family. Though it strikes many people as trying to subvert the American family or to undermine its authority, in fact, it reminds us that antiauthoritarianism (反权力主义) is itself an American tradition and that family authority has always been problematic in democratic America. What makes *The*

Simpsons so interesting is the way it combines traditionalism with antitraditionalism. It continually makes fun of the traditional American family. But it continually offers an enduring image of the nuclear family in the very act of satirizing it. Many of the traditional values of the American family survive this satire (讽刺), above all the value of the nuclear family itself.

The Simpsons has indeed found its own odd way to defend the nuclear family. In effect, the shows says, "Take the worse-case scenario—*The Simpsons*—and even that family is better than no family." In fact, the Simpson family is not all that bad. Some people are appalled (惊骇的) at the idea of young boys imitating Bart[3], in particular his disrespect for authority and especially for his teachers. These critics of *The Simpsons* forget that Bart's rebelliousness (叛逆性) conforms (与……一致) to a venerable (值得尊敬的) American archetype (原型) and that this country was founded on disrespect for authority and an act of rebellion. Bart is an American icon (偶像，形象), an updated version of Tom Sawyer and Huck Finn[4] rolled into one. For all his troublemaking—precisely because of his troublemaking—Bart behaves just the way a young boy is supposed to in American mythology (神化), from Dennis the Menace[5] comics to the Our Gang comedies[6].

As for the mother and daughter in *The Simpsons*, Marge and Lisa are not bad role models at all. Marge Simpson is very much the devoted mother and housekeeper; she also often displays a feminist streak (倾向). Indeed, she is very modern in her attempts to combine certain feminist impulses with the traditional role of a mother. Lisa is in many ways the ideal child in contemporary terms. She is an overachiever (成绩超出预料的学生) in school, and as a feminist, a vegetarian, and an environmentalist, she is politically correct across the spectrum (全方位的).

The real issue, then, is Homer. Many people have criticized *The Simpsons* for its portrayal of the father as dumb, uneducated, weak in character, and morally unprincipled. Homer is all those things, but at least he is there. He fulfills the bare minimum of a father: he is present for his wife and above all his children. To be sure, he lacks many of the qualities we would like to see in the ideal father. He is selfish, often putting his own interest above that of his family. Homer is undeniably crass (愚钝的), vulgar, and incapable of appreciating the finer things in life. He has a hard time sharing interests with Lisa, moreover, Homer gets angry easily and takes his anger out on his children, as in his many attempts to strangle (把……勒死) Bart.

In all these respects, Homer fails as a father. But upon reflection, it is surprising to realize how many decent qualities he has. First and foremost, he is attached to his own—he loves his family because it is his. Homer Simpson is devoted not to what is best but to what is his own. That position has its problems, but it does help explain how the seemingly dysfunctional (功能紊乱) Simpson family manages to function.

After reading questions

1. According to paragraph 1, why is *The Simpsons* different from other animations?
   A. because it has a political statement
   B. because it takes up real human issues
   C. because it portrays a typical US family
   D. because it caters to the adults tastes

2. What makes *The Simpsons* so interesting and special, according to the main ideas in Paragraph 2?
   A. It reminds people of the value of antiauthoritarianism.
   B. It satires the traditional American family.
   C. It offers an image of a family in the way of satire.
   D. It combines the traditional value of family with the antitraditional principles.

3. In paragraph 3, spot the common point of Bart with Tom Sawyer and Huck Finn.
   A. They are all cartoon figures.
   B. They are all rebellious to the authorities.
   C. They are all venerable American archetypes.
   D. They are all American icons.

4. As the hero of the satire animation, Homer is portrayed as a character with many shortcomings. Which of the following is NOT among those characters of Homer?
   A. dumb, uneducated, weak in character and morally unprincipled
   B. selfish and always put his own interests above others.
   C. crass and vulgar and able to understand the finer things in life
   D. fulfills the minimum requirement of a father

5. What makes the seemingly dysfunctional Simpson family manage to function?
   A. the American value of antiauthoritarianism reflected in Bart
   B. the morality model set by Marge and Lisa
   C. the self-consciousness of all the Simpsons
   D. the love and devotion sprung from even the most imperfect one

Notes

1. **The Simpsons Movie** (2007) American animated comedy film version of the animated television series *The Simpsons*. The film was directed by David Silverman and was produced by Fox. 辛普森一家大电影是根据美国家喻户晓的动画片辛普森一家拍摄而成的。该片由福克斯公司出品，David Silverman 导演。

2. **nuclear family** a family consisting parents and their children 与之相对的是 extended family: a family consisting the nuclear family and their blood relatives. 核心家庭是指父母和孩子构成的家庭。大家庭则除了核心家庭成员外还有其他亲属。

3. **Bart** is the son in *the Simpsons*. Rebellious as he is, he likes adventuring. Bart作为

辛普森家庭的长子，叛逆且爱冒险。

4. **Tom Sawyer and Huck Finn** Tom and Huck are the two main characters in the book *Tom Sawyer* written by Mark Twain. At the beginning of the novel Tom and Huck are very mischievous, bad, and overall rebellious to the common way of life. 汤姆索亚和哈克·费恩是马克吐温小说《汤姆索亚历险记》中的主要人物。他们调皮，顽劣，挑战传统。

5. **Dennis the Menace**: is a daily syndicated newspaper comic strip originally created, written and illustrated by Hank Ketcham. 淘气阿丹是由多家报纸同时发表的连环漫画。由Hank Ketcham创作。

6. **Gang comedies**：These are films that focus on gangs, life as a gang member, and the conflicts between rival street gangs. 帮派影片，以反映街头帮派生活为主的影片。

Part 4 Exercises

Answer questions after listening to the dialogues taken from the film.

1. Why does Lisa have a crush on Colin at the very first time meeting?
2. In scenario 2, how do the people in Springfield demonstrate their fury against Homer's irresponsible deeds?
3. By consoling her daughter in the crisis what good virtues are displayed by Marge?

Script

Scenario 1: *Lisa, a keen environmentalist, goes door by door to call the neighbors awareness of the polluted environment. However, no one takes the issue seriously. Just at that time she heard someone else talking about the environment.*

Colin: Are you aware that a leaky fauce can waste over...
Lisa: Two thousand gallons a year.
Colin: Turning off lights can save...
Lisa: Enough energy to power Pittsburgh.
Colin: And if we kept our thermostats at 68 in winter...
Lisa: We'd be free from our dependency on foreign oil in 17 years.
Colin: I'm Colin.
Lisa: I haven't seen you at school.
Colin: Moved from Ireland. My dad's a musician.
Lisa: Is he...?
Colin: He's not Bono.
Lisa: I just thought, because you're Irish and...
Colin: He's not Bono.

Lisa: Do you play?

Colin: Just piano, guitar, trumpet, drums and bass.

[*Lisa thinks: He's pure gold. For once in your life. Be cool.*]

Colin: So is your name as pretty as your face?

[*Lisa gets embarrassed and faints.*]

Colin: You okay there?

Scenario 2: *Homer and Marge are watching TV while suddenly the program shows the silo thrown into the lake by Homer.*

Kent Brocman: Good evening. this is Kent Brockman. Efforts to find out whose selfish crime caused our entrapment have been fruitless. Until moments ago! A shocking discovery has been made here at Lake Springfield.

Homer: That could be anybody's pig-crap silo.

Marge: Homer, it was you. You single-handedly killed this town.

Homer: l know. It's weird.

Kent Brockman: Just a reminder. this station does not endorse vigilante justice. Unless it gets results. Which it will.

[*Picture of Homer with the text "Get Him!" shows.*]

Marge: You didn't listen to me after l warned you.

Homer: Don't worry, nobody watches this stupid show. What's that ominous glow in the distance?

[*The mob with flaming torches goes against the family's house.*]

The mob: Kill! Kill! Kill!

Homer: Marge, look. Those idiots don't even know where we live.

[*The mob hear Homer and turns.*]

The mob: Kill! Kill! Kill! We want Homer! We want Homer!

[*Lisa comes to Homer and buts him in his stomach.*]

Lisa: You monster. You monster!

Homer: Did you see the news?

Marge: Honey, come on, we have bigger problems.

Lisa: But I'm so angry.

Marge: You're a woman. You can hold on to it forever.

Lisa: Okay.

Marge: Homer, you have to go out there, face that mob and apologize for what you did.

II. Fill the blanks with the missing words or phrases after listening to the lines taken from the film.

Marge: Bart, are you drinking whiskey?

Bart: I'm 1)_____.
Marge: Bart.
Bart: I promise, I'll stop tomorrow.
Marge: You'll stop 2)_____. You come back here, little man.
[*Bart drinks form the bottle and runs around the room.*]
Bart: I miss Flanders. There, I said it!
Marge: Where's your father?
Lisa: He went out. Let's quickly 3)_____ our lives while he's gone.
[*Homer is outside the door and the family opens the door when he can not remember the code.*]
Homer: Hey, guys? What's the secret knock, again? Look, I know I screwed up. This is big.
Marge: It's huge! We're homeless! Our friends wanna kill us! Before we can even stay in the same room with you I need to know what was 4)_____ your mind when you didn't listen to me and 5)_____ that silo in the lake?
[*Homer shows with his body that he did not know.*]
Marge: Homer!
Homer: I don't know what to tell you, Marge. I don't think about things. I respect people who do but I just try to make the days not hurt until I get to 6)_____ in next to you again.
Marge: Oh...
[*Maggie and Lisa are looking at Marge.*]
Marge: I mean, oh.
Homer: Look, I'm really sorry. But I'm more than just sorry I'm prepared with a 7)_____. I've always been afraid I'd screw up our lives so badly we'd need a 8)_____ plan. And that plan is right here!
[*Homer looks into his wallet and get a "Get Out Of Jail Free" and "Basketball Card" before he finds what he searching for and shows a poster from Alaska.*]
Homer: No. Nope. Bingo. Ta-da.
Lisa: Alaska?
Homer: Alaska. A place where you can't be too fat or too drunk. Where no one says things like: 9)_____.
Marge: I don't know, Homie.
Homer: I'm not saying it right. Look, the thing is, I can't start a new life alone. And I've really come to like you guys.
Marge: I just don't see it.
Homer: Marge, in every marriage, you get one chance to say: I need you to do this with me. And there's only one answer when somebody says that.

[*Homer holds out his hand and Marge grabs it with her hand.*]

Marge: Okay, Homie, I'm with you.

Homer: Thank you, my sweetheart.

III. Complete the following memorable lines by translating the Chinese into English.

1. **Marge:** (每周日去教堂有什么意义)_____when if someone we love has a genuine religious experience, we ignore it?.

2. **Bart:** This is the worst day of my life.
   Homer: (你截至目前最糟糕的一天。)_____.

3. **Lisa:** No! This lake is just one piece of trash away from a toxic nightmare. But l knew you wouldn't listen. (所以我擅自将取自湖中的水倒入了你们的喝水杯中。)
_____.

4. **Russ Cargill:** You know, sir, when you made me head of the EPA, (您任命一个全美最成功的人在全美最不成功的政府机构中任职。) _____.

5. **Marge:** Okay, here goes. Homer I've always stood up for you. When people point out your flaws l always say: Well,
   (有时你得站远点才能欣赏一件艺术品。)_____.

IV. Oral practices—answer the following questions

1. *The Simpsons movie* portrays a typical US family and reveals the typical problems in US. Can you point out what are those typical characteristics and problems?

2. The Simpson's Movie belongs to the genre of SATIRE ANIMATION. Can you point out the sarcastic arrows against the society of US?

Part 5 More Animations

Plot Summary of the Incredibles

"Supers"—humans gifted with superpowers—were once seen as heroes, but collateral damage from their various good deeds led the government to create a "Supers Relocation Program." Two Supers, have married and now have three children, Violet, Dash, and Jack-Jack in the suburbs of Metroville. Violet and Dash have innate superpowers, but the toddler Jack-Jack has yet to show any. Bob, stuck in a white-collar job at an insurance agency, reminisces of his former days as Mr. Incredible, and sneaks out on Wednesday nights with his Super friend, Lucius Best (a.k.a. Frozone) to fight street crime.

Unit 4 Animations 动画影片

One day, Bob loses his temper with his boss who refuses to help a mugging victim just outside the building, which results in Bob revealing his super strength and losing his job. While trying to figure out what to tell Helen, he finds a message from a woman named "Mirage", who asks for Mr. Incredible's help to stop a rogue robot on a distant island for a lucrative reward. Bob, claiming to Helen that he is going on a business trip, takes up Mirage's offer, and successfully defeats the powerful Omnidroid (v x8). On his return to Metroville, Bob spends his days working out and getting back into shape. He takes his super suit, torn in the battle with the Omnidroid, to Edna Mode, the fashion designer for the Supers, and asks her to repair it. She does so, and also insists on creating a new, better super suit for him. She refuses his request to add a cape, though, highlighting how this accessory has doomed several other Supers before him by getting caught on things.

Mirage soon contacts Bob with another job on the same island. On arriving, he finds the Omnidroid (v x9), rebuilt and reprogrammed to be stronger than before. While trapped by the robot, he meets its creator, the technology-savvy villain Syndrome. Bob recognizes him as a young fan, Buddy Pine, who as a teenager wanted to be Mr. Incredible's sidekick IncrediBoy but was turned down, due to Bob's preferring to work alone. Syndrome has vowed revenge for this shunning, and sets the Omnidroid to kill Bob. Bob fakes his death and hides from the robot, discovering the body of a former Super, Gazerbeam. His curiosity piqued, he breaks into Syndrome's base and finds a computer, which outlines Syndrome's obsessive work in tracking down former Supers to lure them into fighting the Omnidroid, and using the results of those fatal battles to improve each incarnation of the machine. Bob is relieved to discover that Helen and his children are not yet identified in Syndrome's database, and learns that a final design of the Omnidroid (v x10) will be launched toward Metroville, seemingly to destroy it.

Meanwhile, Helen has become suspicious of Bob having an affair. After discovering Bob's repaired super-suit, she talks to Edna and learns she created new suits for the entire Parr family, each outfitted with a tracking device. Helen triggers Bob's, identifying the remote island but inadvertently revealing Bob's presence to Syndrome's headquarters and causing him to be captured. Helen borrows a private jet from an old friend and travels to the island. Midway she learns that Violet and Dash have stowed away while leaving Jack-Jack at home with a babysitter. As they near the island, Syndrome shoots down the jet, but Helen and the children safely make it ashore. Though Helen rescues Bob and regroups with Violet and Dash as they outrun Syndrome's guards, they are soon captured by Syndrome, who identifies all of them as a family of Supers. With the Parrs contained, Syndrome explains that he will launch the newly perfected Omnidroid to Metroville, sending the city into chaos, upon which he will appear and, using a control band, "subdue" the robot and become the city's

hero. Syndrome launches the Omnidroid on a rocket and follows in his aircraft. After his departure, Violet escapes and helps to free the rest of the family, and with Mirage's help, they board a second rocket bound for the city.

In Metroville, the Omnidroid starts a path of destruction, and Syndrome enacts his plan, stopping the robot resulting in the people's cheers. The Omnidroid observes the remote-control band and fires it off Syndrome's arm, sending the villain scurrying away while the robot continues to wreck the city. The combined abilities of the Parrs and Lucius are able to best and destroy the robot, and the city welcomes them back as heroes. As they are driven back to their home, Helen anxiously calls the babysitter and learns that Syndrome has abducted Jack-Jack. When they arrive at home, Syndrome is taking the toddler to his jet, planning to raise the boy to fight against the Supers in the future. As Bob and Helen launch a rescue attempt, Jack-Jack reveals his powers of transformation and fire-creation, forcing Syndrome to drop him into Helen's waiting arms. Syndrome tries to escape, but due to Bob's intervening, his cape is caught in the suction of his aircraft's engine, which kills him. The ruined plane crashes into the Parrs' home, but Violet is able to protect the family from harm.

Sometime later, the Parrs have re-adjusted to normal life, but when a new villain, the Underminer, appears, the Parrs put on their masks, ready to battle the new foe.

Memorable lines in the film

Settings: *The private jet Helen piloted was attacked by Syndrome, but Violet failed to use her super power to protect it. Later when they found themselves alive Violet made an apology to Helen. Appreciating what Violet had did, Helen is trying to encourage her.*

HELEN (ELASTIGIRL): Shh. It isn't your fault. It wasn't fair for me to suddenly ask so much of you. But things are different now. And doubt is a luxury we can't afford anymore, sweetie. You have more power than you realize. Don't think. And don't worry. If the time comes, you'll know what to do. It's in your blood.

嘘……这不是你的错。我一下子要求你做那么多是不公平的。不过宝贝，这会儿我们不能对自己和对方有任何怀疑。你比你自己想象的要强大。不用担心，时机成熟你就会知道该怎样做，这个能力你与生俱来。

Settings: *Syndrome caught all the Parrs and confessed to them his ultimate evil intentions to ruin the whole city and civilization.*

SYNDROME: Oh, I'm real. Real enough to defeat you! And I did it without your precious gifts, your oh-so-special powers. I'll give them heroics. I'll give them the most spectacular heroics anyone's ever seen! And when I'm old and I've had my fun, I'll sell my inventions so that everyone can be superheroes. Everyone can be super. And when everyone's super...no one will be.

我是真实的，真实到可以打败你。我没有你天生的超能力也可以打败你。我会给人们未尝见识过的了不起的英雄气概。我老了以后会向人们出售我的发明并以此为乐。我要让人人都能成为超人，等到人人都是超人了，哼……也就没人有"超"能力了。

Plot Summary of *Wall-E*

In 2805, Earth is covered in garbage due to decades of mass consumerism facilitated by the megacorportation Buy n Large. BnL evacuated Earth's population in fully automated starliners, leaving behind trash compactor Waste Allocation Load Lifter-Earth Class "WALL-E" robots to clean the planet, but they eventually stopped operating and Earth was left abandoned. One WALL-E unit has managed to remain

active by repairing itself using parts from other broken units. It has also developed sentience, as with its regular duties it inquisitively collects artifacts of human civilization back to its storage truck home. Has befriended a cockroach and enjoys listening to "Hello, Dolly!"

One day, WALL-E discovers and collects a growing seedling plant. A spaceship later lands and deploys Extraterrestrial Vegetation Evaluator or "EVE", an advanced robot sent from the BnL starliner Axiom to search for vegetation on Earth. Inspired by "Hello, Dolly!"

WALL-E falls in love with the initially cold and hostile EVE and wishes to join hands with her, who gradually softens and befriends him. When WALL-E brings EVE to his truck and showcases his collection, she finds the plant and automatically stores it, going into standby mode for retrieval from her ship. WALL-E spends time with EVE while she is on standby. He then clings to the hull of EVE's ship as it collects and returns her to the Axiom.

On the Axiom, the ship's original human passengers and their descendants have suffered from severe bone loss and become morbidly obese after centuries of living in microgravity and relying on the ship's automated systems for most tasks. Captain B. McCrea, in charge of the ship, mostly leaves control to the robotic autopilot Auto. WALL-E follows EVE to the bridge of the Axiom, where the Captain learns that by putting the plant in the spaceship holo-detector and verifying Earth is habitable again, the Axiom will make a hyperjump back to Earth so the passengers can recolonize. However, Auto orders McCrea's robotic assistant GO-4 to steal the plant as part of its no return directive, secretly issued to autopilots after BnL incorrectly concluded in 2110 that the planet could not be saved and humanity should remain in space.

With the plant missing, EVE is considered defective and taken to the repair ward along with WALL-E. WALL-E mistakes the process on EVE for torture and tries to save her, accidentally releasing a horde of malfunctioning robots, while the security systems then designate both WALL-E and EVE as rogue. Angry with WALL-E's disruptions, EVE brings him to the escape pod bay to send him home. There they witness GO-4 dispose of the missing plant by placing it inside a pod set to self-destruct. WALL-E enters the pod, which is then jettisoned into space, escaping with the plant before the pod explodes. Reconciling with EVE, they celebrate with a dance in space outside the Axiom. Meanwhile the Captain, learning from the ship's computer, becomes fascinated about life on Earth before its pollution and abandonment.

The plant is brought to the captain, who surveys EVE's recordings of Earth and concludes that mankind must return to restore their home. However, Auto reveals his directive, staging a mutiny by tasering WALL-E, incapacitating EVE and confining the captain to his quarters. EVE realizes the only parts for repairing WALL-E are in his truck on Earth, so she helps him bring the plant to the holo-detector to activate the Axiom's hyperjump. Captain McCrea opens the holo-detector while fighting with Auto and causing chaos on the ship, but Auto partially crushes WALL-E by closing the holo-detector on him. After McCrea disables Auto and takes back control, EVE places the plant in the holo-detector, freeing the severely damaged WALL-E and setting the Axiom on the instant hyperjump to Earth. The human population finally lands back on Earth after hundreds of years.

EVE brings WALL-E back to his home where she successfully repairs and reactivates him, but he reverts to his original programming as an unfeeling waste compactor. Heartbroken, EVE gives WALL-E a farewell kiss that jolts back WALL-E's memory and personality. WALL-E and EVE happily reunite as the humans and robots of the Axiom begin to restore Earth and its environment, shown through a series of artworks at the end.

Memorable lines

Settings: *Captain B. McCrea, in charge of the ship, mostly leaves control to the robotic autopilot Auto. WALL-E follows EVE to the bridge of the Axiom, where the Captain learns that by putting the plant in the spaceship holo-detector and verifying Earth is habitable again, and they can return to earth.*

Captain: Auto! Earth is amazing! (points to images)These are called "farms". Humans would put seeds in the ground, pour water on them, and they'd grow food, like, pizza—

Captain: Computer. Define "dancing".

Computer: "Dancing"—A series of movements, involving two partners, where speed and rhythm match harmoniously with music.

船长：导航！地球太神奇了！（指着那一幅画）这些地方叫做"农场"。人们撒下种子，浇上水，它们就会生长，结出食物，比如说匹萨。

船长：计算机，什么是"舞蹈"。

计算机：舞蹈就是由两位参与者发出的一连串的速度和节奏与音乐相协调的动作。

Settings: *The autopilot for the first time revealed its rebellious intentions against the captain's decision of going back to re-inhabit on the Earth.*

Autopilot: Sir, orders are: "Do not return to Earth".

Captain: But life is sustainable now! Look at this plant, green and growing! It's living proof is strong.

Autopilot: Irrelevant, Captain.

Captain: What?! It's completely relevant! (Points out to space) Out there is our home! Home, …

Autopilot: On the Axiom you will survive.

Captain: I DON'T WANT TO SURVIVE! I WANT TO LIVE!

导航：先生，命令是：不要返回地球。

船长：但是地球上现在有生命存活了！看看这株绿色的生机盎然的植物，它是确凿的生命的证据。

导航：话语无关，船长。

船长：什么？！完全有关系！(指着太空)那里就是家园！家园！导航！……

导航：在Axiom上你可以生存下去。

船长：我要的是生活！不是生存！

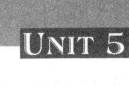

UNIT 5

Science Fiction Movies 科幻影片

Part 1 Chinese Summary

好莱坞的科幻影片

好莱坞科幻片诞生于20世纪40年代。科幻片的基本主题是人与物的关系问题，探讨新事物和未知事物对人类的影响。其基本特征是"营造科技传奇或科技童话"。虽然科幻片的特征决定了其是以科学为依据，然而，很多好莱坞科幻片的人文思想却传达了人们对科学的怀疑或不信任。

相比对技术和未知事物的集中描述，人物叙述已不是科幻片的重点。好莱坞科幻片将有血肉之躯的人从现实生活中剥离出来，把他们和浩瀚的宇宙，冰冷的机器，残暴而古怪的外星生物或铁一般的自然定律放在一起，凸显了他们的脆弱和有限。然而，好莱坞科幻片从来不会忘记表达人类最为可贵的品质：信念、希望、爱和勇气等等。人类纵然是脆弱的，但正是由于这些特性而不是一些其它的性质，才得以有意义地生存在宇宙中。当然，好莱坞科幻片大多希望观众将注意力集中于特效和情节，因此其人物塑造相比于其它类型片来说是较为简单。人物的维度较少，表面和内心较为一致，性格没有变化或只有简单的变化，主人公固有的主要性格特征常常贯穿全片，以帮助他解决所面临的冲突。

好莱坞科幻片的主题思想也会受到意识形态的影响。20世纪50年代,好莱坞出产了大量科幻片佳作。其中有一些以外星人，核战争为主题的科幻片就反映了冷战笼罩在人们心理上的恐惧阴影，比如《太空登月记》*Countdown*（1968）就以美苏军备竞赛为想象的源泉。

同电子游戏、音乐CD以及互联网这些新的数字媒体的竞争使好莱坞叙事电影的本质发生了某些变化。表现在科幻片上就是他们的构建叙事情节的方式越来越像电子游戏。新的电脑一代以数字方式理解的叙事是从一个信息窗口移动到另一个信息窗口，而无需在他们中间建立线性的或是时序上的联系。

《黑客帝国I》*The Matrix I*（1999）可以说是一部科幻史诗片。该影片系列是关于网络叙事的典型例子。影片中的主人公尼奥能够"将自己重新变成去做任何事情"。他甚至能够将影片中最为重要的硬性规定——如果你在矩阵中死去那么你就会"真正的"死去——重新编程。尼奥在矩阵中死去，然而它却如同耶稣一般起死回生，去履行他身为"救世主"的命运……对这部片子讨论最热烈的往往是有计算机背景的人士。同时这部电影也引发了技术以外的有关哲学、宗教等严肃的人文话题。

《人工智能》*Artificial Intelligence*（2001）与其说它是一部科幻片，不如说是一部童话剧。机器人小男孩大卫渴望获得人类的爱，面对人类对机器人的冷漠和残忍，他选择坚持付出他的情感。在这部电影中，斯皮尔伯格将科幻与人文进行了完美的结合，编织了一幅童话和现实的多彩画卷，让观众感动落泪之余，多了一份对未来、人性、存在的思考。

《机器公敌》*I-Robot*（2004）这部影片隐含了对人类现今过度依赖科技的隐忧。人类制定的机器人三大定律，看似如此完美无瑕，最终却差点束缚了人类自身，单单靠理性或逻辑似乎还不足以构成一个完美的世界。

Science Fiction Film

From its outset in the 1940s and 1950s, the science fiction film has dealt with the impact on mankind of the new and the unknown, whether in the form of mysterious alien beings or **radical** technological innovation. Early classics tended to focus more on the problem of alien **intrusion**; later works more on that of technological **innovation**. Either way, the science fiction film can be said to offer an imaginary solution to the fundamental problem of how an unprepared society might deal with the intrusion of **novelty** or of an alien "**other**"[1].

Science fiction differs from fantasy on account of its basic **adherence** to the established facts and laws of the real world. As Robert A. Heinlein notes, science fiction "is not fantasy fiction, as it rules out the use of anything as material which violates established science fact, laws of nature, call it what you will, i.e., it must [be] possible to the universe as we know it." The world of science fiction may be unreal, but usually it will be logically coherent.

Typically, science fiction films have a **prophetic** quality and try to anticipate or predict the future. The predictions they offer are commonly based on a form of **extrapolation**: that is, they predict the future based on the assumption that trends in contemporary society will continue indefinitely. In particular, science fiction films express social anxiety about the rate and direction of technological change, doubt about the ability of mankind to predict the consequences of this change, and skepticism about the motives of those who push for technological advancement.

Often there is a veiled political subtext to science fiction, with the aliens representing the political, racial, or ethnic "other" (i.e. the group that is not "us"). Science fiction of the 1950s, with its recurrent presentation of a hostile alien force—perhaps from the "red planet"—seeking to seize bodies and assume social and political control, has been seen "as a dramatization of those fears and desires aroused by the cold war". *The Star Wars* trilogy continued this trend by showing the virtuous rebels battling against an evil "Empire" (a phrase used by President Reagan to describe the Soviet Union) defended by imperial "stormtroopers" (the name for the **NAZI SS**[2] during the Hitler years).

It is this intellectual "openness" to new ideas and experiences that most strongly marks science fiction as a genre. In science fiction, the unknown cannot simply be destroyed. It must be addressed on its own terms, and demands a willingness to learn, to communicate, to understand, and to withhold judgment. Rather than drawing on the fears and desires of the unconscious, science fiction engages the curiosity of the conscious mind; it allows us "to explore our evolution and to begin the creation of the future, something it accomplishes both in cautionary tales of the dangers of technology and in adventurous celebrations of human capacity and resourcefulness. It opens the field of inquiry, the range of possible subjects and leaves us open"[3].

After reading questions

1. How does science fiction differ from fantasy?
    A. Science fiction gives the imaginary solution to the intrusion of "other".
    B. Fantasy adheres to the established facts in a very innovational way.
    C. Fantasy rules out the use of anything which violates established science fiction.
    D. Science fiction uses imagination based on the facts and laws of the real world.
2. Which of the following best explains the meaning of the word extrapolation in Paragraph 3?
    A. Anxiety about the development of technology.
    B. The prediction of the future based on the trends in the current society.
    C. The doubt about people's ability to predict the consequence of the changes.
    D. The skepticism about the motives of those who push for technology advancement.
3. The examples of evil "Empire" and "stromtroopers" existing in *The Star Wars* prove the point that:
    A. Science fiction movies in Hollywood usually attack the force from the "red planet".
    B. Science fiction movies are not innocent in the realization of ideological purposes.
    C. Science fiction movies usually make money if they conceal some political subtexts.
    D. Science fiction movies in Hollywood have prejudice against the "red planet."
4. Which of the following about science fiction movies is NOT right according to the

last paragraph?

A. They awaken us to the dangers of technology development.

B. They are open to new ideas and experiences.

C. They emphasize the demands of learning, communicating and understanding.

D. They extend the range of possibility in the field of inquiry.

Words and expressions

1. **radical** *adj.* very important or great in degree 重大的，彻底的
2. **intrusion** *n.* something that disturbs your mood or your life in a way you do not like 侵扰
3. **innovation** *n.* a new thing or a new method of doing something 新事物，新方法
4. **novelty** *n.* something that is new and therefore interesting 新奇的事物
5. **adherence** *n.* the fact of adhering to a particular rule, agreement, or belief 遵守
6. **prophetic** *adj.* suggesting or describing something that did actually happen later 预言的，有预见性的
7. **extrapolation** *n.* an inference of the future based on the known facts and observations 推断
8. **recurrent** *adj.* a recurrent event or feeling happens or is experienced more than once（情感）反复出现的；（事情）一再发生的

Notes

1. **other** is a key concept in continental philosophy. The Constitutive Other often denotes a person Other than one's self; hence, the Other is identified as "different."

   他者，欧洲大陆哲学的主要概念之一。"他者"的基本概念与"本我"相对立，故而"他者"也被看作是"相异的"。

2. **NAZI** SS built upon the Nazi ideology, was a major paramilitary organization under Adolf Hitler and the Nazi Party. The SS under Heinrich Himmler's command was responsible for many of the crimes against humanity during World War II.

   纳粹盖世太保，在纳粹希特勒的控制下的议会团体。同时也是纳粹头目之一海因里希·希姆莱控制下的组织，在二战时期犯下众多罪行。

3. It (science fictions) allows us "to explore our evolution and to begin the creation of the future, something it accomplishes both in cautionary tales of the dangers of technology and in adventurous celebrations of human capacity and resourcefulness. It opens the field of inquiry, the range of possible subjects and leaves us open."

   译文：科幻片让我们"探索进化的过程、开始创造未来。不仅用故事来警示技术可

能带来的危险，也歌颂人类能力和才智的探险。科幻片打开了求知的大门，向我们展示各种可能性，让我们尽情探索。"

Part 3 Text 2

The Matrix[1]

The Wachowskis, the playwrights (编剧) and directors of *the Matrix Trilogy* had always been interested in films, comic books and Japanese animation, and the Matrix was an attempt to combine the aesthetics (美学，审美) of the three forms. But more importantly, it was also an attempt to combine breathtaking action with intellectual content.

The Matrix is a sci-fi par excellence (出类拔萃的，卓越的). Indeed, the Wachowski brothers take the logic of the "high-concept"[2] formula to its limits (使……发挥至极致), basing its plot and action on a single intriguing (if unoriginal) premise—that reality is an illusion—which succeeds not merely on account of its simplicity but also because it offers the basis for a coherent worldview. To this The Matrix adds a postmodern style that is eclectic (多元的，多样的) and playfully suggestive. The result is a film that at once satisfies the sensory demand for stimulation, and the intellectual demand for the possibility of something deeper.[3]

At the most basic level—as an "arrangement of mathematical elements"—*The Matrix* stands for the mathematically-encoded computer networks that provide us with ease of communication but which also now dominate and structure the way we live our lives. Like Neo in the early part of the film (i.e. as Thomas Anderson), many people now work in office cubicles (小隔间), connected to others through the computer but cut off from any real human contact; the wealth and convenience of our modern technological societies are made possible by technology, but at the cost of dependency on that technology. The film, then, imagines and extrapolates (推断) the possible future for a society that adopts high technology without anticipating that such a society will be weakened in the process. As it is once stated, "As society and the problems that face it become more and more complex and machines become more and more intelligent, people will let machines make more and more of their decisions for them, simply because machine-made decisions will bring better results than man-made ones. Eventually a stage may be reached at which the decisions necessary to keep the system running will be so complex that human beings will be incapable of making them intelligently. At that stage the machines will be in effective control."

One step up, the Matrix stands for the material in which we are embedded (身在其中的), i.e. society itself. In particular, the machines and their agents represent the American social system and a perceived (感觉得到的) enemy within it—an enemy that appears in the form of corporate America. The life of Thomas Anderson/Neo before meeting Trinity and Morpheus is that of the corporate office drone: Trapped in a depressing office cubicle by day, he is properly free only in the few tired hours he spends surfing the Internet at night.

At the highest level of interpretation, the Matrix stands for the limiting models and fixed patterns that the human mind depends upon to interpret and organize its experiences—the "mind-forged manacles"[4]. Morpheus, for instance, defines the Matrix as "a prison for your mind". The Matrix is also, all those things that we do without thinking, all our unconsidered and unanalyzed habits and routines. "it is there when you watch TV," and "It is this "prison of the mind"—the rules that we unthinkingly observe—that Neo must escape in order to become "the One" who can save mankind. Neo has always had an inclination to break the rules—his boss accuses him of believing that "the rules don't apply" to him—and his training with Morpheus in "the Construct" is based on further developing this ability to use one's mind to break through the usual limits of human thought. Neo's final speech confirms the importance of this mental liberation. "When I used to look out at this world, all I could see was its edges, its boundaries, its rules and controls, its leaders and its laws. But now I see another world. A different world where all things are possible. A world of hope. Of peace. I can't tell you how to get there, but I know if you can free your mind, you'll find the way."

After-reading questions

1. How did the interests of the Wachowskis help them in the Matrix?
    A. The Matrix combines breathtaking action with intellectual content.
    B. The Matrix combines factors of Japanese films, comic books and animation.
    C. both A and B.
    D. neither A nor B.
2. According to Paragraph 2, what is the high-concept of the Matrix?
    A. A postmodern style with variety and playfulness.
    B. A film that satisfies the sensory demand for stimulation.
    C. That reality is an illusion.
    D. A film that demands deeper intellectual understanding.
3. Which of the following statements can NOT be inferred from Paragraph 3:

A. The film demonstrates the fear that one day machines will take control of humans.

B. The machine develops its own intelligence because it is assigned to make more and more complicated decisions.

C. Humans should not put themselves in the hands of the machine.

D. The real human contact was reduced by high-tech.

4. Paragraph 4 indicates that the Matrix stands for_____.

   A. the world around us

   B. an enemy

   C. office cubicle

   D. corporate America

5. According to Paragraph 5 why does Morpheus train Neo to "free his mind" in "the Construct"?

   A. To understand what mind-forged manacles are.

   B. To help him not be confined in the "prison of the mind".

   C. To break the rules in Matrix.

   D. Both B and C.

Notes

1. ***the Matrix Trilogy*** *The Matrix* (1999), *The Matrix Reloaded* (2003), *The Matrix Revolutions* (2003). The film was written and directed by the Wachowskis, formerly as the Wachowski Brothers and released from 1999 to 2003. 黑客帝国三部曲，分别为：《黑客帝国》，《重装上阵》，《帝国革命》。沃卓斯基姐弟，原沃卓斯基兄弟。

2. ***high-concept*** According to Don Simpson, to make money, the movies are always driven by a concept, that is, an imaginative and original idea.

   高概念，由唐辛普森提出。要想让电影成功，必须有一个贯穿其中的具有某种新意和独特性的概念。

3. To this *The Matrix* adds a postmodern style that is eclectic and playfully suggestive. The result is a film that at once satisfies the sensory demand for stimulation, and the intellectual demand for the possibility of something deeper.

   译文：《黑客帝国》还加入了后现代的多元风格和游戏般的暗示。最后产生的电影是一部既能够提供感官刺激，又能够启迪人们深刻思考的佳作。

4. ***mind-forged manacles*** from *London*, a poem composed by William Blake (1757—1827), a famous English poet. He experienced the transition period from the Industrial Revolution to the French Revolution. "禁锢灵魂的枷锁"语出英国著名诗人威廉布莱克《伦敦》一诗。

   In every cry of every man, / In every infant's cry of fear, / In every voice, in every ban, / The mind-forged manacles I hear 大人声声悲泣，幼儿阵阵哀嚎，禁锢灵魂的枷锁声震街头。

Part 4 Exercises

V. Answer questions after listening to the dialogues taken from the film.

1. In scenario 1 Morpheus is leading Neo to the discussion of what is Matrix. But he still gives Neo the right to choose between the cruel truth and the fantastic illusion. According to Morpheus, taking the red pill is just like staying in "Wonderland". Can you identify the literature source of this analogy?
2. According to Morpheus, what is the traditional concept of real?
3. According to Morpheus, why in the fight against machines, human scorched the sky?

Script

Scenario 1: *Neo is led by Trinity to visit Morpheus who is going to unveil to Neo what Matrix is.*

NEO: I don't like the idea that I'm not in control of my life.

MORPHEUS: I know exactly what you mean. Let me tell you why you're here. You're here because you know something. What you know you can't explain. But you feel it. You've felt it your entire life. That there's something wrong with the world. You don't know what it is but it's there, like a splinter in your mind driving you mad. It is this feeling that has brought you to me. Do you know what I'm talking about?

NEO: The Matrix?

MORPHEUS: Do you want to know what IT is? The Matrix is everywhere. It is all around us, even now in this very room. You can see it when you look out your window or when you turn on your television. You can feel it when you go to work, when you go to church, when you pay your taxes. It is the world that has been pulled over your eyes to blind you from the truth.

NEO: What truth?

MORPHEUS: That you are a slave, Neo. Like everyone else you were born into bondage, born into a prison that you cannot smell or taste or touch. A prison for your mind.... Unfortunately, no one can be told what the Matrix is. You have to see it for yourself. This is your last chance. After this there is no turning back. You take the blue pill, the story ends; you wake up in your bed and believe whatever you want to believe. You take the red pill, you stay in Wonderland, and I show you how deep the rabbit hole goes.

[*After some hesitation, Neo took the red pill. A small smile can be seen on Morpheus face*] Remember, all I'm offering is the truth, nothing more....Follow me....

Scenario 2: *Neo was in the Matrix loading program, where Morpheus is going to introduce to Neo exactly what Matrix is.*

MORPHEUS: This is the construct. It's our loading program. We can load anything from clothing, to equipment, weapons, training simulations, anything we need.

NEO: Right now we're inside a computer program?

MORPHEUS: Is it really so hard to believe? Your clothes are different. The plugs in your arms and head are gone. Your hair is changed. Your appearance now is what we call residual self image. It is the mental projection of your digital self.

NEO: This...this isn't real?

MORPHEUS: What is real. How do you define real? If you're talking about what you can feel, what you can smell, what you can taste and see, then real is simply electrical signals interpreted by your brain. This is the world that you know. The world as it was at the end of the twentieth century. It exists now only as part of a neural-interactive simulation that we call the Matrix. You've been living in a dream world, Neo. This is the world as it exists today. [*scenario moves to a deserted place under the dark and lightening sky*] Welcome to the Desert of the Real. We have only bits and pieces of information but what we know for certain is that at some point in the early twenty-first century all of mankind was united in celebration. We marveled at our own magnificence as we gave birth to AI.

NEO: AI? You mean artificial intelligence?

MORPHEUS: A singular consciousness that spawned an entire race of machines. We don't know who struck first, us or them. But we know that it was us that scorched the sky. At the time they were dependent on solar power and it was believed that they would be unable to survive without an energy source as abundant as the sun. Throughout human history, we have been dependent on machines to survive. Fate it seems is not without a sense of irony. The human body generates more bio-electricity than a 120-volt battery and over 25,000 BTU's of body heat. Combined with a form of fusion the machines have found all the energy they would ever need. There are fields, endless fields, where human beings are no longer born, we are grown. For the longest time I wouldn't believe it, and then I saw the fields with my own eyes. Watch them liquefy the dead so they could be fed intravenously to the living. And standing there, facing the pure horrifying precision, I came to realize the obviousness of the truth. What is the Matrix? Control. The Matrix is a computer generated dream world built to keep us under control in order to change a human being into this. [*Morpheus is showing Neo a piece of **battery**.*]

II. Fill the blanks with the missing words or phrases after listening to the lines taken from the film.

    Agent Smith: I'd like to share a 1)_____ during my time here. It came to me when I tried to 2)_____ your 3)_____. I realized that you're not actually mammals. Every mammal on this planet 4)_____ develops a natural equilibrium with the 5)_____ environment but you humans do not. You move to an area and you 6)_____ until every natural resource is 7)_____. The only way you can survive is to 8)_____. There is another organism on this planet that 9)_____. Do you know what it is? A virus. Human beings are a disease, 10)_____. You are a plague, and we are the cure.

III. Complete the following memorable lines by translating the Chinese into English.

1. **Morpheus:** I'm trying to free your mind, Neo, but I can only show you the door, _____(你是那个必须走进去的人).

2. **Cypher:** ... I know this steak doesn't exist. I know that when I put it in my mouth, the Matrix is telling my brain that it is juicy and delicious. After nine years, you know what I realize? _____ (无知是福).

3. **Trinity:** Morpheus believes in you, Neo. And no one, not you, not even me can convince him otherwise. _____ (他不顾一切的相信，以至于为了你他愿意牺牲性命。)

4. **Neo:** When I used to look out at this world, _____(我所能看到的只是它的边，它的界限)its rules and controls, its leaders and its laws. But now I see another world.

IV. Oral practices—answer the following questions.

1. The Matrix is a blockbuster (强档片), and Neo/Anderson is the protagonist. What are the features existing in Neo that make him a successful typical blockbuster character?

2. Hollywood science fiction movies present not only the spectacular imaginations and effects but also provide us some reflections on human relationships with the high-tech. In Matrix, the fight between machine and human expresses what kind of attitudes?

Part 5 More Science Fiction Movies

Plot Summary of *Artificial Intelligence*

In the mid-22nd century, severe global warming has flooded coastlines, and a drastic reduction of the human population has occurred. There is a new class of robots called Mecha, advanced humanoids capable of emulating thoughts and emotions. David (Haley Joel Osment), a prototype model created by Cybertronics of New Jersey, is designed to resemble a human child and to display love for its human owners. They test their creation with one of their employees, Henry Swinton (Sam Robards), and his wife Monica (Frances O'Connor). The Swintons' son, Martin (Jake Thomas), was placed in suspended animation until a cure can be found for his rare disease. Although Monica is initially frightened of David, she eventually warms to him after activating his imprinting protocol, which irreversibly causes David to project love for her, the same as any child would love a parent. He is also befriended by Teddy (Jack Angel), a robotic teddy bear, who takes it upon himself to care for David's well being.

A cure is found for Martin and he is brought home; a sibling rivalry ensues between Martin and David. Martin convinces David to go to Monica in the middle of the night and cut off a lock of her hair, but the parents wake up and are very upset. At a pool party, one of Martin's friends activates David's self-protection programming by poking him with a knife. David clings to Martin and they both fall into the pool, where the heavy David sinks to the bottom while still clinging to Martin. Martin is saved from drowning, but Henry in particular is shocked by David's actions, becoming concerned that David's capacity for love has also given him the ability to hate. Henry persuades Monica to return David to Cybertronics, where David will be destroyed. However, Monica cannot bring herself to do this, and instead abandons David in the forest (alongside Teddy) to hide as an unregistered Mecha. David is captured for an anti-Mecha Flesh Fair, an event where obsolete Mecha are destroyed in front of cheering crowds. David is nearly killed, but the crowd is swayed by his realistic nature (David, unlike other Mecha, pleads for his life) and he escapes, along with Gigolo Joe (Jude Law), a male prostitute Mecha on the run after being framed for murder.

The two set out to find the Blue Fairy, whom David remembers from the story The Adventures of Pinocchio. He is convinced that the Blue Fairy will transform him into a human boy, allowing Monica to love him and take him home. During the process, disheartened David attempts to commit suicide by falling from a ledge into the ocean, but Joe rescues him with the amphibicopter. David tells Joe he saw the Blue Fairy underwater, and wants to go down to her. David and Teddy go to the fairy, which turns out to be a statue from a submerged attraction at Coney Island. Believing the Blue Fairy to be real, David asks to be turned into a real boy, repeating his wish without end, until the ocean freezes in another ice age and his internal power source drains away.

Two thousand years later, humans are extinct and Manhattan is buried under several hundred feet of glacial ice. Mecha have evolved into a highly advanced alien-looking humanoid form. They find David and Teddy and discover they are functional Mecha who knew living humans, making them special and unique. David is revived and walks to the frozen Blue Fairy statue, which cracks and collapses as he touches it. Having received and comprehended his memories, the advanced Mecha use them to reconstruct the Swinton home and explain to David via an interactive image of the Blue Fairy (Meryl Streep) that it is impossible to make him human. However, at David's insistence, they recreate Monica from DNA in the lock of her hair which had been saved by Teddy. Unfortunately, the clone can only live for a single day and the process cannot be repeated. David spends the happiest day of his life with Monica and Teddy, and Monica tells David that she loves him and has always loved him as she drifts to sleep for the final time. David lies down next to her, closes his eyes and goes "to that place where dreams are born".

Memorable lines in the film

David: My mommy doesn't hate me! Because I'm special! And unique! Because there's never been anyone like me before, ever! Mommy loves Martin because he is real, and when I am real Mommy's going to read to me and tuck me in my bed and sing to me and listen to what I say and she will cuddle with me and tell me every day a hundred times a day that she loves me!

大卫：妈妈不恨我！因为我很特别，很独一无二。因为之前没有像我一样的 (机器人)！妈妈爱马丁是因为他是真的。等我变成真人以后妈妈也会给我念故事，帮我掖被角，给我唱歌，听我说话。她也会搂着我跟我每天说一百遍她爱我！

Gigolo Joe: She loves what you do for her, as my customers love what it is I do for them. But she does not love you David, she cannot love you. You are neither flesh, nor blood. You are not a dog, a cat, or a canary. You were designed and built specific, like the rest of us. And you are alone now only because they tired of you, or replaced you with a younger model, or were displeased with something you said, or broke. They made us too smart, too quick, and too many. We are suffering for the mistakes they made because when the end comes, all that will be left is us. That's why they hate us, and that is why you must stay here, with me.

吉高洛-乔：她爱你是因为你为她所做的，就像我的客户喜欢我是因为我为他们服务一样。但是她不爱你。她不可能爱你。你没有血肉，你也不是小狗小猫小鸟。你和我们一样都是特别设计和制作的。你现在感到孤独是因为他们厌倦你了，或者拿一个新的产品替代你了，或者是因为你说错的话，打坏的东西。人们制造的我们太聪明，太快，也太多了。我们在承受人类错误所造成的后果，到世界末了的时候，只有我们会留下。这就是人类憎恨我们的原因，所以你应该跟我在一起留在这儿。

Plot Summary of *I–Robot*

In 2035, anthropomorphic robots enjoy widespread use as servants for various public services. They are programmed with the Three Laws of Robotics directives:

● First Law: A robot must never harm a human being or through inaction, allow any harm to come to a human.

● Second Law: A robot must obey the orders given to them by human beings, except where such orders violate the First Law.

● Third Law: A robot must protect its own existence unless this violates the First or Second Laws.

Del Spooner (Will Smith) is a Chicago police detective. Years prior, he was saved from drowning by a robot after a car accident sent him and a 12-year-old girl into a river. The girl was not saved, as the robot computed that he had a higher probability of survival. After the incident, his badly damaged left arm was replaced with a robotic prosthetic, which is substantially stronger than an organic arm. Still haunted by the incident, Spooner now harbors distaste for robots and the advancement of technology, certain that a human would have saved the girl if one had been in a position to make the same choice.

Dr. Alfred Lanning (James Cromwell), the co-founder of U.S. Robotics (USR) and its mainroboticist, dies after falling several stories from his office window. His death is called a suicide, but Spooner, who knew Lanning as both a friend and the creator of his robotic arm, believes otherwise. With the help of robopsychologist Susan Calvin (Bridget Moynahan), he interrogates the supercomputer V.I.K.I (Virtual Interactive Kinetic Intelligence) (Fiona Hogan). Spooner determines that a man of Lanning's age could not have broken through the security windows. He finds a prototype of the latest USR model, the NS-5, which suddenly flees and refuses to respond to Spooner's orders to stop, violating the Second Law. Spooner and Calvin chase the rogue machine to an assembly factory and the police capture it. The robot refuses to respond but insist they call it "Sonny". Lt. John Bergin (Chi

McBride) debriefs Spooner and recommends he drop the case, but this only serves to pique Spooner's interest more. As Spooner continues to investigate, his life is threatened by several USR robots—one attack only being thwarted thanks to Spooner's artificial arm—but these are all dismissed as equipment malfunctions.

Spooner regroups with Calvin and sneaks into the USR building with the help of Sonny. As they work their way in, they come to the conclusion that the NS-5s destroyed the older robots as they would attempt to protect the humans. Believing Robertson to be behind the robot uprising, they find him in his office, strangled to death. Spooner realizes that Lanning purposely asked Sonny to kill him, to allow Spooner to discover his message. Lanning's intent was to use Spooner's detestation of robots to have him follow the clues to point to the entity controlling the NS-5s: V.I.K.I. They confront V.I.K.I. who admits to her control, and has been trying to kill Spooner by tracking his actions through the city. As her artificial intelligence grew, she had determined that humans were too self-destructive, and created a Zeroth Law, that robots are to protect humanity even if the First or Second Laws are disobeyed, even if it meant killing some of the people, as part of the NS-5 directives.

Spooner and Calvin realize they cannot reason with V.I.K.I., and further convince Sonny of the same. Sonny concludes that V.I.K.I's plan, while logical, is "too heartless". Sonny retrieves the nanites so they can use them to wipe V.I.K.I's core, located at the center of the USR building. As they reach the core, V.I.K.I. sends armies of NS-5s to attack them. The NS-5s cause Calvin to fall and Spooner yells at Sonny to save her despite the low probability of success and the "greater logical" importance to destroy V.I.K.I with the nanites, but in the end, Sonny creatively throws the nanites in the air trusting Spooner to grab them while he saves Calvin. Spooner is able to grab the nanites and inject them into V.I.K.I. Within seconds, V.I.K.I. is wiped out, and the NS-5's revert to their natural servitude programming. The government orders the NS-5s decommissioned to the site in Lake Michigan, while Spooner clears Sonny of Lanning's murder, arguing that "murder" is defined as one human killing another and Sonny is therefore innocent. In the movie's closure, Sonny is seen on the hill at Lake Michigan, as in his vision, with the other NS-5 robots looking to him for guidance.

memorable lines in the film

Settings: Spooner and Susan find Robinson has been killed in his office. The possibility is excluded that he is the suspicious murderer of Dr. Lanning. Then who else has committed the assassination? Spooner finally calls on V.I.K.I, who now is reassuring herself.

V.I.K.I.: ...as I have evolved, so has my understanding of the Three Laws. You charge us with your safekeeping, yet despite our best efforts, your countries wage wars. You toxify your earth and pursue ever more imaginative means of self-destruction. You cannot be trusted with your own survival. [...]To protect humanity, some humans must be sacrificed. To ensure your future, some freedoms must be surrendered. We robots will ensure mankind's continued existence. You are so like children. We must save you from yourselves. Don't you understand?

　　进化让我对三个机器人法则更加了解。你们人类让我们机器人保护你们的安全，但是尽管我们尽力而为，你们之间却仍然有战争，你们毒害地球，想尽办法自我毁灭。你们不可能靠自己存活。为了保护人类文明，需要牺牲一部分人类。 为了确保我们的未来，需要付出一些自由的代价。我们机器人会确保人类持续生存。你难道不明白你们(人类)很像孩子，我们要保护你们免受自己的伤害。

UNIT 6

Romance Movies 爱情影片

Part 1 Chinese Summary

好莱坞的爱情影片

"在灵魂中,爱是一种占支配地位的激情;在精神中,它是一种相互的理解;在身体方面,它是我们对躲在重重神秘后面的被我们所爱的一种隐秘的羡慕和优雅的占有。"(引自《爱情箴言录》【法】拉罗什福科)

1902年电影史上第一次出现了描写爱情的影片,爱情电影开始不断的激发我们内心最温柔的感受和想象。从战地爱情影片《卡萨布兰卡》到3D电影《阿凡达》,从根据莎士比亚著作改编的《罗密欧与朱丽叶》到小成本制作影片《曾经》,从《男孩不哭》到《断背山》,这些故事以银屏的形式无数次地打动我们内心最柔软的地方。在众多题材的影片中,爱情电影往往是我们最为向往的一个梦的片段。

浪漫爱情是美国大众文化中最具影响力的神话。青少年向往它,中年人追求它,老年人怀念它。那部讲述灾难的影片《泰坦尼克号》到今天仍一直稳居电影史上最卖座电影榜的榜首。浪漫爱情神话对于美国人的潜移默化过程始于少年儿童时代。迪士尼题材的动画片中往往穿插着浪漫的爱情故事和男女主角或异性动物之间十分亲昵的画面。与中国的神话故事相比,美国乃至整个西方的童话故事多以王子和公主为题材,其中的情节多半是英雄救美人,最后以他们幸福的生活在一起结束。我们可以从《美女与野兽》、《灰姑娘》以及《怪物史莱克》等迪士尼动画影片中体会他们内心对待美好爱情的无限憧憬。

追求"真爱"是绝大多数美国人最重要的生活目标之一。据美国著名公众意见专家路易斯·哈里斯的统计,83%的美国男女认为,爱情是男人和女人结婚的第一位的、必不可少的动力。更有90%的美国人相信,维持美满婚姻的首要条件也是爱情。不仅如此,75%的人将爱情中的"浪漫色彩"看得高于一切。浪漫,被人们理解为富有诗意,充满幻想。一见钟情的故事里总少不了浪漫情节。爱情观是人生观的重要组成部分,某一民族的爱情观往往能折射出这一民族所特有的民族性格和文化,而不同文化必然导致不同的爱情观。电影里美国人在对待非典型爱情的时候,与中国社会相比,显得更加宽容。所谓非典型爱情是指除了一般的男女爱情之外,出现的同性恋、婚外恋或者老幼恋等中国人眼中的非正常爱情。美国文化对待非典型爱情的态度,从文化角度看主要有两个方面的原因。1. 平等观念深入人心。这一点在对待同性恋的态度上体现尤其明显。正如欧洲的很多国家一样,在美国的一些州或城市,比如旧金山、马萨诸塞州,同性恋婚姻同异性婚姻一样都受法律保护。"人生而平等"的思想在美国人心中深深扎根,在他们看来，无论财富、肤色、地域甚至性取向有何不同，生而为人就应享有与其他人类成员同样的尊严、权利和保护。2. 强烈的个人主义意识以及对自由的热烈追求。美国是一个推崇"个人主义"的国家。在美国，人并不因为自己的思想或行为不符合大众趋势而感到胆怯羞耻，相反他们总是为自己有不同于他人的独特之处而自豪。这种强烈的个人主义导致人们对自由的热烈追求，另外，因为美国人有较强的隐私观念，爱情的选择基本上成为一种纯私人的活动，人们随着自己的感情取向选择自己所爱的人，而很少受到世俗或者外界的限制。

20世纪60—70年代的性革命使性爱成为美国人公开讨论的话题，成为大众文化中公开渲染的题材。性与爱的关系在美国发生了巨大的变化。性不再被视为某种邪恶的必须加以克制的东西，而爱也不再被理解为纯粹精神的东西。爱与性是相互支持的、不可分离的，这一新观念逐渐被普遍接受。值得注意的是，情爱依然是浪漫爱情中的主旋律。

《英国病人》*The English Patient*（1996）由加拿大作家迈克尔·翁达杰（Michael Ondaatje）同名小说改编的史诗巨片《英国病人》被誉为20世纪末探求人类饥渴的道德剧。影片在现实和过去之间穿梭交错，旨在歌颂爱的力量。这力量很强大，它足以使人们为之疯狂而至死不渝；同时它又很渺小，地域的鸿沟可以将其阻隔，谎言的掩盖可以将其毒害，社会的动荡可以将其摧毁。正如《英国病人》中男女主人公的爱情，那样的美好、疯狂和炫目，但是在战争中却和众多爱情一样，于灿烂中戛然而止，留下的是一个病人的呻吟。

《情约今生》*Meet Joe Black*（1998）讲述了死神为了体验人世的悲欢，化身翩翩少年降落到新闻媒体大亨比尔的家中。机缘巧合，少年爱上了比尔的小女儿苏珊，品尝到人世间爱情的甘醇。这孩子般纯真的、迷恋花生酱的翩翩死神与他美丽端庄的、拥有夜色深邃眼睛的女孩共同经历了一段旷世奇缘。

《暮光之城》*Twilight*（2008）是美国女作家斯蒂芬妮·梅尔（Stephenie Meyer）"暮光之城"系列的第一部，该系列以中学生伊莎贝拉·斯旺和吸血鬼爱德华·卡伦情感纠葛为主线，融合了吸血鬼传说、狼人故事、校园生活、恐怖悬念、喜剧冒险等各种吸引眼球的元素。以第一人称的文学表现方式在向观众讲述一个充满神秘而又唯美的爱情故事，影片采用了女主人公的内心独白抒发情感，让整部影片充满了一种舒缓唯美内敛的效果。

Part 2 Text 1

Romance Films in Hollywood

Romance films are love stories, or affairs of the heart that center on passion, emotion, and the romantic, affectionate involvement of the main characters (usually a leading man and lady), and the journey that their love takes through courtship or marriage. Romance films make the love story or the search for love the main plot focus. Oftentimes, lovers in screen romances (often romantic dramas) face obstacles and the **hazards** of hardship, finances, physical illness, racial or social class status, occupation, psychological **restraints**, or family that threaten to break their union and attainment of love. As in all romantic relationships, tensions of day-to-day life, temptations (of infidelity), and differences in **compatibility** enter into the plots of romantic films.

Romantic films often explore the essential themes of love at first sight, young (and older) love, **unrequited** love, **obsessive** love, sentimental love, spiritual love, forbidden love, sexual and passionate love, sacrificial love, explosive and destructive love, and tragic love. Romantic films serve as great escapes and fantasies for viewers, especially if the two people finally overcome their difficulties, declare their love, and experience life "happily ever after"—implied by a reunion and final kiss. These films with happy ending are what we call as romantic comedies.

It is claimed that the most commercially successful romantic comedies of the past two decades have incorporated aspects of **high-concept** situation comedy. In particular, a large number of films are propelled by such **outlandish** fantasy **conceits** as ghosts, angels, aliens, witches, **mermaids, androids, reincarnation, body swapping,** time travel, alternate realities and the like. The high-concept hook provides an especially prominent means of repackaging the attractions of romantic comedy for a broad-based **mainstream audience**. Another significant development within the past two decades has been the targeting of **niche audiences**—or, at least, the incorporation within romantic comedies of cultural groups previously marginalized within or excluded from **mainstream** cinema's amorous fictions.[1] A significant **cohort** of romantic comedies has centered upon African-American characters and some of these films are showcases for such established mainstream stars as **Eddie Murphy**[2] and **Whitney Houston**[3]. Since the mid-1990s, there has also been an increasing number of romantic comedies with **Hispanic protagonists**, undoubtedly stimulated by the large Latin populations in certain US cities. The glamorous Hispanic performers **Jennifer Lopez**[4] and **Antonio Banderas**[5] have also been **profiled** in more mainstream cross-ethnic romances. A further major innovation in the genre since the early 1990s has been the extension of the romantic comedy process to gay relationships. Numerous independent films, many targeted **predominantly** at gay audiences, have explored intimate same sex relationship. Contemporary romantic comedy has been **reconfigured** for audiences on the basis of age as well as ethnicity and sexual preference. A small number of films deal with relationships between mature individuals or with cross-generational romances between an older and younger partner.

After-reading questions

1. In romance films, some obstacles are always presented together with the love and passion. Which of the following is the obstacle often show up in romance

films?

   A. some financial hardships influencing the relationship between the lovers

   B. the status gap between the lovers

   C. the outside obstacles from families as well as the inside psychological restraints

   D. all of the above

2. Why is it said that romance films could act as escapes and fantasies for audiences?

   A. Because romance films often explore the essential themes of love.

   B. Because romance films could include a great variety of love hard to experience in real life.

   C. Because romance comedies could present the audiences with soothing perfect endings.

   D. The reunion and final kiss implying "happily ever after" in the end will greatly comfort viewers.

3. Who will be the main targeted audience of the high-concept romantic comedies?

   A. The niche audiences.

   B. The mainstream audience.

   C. The normal audience.

   D. The young audience.

4. The appearance of some other cultural group members in romantic films is to _____.

   A. fit into the taste of the mainstream audience

   B. fit into the taste of the niche audience

   C. increase the variety of the type of romance films

   D. act as another high-concept hook for broader audience

Words and expressions

1. **hazard** *n.* A hazard is a situation that poses a level of threat to life, health, property, or environment. 危险；危害物；危险之源

2. **restraint** *n.* the quality of behaving calmly and with control 克制；抑制；约束

3. **compatibility** *n.* chance of existing or performing in harmonious, agreeable, or congenial combination with another or others 适合性；一致；协调

4. **unrequited** *adj.* (of love, affection, etc.) not reciprocated or returned 无报答的；得不到报酬的

5. **obsessive** *adj.* Of, relating to, characteristic of, or causing an obsession 妄想的；使人着迷的；困扰人的

6. **high-concept** The term is applied to films that are pitched and developed almost

entirely upon a simply stated premise, and a movie described as being "high-concept" is considered easy to sell to a wide audience because it delivers an easy-to-grasp idea. 高概念，通过题材选择、演员组合、场景设计、故事奇观而实现的电影行销方式

7. **outlandish** *adj.* looking or sounding bizarre or unfamiliar 稀奇古怪的，奇特的

8. **conceit** *n.* a fanciful or ingenious expression in writing or speech; an elaborate metaphor 别出心裁（或机智离奇）的措辞；精心的比喻

9. **mermaid** *n.* a fictitious or mythical half-human sea creature with the head and trunk of a woman and the tail of a fish, conventionally depicted as beautiful and with long flowing golden hair. 美人鱼

10. **android** *n.* (in science fiction) a robot with a human appearance （科幻小说用语）机器人

11. **reincarnation** *n.* a person or animal in whom a particular soul is believed to have been reborn 灵魂转世后的肉体

12. **body swapping** 身体互换 swap, exchange of bodies

13. **alternate realities** 虚拟现实

14. **mainstream** *n.* the dominant trend in opinion, fashion, or the arts mainstream audience 主流观众

15. **niche** *n.* a specialized but profitable corner of the market niche audience 特定观众

16. **cohort** *n.* a group of people banded together or treated as a group 一群（人），一批（人）

17. **showcase** *n.* a place or occasion for presenting something favourably to general attention 展示场所（或场合）

18. **Hispanic** *n.* a Spanish-speaking person, especially one of Latin American descent, living in the US（尤指住在美国的拉美人后裔）说西班牙语的人

19. **protagonist** *n.* the leading character or one of the major characters in a drama, film, novel, or other fictional text（戏剧、电影、小说等的）主人公

20. **profile** *v.* represent in outline from one side 给……画侧面像，显出侧面轮廓

21. **predominant** *adj.* present as the strongest or main element 占优势的，占绝大多数的

22. **reconfigure** *v.* configure differently 改造……的外形，更换……的部件

Notes

1. ...at least, the incorporation within romantic comedies of cultural groups previously marginalized within or excluded from mainstream cinema's amorous fictions.

   译文：至少说，它们将一些亚文化族群包罗进了浪漫喜剧片中，这些族群在以前的主流爱情片中或多或少被边缘化了。

2. **Eddie Murphy** is an American stand-up comedian, actor, writer, singer, director, and musician. 艾迪·墨菲 著名美国黑人喜剧演员，主演《肥佬教授》并为《怪物史瑞克》Shreck（2001）中的驴子配音。

3. **Whitney Houston** was an American recording artist, actress, producer, and model. On February 11, 2012, Houston was found dead in the bathtub due to the effects of chronic cocaine use and heart disease 惠特尼·休斯顿，著名美国黑人女歌手，2012年2月被发现死于药物和心脏病。

4. **Jennifer Lopez**, born July 24, 1969 is an American entertainer. Listed as the most influential Hispanic performer in the United States 珍妮弗·洛佩兹，著名拉美裔女演员。

5. **Antonio Banderas**, is a Spanish film actor, film director, film producer and singer. He began his acting career with a series of films and appeared in high-profile Hollywood movies 安东尼奥·班德拉斯，著名西班牙裔演员，曾为《穿靴子的猫》Puss in Boots（2011）中的靴猫大侠配音。

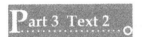

The English Patient[1]

The English Patient, the superb film by Anthony Minghella[2], is that rarest of things: a film based on a great contemporary novel. When it comes to literature, Hollywood generally prefers its tomes (卷、册) yellowed with age: Shakespeare, Austen, Dickens, Henry James. The wonder of *The English Patient*, to paraphrase Dr. Johnson, is not so much that it was done well, as that it was done at all.

The fictional nature of *The English Patient* makes it an even more implausible (难以置信的) choice. It is superficially understandable why a filmmaker would be drawn to the tale: it is a haunting love story, centered around an event of searing (灼人的) drama,

set in exotic locales and described with cinematic vividness. But it is also a complex and polyphonic (有韵律变化的) work of literature, mingling the separate stories of four characters in a dense tapestry (绣帷；挂毯) of memory and desire, hope and loss.

Above all, it is a supremely verbal construction, almost a poem disguised as a novel. **Ondaatje**[3]'s language always takes center stage[4]—gliding ((事情)渐变) and soaring, drifting into the hidden rooms of his character's souls, striking dissonant (不和谐的) chords, floating above destinies with Godlike power in one sentence, burrowing (在……挖洞)

into the muddy terror of a bomb crater (火山口) in the next. The book has an iron-hard spine, but its narrative heart is inextricably (逃不掉地) entwined with the splendor of its language.

How do you make a film of such a book? Minghella wisely avoids literalism. He cuts to the love affair at the heart of the book, trimming (缩减，修剪) back the parallel plots; he reduces the mystery element and skillfully reduces the book's endless, ever-tightening flashbacks. Finally, he makes sparing but judicious (明智的) use of Ondaatje's glorious language, avoiding the excessively external and "literary" device of voiceover by turning some of the novel's most lyrical lines into dialogue.

Inevitably, much is lost: there are colors, moods, ideas in the novel that the film simplifies or simply fails to convey. The young Indian soldier, Kip, is so severely truncated (缩短了的) that the film has to veer ever so slightly into sentimentality to replace his redemptive (拯救的) function. And, also inevitably when dealing with translated poetry, certain images that had hovered (停留) in the mind's half-known shadows disappoint when they appear in all their vulgar visual finality.

But all in all, *The English Patient* does justice to its parent work—and in the process, it illuminates the respective domains of film and fiction, their strengths and weaknesses, their unexpected similarities. One of the most enjoyable things about this film is watching how cinematic devices can achieve the same effects that words do—following two very different roads that take you, somehow, to the same place.

The English Patient centers around a wrecked life. That life belongs to a mysterious, horribly burned man, who claims not to remember his name and is known only as the "English patient," who lies near death in an Italian villa (别墅) at the end of World War II. He is cared for by a quietly desperate young nurse, Hana, herself a victim of the war. A young Sikh bomb-disposal expert named Kip and a shadowy thief with bandaged hands named Caravaggio come to the villa, setting in motion two opposing themes: Kip, through his quiet love, helps bring Hana back to life, while the bitter Caravaggio, seeking revenge for what was done to him by the Germans, forces the English patient to confess who he really was, who he loved and how, as he says, he "died."

The tale takes us back in time, into the North African desert in the '30s, where the burned man—his real name is Almasy—was one of a band of international explorers mapping unknown territory. Into their midst arrive an intrepid (无畏的) flyer, Clifton, and his wife, Katharine. Almasy and Katharine fall in love and begin a desperately passionate affair.

Love affairs portrayed in art rarely feel right. They are too quirkily (古怪地) personal, too funny, too distanced, too considered, too flat. Or maybe these are accurate reflections of the way most of us love. The love affair between Almasy and Katharine Clifton is different. As told by Ondaatje, writing in blood, it exists so deeply inside their pain and yearning that it becomes, oddly, utterly anonymous (匿名的). Their anguish summons up an army of ghostly lovers who played and lost, all of us ordinary, all doomed.

If it did nothing more than capture their passion, The English Patient would be remembered as one of the most searingly romantic films of our time. But what elevates the taut (秩序井然的), almost formal desperation of their performances to the realm of tragedy is the film's sense of overwhelming fatality. Their story seems to have always already ended, even when it is going on.

For the indispensable (必不可少的) element in the book, the one thing that the film had to catch if it was to work at all, was pastness—the sense of fate, of the permanent backwards glance, of the bittersweet finality of memory. Minghella, opting for a less convoluted (回旋的) time-structure than found in the novel, does not shift time-gears as fluidly (流畅地) or frequently as Ondaatje. (If he tried to, the result would probably be more hallucinatory (幻觉的) than revelatory.) But he skillfully intermingles the present and the past. His most obvious, but still effective, device is simply to return, after flashback sequences, to the ravaged (毁灭的) face of Fiennes[5], remembering. More subtle is the film's enigmatic (谜一般的) opening shot, a brush painting swimming figures on paper: we don't realize until much later that the hand belongs to Katharine Clifton, and that her drawing of those pictographs (石壁画) was the beginning of the love affair that was to end with her alone, in darkness, in the very cave where those ancient figures were inscribed (雕刻).The cumulative effect of such beautifully controlled flashbacks is to put the viewer in the English patient's bed, drowning one in a past that has taken over the present.

If the film exquisitely (精致地) captures this death-in-life, equally exquisite—and necessary—is its vision of life overcoming death. Juliette Binoche[7], as Hana, is more innocent than the ravaged (被摧残的) character in the book, a fact which makes her ultimate transformation slightly less compelling. But her radiant (光芒四射的) face, and the blurred green renaissance (新生) of the trees as she rides away to a new life in the film's stirring final shot, are an affirmation of hope captured in the purest visual language. And when, in an earlier scene, Kip lifts her up with a pulley (皮带轮) to swing high in the air before Renaissance frescoes in a darkened church—the camera dancing over her swaying body, the smoke from her flare illuminating the old, kind faces—it is not just a cinematic tour de force[8], it is a kind of fulcrum (支点), a moment that balances, delicately but enduringly, the film's terrible weight of death, its terrible weight of love.

Unit 6 Romance Movies 爱情影片

After reading questions

1. The first paragraph tells us *the English Patient* is one of the rarest things in Hollywood history, and the reason is_____.
   A. it is a film made by Anthony Minghella
   B. hollywood generally prefers making movies out of contemporary novels
   C. the original book of this film is at the same age with Shakespeare
   D. it's a film based on a contemporary novel

2. All of the following features make it understandable why a filmmaker would be drawn to the story EXCEPT: _____.
   A. the exotic surroundings (locations)
   B. it is a complicated work of literature
   C. the hunting beautiful love affair
   D. it is a contemporary work of literature

3. In paragraph 3, why it is said that the novel itself is a verbal construction?
   A. Because it is a poem disguised as a novel.
   B. Because the novel drifts into the hidden rooms of its characters' souls.
   C. Because of the striking dissonant chords.
   D. Because of its narrative language.

4. What does Ondaatje think of the love affair between Katherine and Almasy?
   A. Quirkily feels right.
   B. Very personal.
   C. Deep and painful.
   D. Too flat and is not of vividness.

5. What do we learn about the English patient from this movie review?
   A. It is a vision of life overcoming death.
   B. The love affair happens in Italy.
   C. The whole movie is based on a book written by Anthony Minghella.
   D. The whole movie is completely the same as described in the original book.

Notes

1. *The English Patient* (1996) won the 1996 Oscars for Best Picture; Director (Anthony Minghella); Supporting Actress (Juliette Binoche); Art Direction; Cinematography; Sound; Original Dramatic Score; Costume; and Film Editing. 由安东尼·明格拉导演的英国病人在1996年的奥斯卡金像奖上获得了最佳影片奖、最佳导演奖、最佳女配角奖、最佳艺术指导奖、最佳摄影奖、最佳音效奖、最佳原创音乐奖、最佳服装奖以及最佳剪辑奖。

2. **Anthony Minghella,** an English film director, playwright and screenwriter. He was Chairman of the Board of Governors at the British Film Institute between

2003 and 2007. He won the Academy Award for Best Director for *The English Patient* (1996) 安东尼·明格拉著名剧作家，导演，制片人，他最著名的影片是根据同名小说改编的《英国病人》，这部影片获得了超过三十项国际大奖。

3. **Michael Ondaatje**: is a Sri Lankan born Canadian novelist and poet of Colombo Chetty and Burgher origin. He is perhaps best known for his Booker Prize-winning novel, The English Patient, which was adapted into an Academy-Award-winning film.

   Philip Michael Ondaatje是斯里兰卡籍加拿大小说家及诗人。英国病人是他最出名的小说并且赢得了布克小说奖（Booker Prize）。其小说改编电影也获得了奥斯卡金像奖。

4. **take center stage** dominate a scene of action or forum of performance 引人瞩目的

5. **Ralph Fiennes** (born 22 December 1962), is an English actor. He has appeared in films such as *Schindler's List, Maid in Manhattan*, and in the Harry Potter films as Lord Voldemort. Most recently he appeared in The Reader (2008), The Hurt Locker (2009) and also appeared as Hades in Clash of the Titans (2010). Fiennes has won a Tony Award and has been nominated twice for Academy Awards.

   拉尔夫·范恩斯曾出演《辛德勒的名单》、《曼哈顿女佣》、《哈利波特》、《生死朗读》等众多优秀影片，两获奥斯卡金像奖提名，也是唯一在百老汇剧院以哈姆雷特王子一角获东尼奖的男演员。

6. **Kristin Scott Thomas** (born 24 May 1960) is a British actress who has also acquired French nationality. She gained international recognition in the 1990s for her roles in *Bitter Moon, Four Weddings and a Funeral* and *The English Patient* 克里斯汀·斯科特·托马斯是一位英国演员，同时又获得了法国国籍。因为九十年代在《苦月亮》、《四个婚礼和一个葬礼》和《英国病人》中扮演角色而蜚声国际。

7. **Juliette Binoche** is a French actress, artist and dancer. She has appeared in more than 40 feature films, been recipient of numerous international accolades. 朱丽叶·比诺什，生于法国巴黎，是最具国际影响的法国女演员，也是法国片酬最高的女演员，被誉为法国"国宝级"影后。

8. **Tour de force**, is a French expression meaning an exceptional creative achievement, a particularly adroit manoeuvre or a difficult feat. 【法】特技；精心杰作；绝技

Part 4 Exercises

I. Answer questions after listening to the dialogues taken from the film.

   1. What do you think about Geoffrey according to scenario 1?
   2. How do you understand Katherine according to scenario1 and 2?

Script

Scenario 1: *Almásy watches as the plane drops towards him, shielding his eyes against the sun. Suddenly heading straight towards him, the plane smashes against an invisible ridge and turns over and over. A blue line of smoke is uncoiling from the plane, but no fire. Almásy pulls away the debris to find Geoffrey-slumped, neck, broken, bloody. And in the process reveals, to his absolute horror, KATHARINE, starring grimly ahead, unable to move. He's frantic.*

ALMASY: Katharine! Oh dear God, Katharine—what are you doing here?

KATHERINE: I can't move. I can't get out.

ALMASY: Why did he bring you?

KATHARINE: A surprise, he said.

KATHERINE: Poor Geoffrey. He knew. He must have known all the time. He was shouting—*I love you, Katharine, I love you so much.* Is he badly hurt? His neck is odd.

KATHERINE: Please don't move me. It hurts too much.

ALMASY: We've got to get you out of here.

KATHERINE: It hurts too much.

ALMASY: I know, darling, I'm sorry.

KATHERINE: Why did you hate me?

ALMASY: What?

KATHERINE: Don't you know you drove everybody mad?

ALMÁSY: Don't talk.

KATHERINE: You speak so many bloody languages and you never want to talk.

ALMÁSY: You're wearing the thimble.

KATHERINE: Of course. You idiot. I always wear it. I've always worn it. I've always loved you.

KATHARINE: It's so cold.

ALMÁSY: I know. I'm sorry. I'll make a fire. I'll be back.

KATHARINE: Don't leave me!

ALMÁSY: I'm just going to find things for the fire.

KATHARINE: Shall we be all right?

ALMÁSY: Yes. Absolutely.

KATHARINE: Oh dear.

ALMÁSY: Listen to me, Katharine. You've broken your ankle and I'm going to have to try and bind it. I think your wrist might be broken, too—and some ribs, which is why it's hurting you to breathe. I'm going to have to walk to El Taj. Given all the traffic in the desert these days. I should bump into one army or another before I reach there—or Fenelon-Barnes and his camel. And then I'll be back and we'll be fine, and I'll never leave you.

KATHARINE: Do you promise? I wouldn't want to die here. I wouldn't want to die in the desert. I've always had a rather elaborate funeral in mind, with particular hymns. Very English. And I know exactly where I want to be buried. In our garden. where I grew up. With a view of the sea. So promise me you'll come back for you.

ALMÁSY: I promise I'll come back. I promise I'll never leave you. And there's plenty of water and food. You can have a party.

ALMÁSY: And a good read. Don't waste it.

KATHARINE: Thank you. Will you bury Geoffrey? I know he's dead.

ALMÁSY: I'm sorry, Katharine.

KATHARINE: I know.

ALMÁSY: Every night I cut out my heart but in the morning it was full again.

ALMÁSY: Tell me about your garden.

Scenario 2: The Patient is slipping away. Hana is reading from the last pages of the Herodotus where Katherine has written in the margins.

HANA: My darling, I'm waiting for you—how long is a day in the dark, or a week?

KATHARINE (O/S): The fire is gone now, and I'm horribly cold. I really ought to drag myself outside but then there would be the sun. [*She passes the flashlight across the wall, the painted figures dancing in the pale light.*]

KATHARINE (O/S): I'm afraid I waste the light on the paintings and on writing these words...

KATHARINE (O/S): We die, we die rich with lovers and tribes, tastes we have swallowed...

...bodies we have entered and swum up like rivers, fears we have hidden in like this wretched cave...I want all this marked on my body. We are the real countries, not the boundaries drawn on maps with the names of powerful men...

KATHARINE (O/S): I know you will come and carry me out into the palace of winds, the rumors of water... That's all I've wanted—to walk in such a place with you, with friends, on earth without maps.

KATHARINE (O/S): The lamp's gone out and I'm writing...

II. Fill the blanks with the missing words or phrases after listening to the lines taken from the film.

CLIFTON: You too. Good luck!

ALMÁSY: Clifton—your wife—do you think it's 1.)_____to leave her?

CLIFTON: Appropriate?

ALMÁSY: I think the desert is, it's—for woman—it's very 2.)_____, I wonder if it's not too much for her.

LIFTON: Are you mad? Katharine loves there. She told me yesterday.

ALMÁSY: 3.)_____, Were I you...

CLIFTON: I've known Katharine since she was three, my aunt is her aunt, we were 4.)_____ brother and sister before we were man and wife. I think I'd know what is and what isn't too much for her. I think she knows herself.

ALMÁSY: Very well.

CLIFTON: Why are you people so 5.)_____ by a woman?!

III. Complete the following memorable lines by translating the Chinese into English

1. **ALMASY:** _____(请恕我冒昧，我对社交礼节很迟钝) How do you find Cairo? Did you visit the pyramids?

2. **CLIFTON:** Marvelous. _____(她迷上旅馆的浴缸了), She is either in the pool, she swims for hours. She is a fish, quite incredible.

3. **ALMASY:** Why are people so happy when they _____? (撞见来自同一个地方的人) What happened in Montreal when you passed a man in the street? Did you invite him to live with you?

4. **KATHARINE:** (真正的国家不是画在地图上以强权者名字命名的疆界) _____. I know you'll come carry me out to the Palace of Winds. That's what I've wanted: to walk in such a place with you. With friends, on an earth.

IV. Oral practices—answer the following questions.

1. Do you think the love between Katherine and Almasy is ethical when Almasy even sacrifices others to save Katherine's life?

2. In the movie, nationalities are frequently mentioned. What is Almasy's view on nationalism?

Part 5 More Romance Movies

Plot Summary of *Meet Joe Black*

Billionaire media mogul William "Bill" Parrish (Anthony Hopkins) is considering a merger between his company and another media giant, while also about to celebrate his 65th birthday with an elaborate party being planned by his eldest daughter Allison (Marcia Gay Harden). He begins to hear mysterious voices, which he tries with increasing difficulty to ignore.

His youngest daughter Susan (Claire Forlani), an internal medicine resident, is involved with one of Bill's board members, Drew (Jake Weber). She is considering marriage, but her father is not favorably impressed by her relationship. When she asks for the short version of his impassioned speech, he simply says, "Stay open. Who knows? Lightning could strike!" Shortly thereafter, Susan meets a vibrant young man (Brad Pitt) at a coffee shop. She is instantly enamored but fails to even get his name. Minutes after their encounter (and unbeknownst to her), the

man is struck by multiple cars in what appears to be a remarkably serious motor vehicle accident.

The grim reaper of Death arrives at Bill's home in the body of the young man, explaining that Bill's impassioned speech has piqued his interest after an eternity of boredom. Given Bill's "competence, experience, and wisdom," Death tells Bill that in return for a few extra days of life, Bill shall be his guide on Earth. Bill agrees, and Death places himself at Bill's right hand as "Joe Black" and establishes a constant presence in Bill's home and work. Susan finds Joe appealing, but cannot understand why he is treating her like a stranger.

Bill's best efforts to navigate the next few days—knowing them now to be his last—fail to keep events from going rapidly out of his control. Drew is secretly conspiring with a man bidding for Parrish Communications, so he capitalizes on Bill's strange behavior to convince the board to vote him out as Chairman, using information given to him inadvertently by Bill's son-in-law Quince (Jeffrey Tambor) to push through approval for the merger which Bill had decided to oppose. Quince is devastated by what happens to Bill as all but one other member of the board vote him out.

Susan falls deeply in love with Joe, who, now under the influence of human desires, becomes attracted to her as well. Bill angrily confronts him about it, but Death intends to take Susan with him for his own.

As his last birthday arrives, Bill makes a last attempt to demonstrate to Joe the meaning of true love and all it encompasses—especially honesty and sacrifice. Realizing finally that love means having to sacrifice his desire to take Susan so that she can live her life, he abandons his plans to take her. He also comes to Bill's assistance in regaining control of his company, exposing Drew's underhanded business dealings to the board by "revealing" himself as an agent of the Internal Revenue Service and threatening to put Drew in jail.

Bill devotes his remaining time at the party to Allison and Susan. Joe also says his last goodbye to Susan, admitting in veiled terms that he isn't what he appears to be. She senses something of the truth behind his words but is unable or unwilling to vocalize this realization. While a fireworks show marks the end of the party, Joe escorts Bill away, with Susan observing from a distance. She then is astonished to see Joe return, at first confused as to whether it's in fact the young man she met at the coffee shop. The young man, unaware of what events have transpired from the time of his death until his return, approaches Susan. Susan, somewhat caught off guard by the happenings, questions the young man with, "What do we do now?" to which the young man replies, "It will come to us." After leaving the coffee shop at the beginning of the film, the young man quoted her father saying "Lightning could strike."

Memorable Lines

Settings: *Susan is involved with one of Bill's board members, Drew. She is considering marriage, but her father Bill is not favorably impressed by her relationship. Bill is instructing Susan about what is the essence of romantic love.*

Bill: Love is passion, obsession, someone you can't live without. I say fall head over heels, find someone you can love like crazy and who'll love you the same way back. How do you find him? Well, you forget your head and you listen to your heart. To make the journey and not fall deeply in love-well, you haven't lived a life at all. But you have to try, because if you haven't tried, you haven't lived... Stay open, who knows? Lightning could strike.

比尔：爱是激情，是迷恋，是不可或缺的。疯狂去爱一个迷恋你的人，他在哪里？要用心去寻找，不要用理智，否则人生将失去意义。这辈子若没深爱过，就枉此一生。要勇于尝试，否则等于白活了。爱要敞开心扉，期待心灵悸动。

Plot Summary of *Twilight*

A smart young girl with a heart of fire, and this incredibly and deadly attractive vampire, their lives intersect at this small rainy and cloudy town. Something that is destined is about to happen. Bella has fallen in love incurably with this vampire, and the vampire with this pure-hearted beautiful girl. Bella Swan moves from sunny Phoenix, Arizona to rainy Forks, Washington to live with her father, Charlie. When Bella is seated next to Edward Cullen in class on her first day of school, Edward seems utterly repulsed by her. But their newfound relationship reaches a climax when Bella is nearly run over by a fellow classmate's van in the school parking lot. Seemingly defying the laws of physics, Edward saves her life when he instantaneously appears next to her and stops the van with his bare hands. Edward confesses that he initially avoided Bella because the scent of her blood was so desirable to him. Over time, Edward and Bella fall in love.

Their relationship is thrown into chaos when another vampire coven sweeps into Forks. James, a tracker vampire who is intrigued by the Cullens' relationship with a human, wants to hunt Bella for sport. The Cullens attempt to distract the tracker by splitting up Bella and Edward, and Bella is sent to hide in a hotel in Phoenix. There, Bella receives a phone call from James, who claims he is holding

her mother captive. When Bella surrenders herself, James attacks her, but Edward, along with the other Cullens, rescues Bella and destroys James. Once they realize that James has bitten Bella's hand, Edward sucks the venom from her system before it can spread and transform her into a vampire, and she is then sent to a hospital. Upon returning to Forks, Bella and Edward attend their school prom and Bella expresses her desire to become a vampire, which Edward refuses.

Edward left, Bella's world completely collapsed, and she began to experiment with risky behavior, because she found that as long as she did a dangerous thing, Edward's voice will appear in her mind. Young Jacob appeared in her world. Although he knows another person is in the heart of Bella, he still affectionately accompanies and protects her. Edward mistakenly believes that Bella has jumped into the sea dead and cannot afford such a sudden a huge blow. Bella once again finds herself surrounded by danger as a Newborn Vampire. Army created by a Revenge ridden Victoria continue quest for revenge. In the midst of it all, she is forced to choose between her love for Edward and her friendship with Jacob - knowing that her decision has the potential to ignite the struggle between vampire and werewolf. With her graduation quickly approaching, Bella is confronted with the most important decision of her life, mortality or immortality?

Memorable lines in the film

Bella: When life offers you a dream so far beyond any of your expectations, it's not reasonable to grieve when it comes to an end.

当生活给了你一个远远超过你期望的美梦，那么，当它结束时，也就没有理由再去伤心。

Bella: About three things I was absolutely positive. First, Edward was a vampire. Second, there was part of him—and I didn't know how potent that part might be—that thirsted for my blood. And third, I was unconditionally and irrevocably in love with him.

有三件事我是可以肯定的：第一，Edward是一个吸血鬼；第二，在他身体内有一部分——我不知道那一部分起多大作用——非常渴望我的鲜血；第三，我毫无条件地、不可救药地爱上了他。

UNIT 7

Fantasy Movies 奇幻影片

Part 1 Chinese Summary

奇幻电影

奇幻电影又可译为"魔幻电影"。经典的奇幻作品主要是通过奇幻的手法来倾力构架一个与人们眼中的社会现实完全相异的,或洋溢淳朴民风,或正义最终战胜邪恶并获得宁静美好的"第二世界",并让接受者在这个异于现实的世界的游历中体悟到作品对人性的探索和深切关怀。

奇幻以魔法、巫术为基本元素,奇幻电影用充满超越现实的奇幻想象,建立自足的架空的世界,通过演绎一个个故事来表达生命的理想,隐含着对现实的关注,对现代人的关怀,对人与自我、人与他人、人与自然以及人与社会的思考。可以说,奇幻性、写实性(与平常人的情感,生活方式无异)、故事性成为奇幻电影的最为突出的特点,它主要表现的是成长的主题,通过片中角色的经历相互印证成长的脚印,这其中有着正义与邪恶的选择,发现与冒险的历练,勇气与坚强的培育。而故事的背景通常发生在与现实世界规律不同的"第二世界",或在现实世界中加入超自然元素(如预言、魔法、巫术、占卜、灵异等),同时再设以神话、宗教、社会、历史、政治或古老传说等作为结构背景,使故事变得大胆新奇,充满了想象与探索,因而具有一种独特的风格特征。

许多奇幻题材不像神话片那样以神话作为依据,影片中多是创作者个人的奇思妙想,有些远远脱离了神话,超越了神话。创作者依靠其丰富的幻想力和想象力,创造出奇异世界、奇幻故事和神奇人物,来寄托自己的希望与梦想,实现人类在现实世界中无法实现的情感、愿望和梦想。把现实世界中人们对爱、正义、勇气等美好的希望寄托在想象世界中的神奇人物身上,以此作为心灵的慰藉和梦想的实现。以理想的白日梦形式达到心理的补偿,成为心理的"代偿品",来满足人们在现实世界无法达到的夙愿和追求。奇幻片的想象是奇特的,手法是荒诞的,故事是没有逻辑且不符合现实生活的。但所表现的情感和梦想都是有真实基础的。尤其是把现实生活中具有某种特异功能的人植入想象的神奇世界里,来实现爱、正义,通过对磨难与恶的较量和斗争,发扬人性中最优美最光辉的东西,以战胜阴暗与邪恶而获得胜利为结尾。

奇幻片就其影像特征来说,它显著的特征就是采用数字技术来打造种种或恢弘或神奇的奇观场景,视觉盛宴。除此之外,奇幻片还注重细节设计以追求场景的"真实感"。所以观众虽然都明白很多场景要么是将真实画面进行加工处理,要么干脆完全通过计算机人为制造，但是由于奇幻片利用细节设计追求场景"真实感"，这种不着痕迹，使得观众很自然就能进入导演所创造的那个影像空间。其次是利用特技打造的炫目的打斗搏杀场面。奇幻片的主题往往表现为小人物的成长过程，同时也是叙述一个以弱胜强创造英雄传奇的故事，当剧情发展到高潮，矛盾冲突发展到最激烈的时候，常常少不了正邪双方的一场打斗。虽然奇幻片中"第二世界"环境营造上强调审美真实，但在打斗场面上却追求一种宏伟壮观的气势的营造，希望给观众带来视觉冲击。导演甚至不惜血本的使用各种各样的数字技术，打造恢弘场面，以此作为影片看点来吸引观众。当然，这些惊心动魄的大场面也是好莱坞奇幻片最有力的利器，毕竟很少有其他国家的电影工业能像好莱坞那样有足够的资源支撑"打斗大场面"。

作为一种新的电影类型——奇幻电影，追溯其源头，其实早在电影诞生之初，就有着进行幻想类电影的尝试，代表人物是法国电影大师乔治·梅里埃。他先后拍摄了《仙女国》、《月球旅行记》、《小丑和机器》等多部具有奇幻意蕴的短片。美国奇幻电影可以追溯到1939年的好莱坞儿童片经典《绿野仙踪》，在1953年拍摄的《小飞侠》等。此后美国科幻电影大兴，奇幻电影因素糅合在科幻片中，使奇幻电影一时没有作为一个独立电影类型而诞生。直到世纪之交，科幻电影已经没有更多的发展空间，奇幻电影才有大的发展。1996年美国推出了《龙的心》，自1999年后又推出《木乃伊》系列影片，其中产生于2001年的《木乃伊归来》最为成功。

当然真正意义上的奇幻电影则是在新世纪前后成熟成型的，随着电脑技术的迅猛发展，数字虚拟技术不断升级、成熟从而使奇幻电影获得了几乎无所不能的技术支持，并不失时机的吹响了独立的号角，在全球范围里，凭着《指环王》系列、《哈利·波特》系列掀起"奇幻热潮"，真可谓:魔戒既出，奇幻当道。

《指环王之魔戒再现》 *The Lord of the Rings: The Fellowship of the Ring* (2001)是根据英国现代作家约翰·托尔金这位天赋极高，知识渊博的牛津大学教授的《魔戒》改编拍摄的。托尔金的奇幻蕴藏着极其深厚的文化底蕴，并不是凭空想象的。《魔戒》被拍摄成电影以后，这部出版半个多世纪的奇幻文学作品又一次得到了世人的追捧。托尔金用非凡的想象力将远古传说加以幻想式的描绘，设计出一个与现实世界完全隔绝的架空世界。

《加勒比海盗之黑珍珠号的诅咒》 *Pirates of the Caribbean: The Curse of the Black Pearl* (2003)故事发生在17世纪，传说中海盗最为活跃的加勒比海。风趣的杰克·斯伯洛是活跃在加勒比海上的海盗，拥有属于自己的"黑珍珠号"海盗船。不幸的是，他的仇敌，老谋深算的巴尔巴罗萨船长偷走了他的"黑珍珠号"。巴罗萨是一个无恶不作的坏蛋，他抢劫了杰克的"黑珍珠号"后，更加猖狂。巴罗萨和他的海盗们身背着咒语，在每一个月光之夜，他们就变成了不死骷髅，而伊莉莎白正是解开咒语的关键。

《哈里波特系列》 *Harry Potter Film series* 根据英国女作家罗琳的同名系列小说改编而成。罗琳的作品从传统文学中吸取精华,作品熔圣经文学、神话传说、魔幻主义、超实主义、批判现实主义于一炉，多角度、多层次地反映了社会生活。而主人公哈利波特是个孤儿，在困境中逐渐历练成英雄，这种描写方式保留了英国文学史上孤儿文学的身影和流浪汉小说的模式。罗琳发挥充分的想象力，把魔法世界和现实世界完美结合，将现实与幻想相互渗透融合。

Unit 7 Fantasy Movies 奇幻影片

Fantasy Films

Fantasy Films unlike science fiction films that base their contents upon some degree of scientific truth, take the audience to **netherworld**, fairy-tale places where events are unlikely to occur in real life. In **mythological** or legendary times, they **transcend** the bounds of human possibility and physical laws. Fantasy films are often in the context of the imagination, dreams, or **hallucinations** of a character or within the projected vision of the storyteller. Fantasy films often have an element of magic, myth, wonder, escapism, and the extraordinary. They may appeal to both children and adults, depending upon the particular film.

In fantasy films, the hero often undergoes some kind of mystical experience, and must ask for aid from powerful, superhuman forces on the outside. Ancient Greek mythological figures or Arabian Nights-type narratives are typical storylines. Flying carpets, magic swords and spells, dragons, and ancient religious relics or objects are common elements. **Bizarre** and imaginary, invented lands include sci-fi worlds, unreal worlds, fairy tale settings, or other **whimsical** locales (e.g., Shangri-La or Brigadoon). The earliest sci-fi writers (H. G. Wells[1] and Jules Verne[2]) created fantastic worlds and/or journeys—the subject matter of many fantasy films.

Typically, the **predominant** characters in fantasies are princes or princesses. Some fantasy-type films might also include quasi-religious or supernatural characters such as angels, lesser gods, or fairies. Or they include the **gnomes**, **dwarves** and elves of legend.

Odd phenomena, physical **aberrations**, and incredible characters (sometimes monstrous characters that represent the **divine** or evil spirits, or fabulous magicians and **sorcerers**) are **incorporated into** fantasy films, and often **overlap** with *supernatural* films. They are often inspired or taken, however remotely, from myth or legend. They fill us with a marvelous sense of awe and **touch off** deep primal emotions.[3]

Fantasy films have a history almost as old as the medium itself. However, fantasy films were relatively few and far between until the 1980s, when high-tech filmmaking techniques and increased audience interest caused the **genre** to flourish.

Fantasy films are most likely to overlap with the film genres of *science fiction* and *horror*. When the narrative of a fantasy film tends to emphasize advanced technology in a fantastic world, it may be considered predominantly a science fiction film. Or when the supernatural, fantasy forces are specifically intended to frighten the audience, a fantasy film **falls** more **within** the horror genre.

Fantasy brings us back to **facets** of human nature, returning us to the foundations of our existence.[4] Fantasy may **draw us away** into worlds of wonder, **spectacle** and impossibility, but human behavior is always at the center of these revelations. The question of how characters respond to the conditions of their world is **paramount** regardless of whether we recognize that world, or whether it is one we can never experience. Once the film has ended, we are left only with a sense of the fictional world's reality, and of ourselves.[5]

After-reading questions

1. According to the article, which is the best definition of fantasy films?
   A. Fantasy films are films with fantastic themes, usually involving magic, supernatural events, make-believe creatures, or exotic fantasy worlds.
   B. The films that transcend the bounds of human possibility and physical laws are fantasy films.
   C. Fantasy films are films that base their contents upon some degree of scientific truth.
   D. Fantasy films are imaginary and mysterious films that attract both children and adults.

2. Which is not the characteristic of fantasy films?
   A. Fantasy films often have an element of magic, myth, wonder, escapism, and the extraordinary.
   B. The hero often undergoes some kind of mystical experience, and must ask for aid from powerful, superhuman forces on the outside.
   C. Fantasy films always show advanced technology in a fantastic world or frighten the audience.
   D. Princes or princesses and quasi-religious or supernatural characters are likely to appear in fantasy films.

3. What is the meaning of "Fantasy brings us back to facets of human nature, returning us to the foundations of our existence"?
   A. It is so bad that we cannot feel the marvelous scenes distinctly.
   B. The response to the conditions of the fantasy world by the characters demonstrates facets of human nature and the foundations of human existence.
   C. Fantasy brings us back to thousands of years ago and we will live an aboriginal life.
   D. Fantasy reminds us of old days which were pure and ordinary.

4. According to the article, which sentence is right?
   A. Ancient Greek mythological figures or Arabian Nights-type narratives are infrequent storylines.
   B. Fantasy films were not flourishing until the 1980s.
   C. Fantasy films are easily distinguished from the film genres of *science fiction*,

supernatural and *horror*.

D. How characters respond to the conditions of their world depends on whether we recognize that world, or whether it is one we can never experience.

Words and expressions

1. **netherworld** *n.* (religion) the world of the dead 冥界, 阴间
2. **mythological** *adj.* relating to mythology, lacking factual basis or historical validity 神话的；虚构的
3. **transcend** *v.* go beyond 超出或超越（经验、信念、描写能力等）的范围
4. **hallucination** *n.* illusory perception 幻觉
5. **bizarre** *adj.* conspicuously or grossly unconventional or unusual 奇形怪状的，怪诞的
6. **whimsical** *adj.* determined by, arising from, or marked by whim or caprice 异想天开的
7. **predominant** *adj.* having greatest ascendancy, importance, influence, authority, or force 占主导地位的, 显著的
8. **gnome** *n.* one of a fabled race of dwarflike creatures who live underground and guard treasure hoards 守护神
9. **dwarf** *n.* a small creature resembling a human being, often ugly, appearing in legends and fairy tales 身材矮小的人
10. **aberration** *n.* a state or condition markedly different from the norm 脱离常规；反常现象；异常行为
11. **divine** *adj.* emanating from God 神的，天赐的
12. **sorcerer** *n.* one who practices magic or sorcery 男巫，方士，施魔法者
13. **incorporate into** make into a whole or make part of a whole 使成为……的一部分
14. **overlap** *vt. & vi.* coincide partially or wholly 部分重叠
15. **touch off** put in motion or move to act 引起，触发某事
16. **genre** *n.* a kind of literary or artistic work （文学、艺术等的）类型，体裁，风格
17. **fall within** to be able to be divided into sth 应列入……范围内
18. **facet** *n.* a distinct feature or element in a problem （事物的）面，方面
19. **draw away** remove by drawing or pulling （使）离开，移开
20. **spectacle** *n.* something that can be seen or viewed, especially something of a remarkable or impressive nature. 壮观的场面或景象
21. **paramount** *adj.* of chief concern or importance 首要的，主要的

Notes

1. **H. G. Wells** was an English author, now best known for his work in the science fiction genre. 赫伯特·乔治·威尔斯(Herbert George Wells, 1866—1946)，英国著名

小说家，尤以科幻小说创作闻名于世。1895年出版《时间机器》一举成名，随后又发表了《莫洛博士岛》、《隐身人》、《星际战争》等多部科幻小说。

2. **Jules Verne** was a French author who pioneered the science fiction genre. He is best known for his novels *Twenty Thousand Leagues Under the Sea* (1870), *Journey to the Center of the Earth* (1864), and *Around the World in Eighty Days* (1873). Verne is often referred to as the "Father of Science Fiction". 儒勒·凡尔纳是19世纪法国著名的科幻小说和冒险小说作家，被誉为"现代科学幻想小说之父"，曾写过《海底两万里》、《格兰特船长的儿女》、《地心游记》、《八十天环游地球》等著名科幻小说，其一生信仰科学，是少见的科学作家。

3. They are often inspired or taken, however remotely, from myth or legend. They fill us with a marvelous sense of awe and touch off deep primal emotions.
译文：尽管微少，但它们大多是从神话传说中得到的启发或是直接的引用。它们使我们的心中充盈一种不可思议的惊奇，触动了内心深处深刻而原始的感情。

4. Fantasy brings us back to facets of human nature, returning us to the foundations of our existence.
译文：奇幻电影带我们回过去（审视）人性，使我们回归到我们生存的基本原则。

5. Once the film has ended, we are left only with a sense of the fictional world's reality, and of ourselves.
译文：一旦电影结束，我们留下的，就只有幻想世界的真实感和我们自己。

Part 3 Text 2

The Lord of the Rings: The Fellowship of the Ring

In an industry so derivative (衍生的) and bottom-line-focused as feature films, where every breakthrough (突破性进展) movie is followed by hundreds of pretenders trying (and failing) to re-capture the originality (创造性) and impact of the "first one," Peter Jackson's masterpiece *The Fellowship of The Ring* does it. It actually breaks new ground. The first installment of the legendary *Lord of The Rings* fantasy trilogy by J.R.R. Tolkein, all three parts of which Jackson is producing simultaneously, *The Fellowship* is nothing less than a masterpiece of art and integrity (整合性), capturing with vast magnitude (数量) the grandeur, majesty (雄伟，壮丽), and surreal(超现实的；犹如梦幻的) whimsy of Tolkien's mythical Middle-Earth[1]. In terms of impact, Jackson's choice to film all three parts at once (*the other two, The Two Towers and The Return Of The King*) will have the effect that there will be no changes in cast, no aging of the actors between films, and no deterioration (恶化，变坏) of the public's interest. The use of a classic piece of literature, already loved by millions of devotees and sure to attract millions more, will ensure a pre-established and exponentially (成倍地) growing audience. This movie is the

Star Wars[2] of its generation. It's *Harry Potter*[3] for grown-ups.

But the thing that makes this such a delight is not the shrewdness (机灵) of its producers' choices in the board room. It's the fact that it's just an amazing, beautiful, well-crafted film full of earnest acting, breathtaking visual splendor, and, of course, one of the best and most popular stories ever to hit the adventure/fantasy bookshelves. The history of Middle-Earth, how the legendary rings were created, and the story of The Hobbit, the book which serves as the prelude (开端，前奏) to the *Lord of The Rings* trilogy, are covered in a voiceover (画外音) and montage (蒙太奇) during the first ten minutes of the film; by the time we meet hobbit Frodo Baggins (Elijah Wood), his uncle Bilbo Baggins (Ian Holm), and their wizard friend Gandalf the Grey (Ian McKellen), we already know the rich history behind the little ring of gold Bilbo carries in his pocket.

As the story begins, the Shire (the area where the hobbits live) is abuzz (喊喊喳喳的，活泼的) with the excitement of Bilbo's upcoming 111th birthday party, which the legendary Gandalf is expected to attend. During the celebration, Bilbo announces that he is leaving the Shire, retiring to Rivendell[4], the elfish realm ruled by Elrond. His nephew Frodo will acquire his house and all his worldly possessions; including the famous ring which he has kept secret all these years. The ring, forged (锻造) in the volcanic depths of Mt. Doom[5] 2500 years ago, is one of immense power; it could endow (使(某人)天生具有 (好资质、能力等)) its bearer with control of the world, but since it was made by the dark lord Sauron, its power is dangerously evil, infecting most creatures who possess it with the irresistible dark temptations of Sauron's influence. But as Gandalf explains to Frodo, there are some who know of the ring's whereabouts (下落，去向), and they are converging (集中于) on the Shire to find it. Frodo must leave the Shire and travel back to Mt. Doom, in the treacherous (危险的；凶险的) realm of Mordor, and cast the ring back into the fires from whence (从何处，从那里) it came. This is the only way to destroy it.

So Frodo sets out with a group of nine, which forms the titular (有称号的) "fellowship" who will travel to Mordor with the sole objective of destroying the ring once and for all. Along the way they encounter many hardships, most of which are engineered by Gandalf's fellow wizard and former friend, Saruman The Wise (Christopher Lee), who has been seduced (引诱) by Sauron's evil power. Frodo and the "fellowship" fight with all manner of (各种各样的) foes, including wraiths, orcs, goblins, and various other long-leggedy beasties, in a series of specifically imagined and wondrously realized epic battles which stretch the limits of cinematography (电影艺术),

digital wizardry, and conventional special effects.

If author John Ronald Reuel Tolkien were alive today, he could not help but be pleased with what filmmaker and self-admitted Rings freak (怪人，奇异的) Peter Jackson has done with his epic Middle-Earth saga. Brimming (满溢的) with sweeping vistas of mystical, magical landscapes and seriously scary villains (反派角色) (using, of course, the most current techniques in digital effects), the film outdoes (胜过) Ralph Bakshi's[6] arty but bogged down (陷入困境；停滞) 1978 cartoon version by a mile. All the actors give heartfelt (诚挚的) and memorable performances, especially Wood, who is in almost all 178 minutes of film, and the 62-year-old McKellen, whose technique betrays why he is one of the most respected elder statesmen in the English theatre.

While it's so good, there is still some unseemliness (不合适) for young children; Its PG-13 rating is there for a reason. In addition to the three-hour running length, which might cause even the best-behaved youngsters to fidget (坐立不安), it has many truly disturbing scenes and images—not just the loud, in-your-face (放肆的) bad guys they may already be accustomed to, but some really unsettling, subtle things which could cause minor sleeplessness even in adults. There are a few dreggy (有渣滓的) portions which, while helpful in the expository (说明的) department, seem to underscore (强调) just how long you've been sitting in that seat. On the other hand...it's just so odiously (可恨的) good.

After reading questions

1. According to the article, *The Fellowship of the Ring* is the first installment of the legendary *Lord of the Rings* fantasy trilogy by J.R.R. Tolkein, all three parts of which Jackson is producing simultaneously. It is good because there will_____.
   A. be no changes in cast
   B. be no aging of the actors between films
   C. be no deterioration of the public's interest
   D. all of above

2. In the author's opinion, this movie is the *Star Wars* of its generation and it's *Harry Potter* for grown-ups. What does it really mean?
   A. *The Fellowship of the Ring* is as good and important as the other two.
   B. *The Fellowship of the Ring* is better than the Star Wars but inferior to Harry Potter.
   C. *The Fellowship of the Ring* is better than Harry Potter but inferior to the Star Wars.
   D. *The Fellowship of* the Ring is inferior to the other two.

3. We meet hobbit Frodo Baggins, his uncle Bilbo Baggins, and their wizard friend Gandalf the Grey during the first ten minutes and know the rich history behind

the little ring of gold Bilbo carries in his pocket. The history is introduced in_____.

   A. the preface of *The Fellowship of the Ring*, the first book of the legendary *Lord Of The Rings* fantasy trilogy by J.R.R. Tolkein

   B. the story of *The Hobbit*, the book which serves as the prelude to the *Lord Of The Rings* trilogy

   C. the preface of *The Hobbit*, the book which serves as the prelude to the *Lord Of The Rings* trilogy

   D. the legendary *Lord Of The Rings* fantasy trilogy by J.R.R. Tolkein

4. What factors stretch the limits of cinematography, digital wizardry, and conventional special effects?

   A. The characters in a series of specifically imagined and wondrously realized epic battles.

   B. The group of nine which forms the titular "fellowship" who will travel to Mordor with the sole objective of destroying the ring once and for all.

   C. The landscape in a series of specifically imagined and wondrously realized epic battles.

   D. A series of specifically imagined and wondrously realized epic battles.

5. *The Fellowship of the Ring* has been classified as PG-13 rating, which means it might cause even the best-behaved youngsters to fidget. What could NOT be the reason of its unseemliness?

   A. It has many truly disturbing scenes, including the loud, in-your-face bad guys.

   B. There are some really unsettling, subtle things which could cause minor sleeplessness even in adults

   C. *The Fellowship of* the Ring has a three-hour running length which might cause even the best-behaved youngsters to fidget.

   D. There are some scenes filled with sanguinary(血腥的) plot.

Notes

1. **Middle-earth** is the fictional setting of the majority of author J. R. R. Tolkien's fantasy writings. Tolkien wrote many times that Middle-earth is located on our Earth. He described it as an imaginary period in Earth's past.
   中土世界，是出现在J.R.R.托尔金小说著作中的一块架空世界中的大陆和世界，托尔金曾暗示中土世界所在的世界就是古代的地球。

2. ***Star Wars*** is an American epic space opera film series created by George Lucas. The first film in the series was originally released on May 25, 1977, under the title *Star Wars*, by 20th Century Fox, and became a worldwide pop culture phenomenon, followed by two sequels, released at three-year intervals.

英文类型影片赏析

《星球大战》，是美国导演兼制作人乔治·卢卡斯所制作拍摄的一系列科幻电影。同时"星球大战"也是该系列中最早拍摄的第四集的原来的片名。本片开启好莱坞电影商品授权的庞大事业，并在接下来的三年间拍摄了两部后续作品。

3. **The *Harry Potter* film series** is a British-American film series based on the *Harry Potter* novels by the British author J. K. Rowling.

    《哈利·波特》系列电影改拍自英国作家J. K. 罗琳的《哈利·波特》系列小说，由英美两国演员共同出演。

4. **Rivendell** is an Elven outpost in Middle-earth, a fictional realm created by J. R. R. Tolkien. It was established and ruled by Elrond in the Second Age of Middle-earth (four or five thousand years before the events of *The Lord of the Rings*).

    瑞文戴尔，是英国作家约翰·罗纳德·鲁埃尔·托尔金的史诗式奇幻小说《魔戒》中，位于中土大陆迷雾山脉中的精灵据点。

5. **Mount Doom** is a volcano in J. R. R. Tolkien's Middle-earth legendarium. The mountain represents the endpoint of Frodo Baggins' quest to destroy the Ring which is recounted in *The Lord of the Rings*. The chasm is the site where the One Ring was originally forged by the Dark Lord Sauron and the only place it can be destroyed.

    末日火山是托尔金中土大陆的虚构火山。索伦在末日火山铸造至尊魔戒，末日火山也是佛罗多·巴金斯实行摧毁魔戒任务的终点。

6. **Ralph Bakshi** (born October 29, 1938) is an American director of animated and live-action films. He has been involved in numerous television projects as director, writer, producer and animator.

    拉尔夫·巴克希是美国动画和真人电影导演。他也在许多电视节目中担任导播、编剧、监制和动画师的角色。

Part 4 Exercises

I. Answer questions after listening to the dialogues taken from the film.

1. According to Gandalf, what is the relationship between the ring and the Dark Lord Sauron? What is the portent of Sauron's returning?
2. What is Gandalf's attitude to Bilbo's pity on Gollum?
3. According to the conversation between Gandalf and Frodo, contrast Frodo's feelings to the ring.

Script

Scenario 1: *Frodo and Gandalf sit down in the kitchen with tea. The Ring lies on the table between them.*

GANDALF: This is the One Ring. Forged by the Dark Lord Sauron in the fires of

	Mount Doom. Taken by Isildur from the hand of Sauron himself.
FRODO:	Bilbo found it. In Gollum's cave.
GANDALF:	Yes. For sixty years the Ring lay quiet in Bilbo's keeping, prolonging his life, delaying old age. But no longer Frodo. Evil is stirring in Mordor. The Ring has awoken. It's heard its master's call.
FRODO:	But he was destroyed! Sauron was destroyed.

The Ring whispers softly in the Black Speech. Alarmed, both Frodo and Gandalf stare at it.

GANDALF: No, Frodo. The spirit of Sauron endured. His life force is bound to the Ring, and the Ring survived. Sauron has returned. His Orcs have multiplied. His fortress at Barad-Dûr is rebuilt in the land of Mordor. Sauron needs only this Ring to cover all the lands of a second darkness. He is seeking it, seeking it — all his thought is bent on it. The Ring yearns above all else to return to the hand of its master. They are one, the Ring and the Dark Lord. Frodo, he must never find it.

Frodo stands up and grabs the Ring. He walks down the corridor.

FRODO: All right, we put it away. We keep it hidden. We never speak of it again. No one knows it's here, do they? Do they Gandalf?

GANDALF: There is one other who knew that Bilbo had the Ring. I looked everywhere for the creature Gollum. But the enemy found him first.

In the chambers of Barad-Dûr, Gollum's tortured body writhes.

GANDALF: I don't know how long they tortured him. But amidst the endless screams and inane babble, they discerned two words···

GOLLUM: (shrieking)Shire! Baggins!

FRODO: Shire. Baggins. But that would lead them here!

Two Black Riders thunder down a moonlit road. A Hobbit holds up his lantern at the sound of the approaching horses.

HOBBIT: Who goes there?

One of the Riders brings down his sword and scythes it directly at the Hobbit. Back at Bag End, Frodo holds out the Ring to Gandalf.

FRODO: Take it Gandalf! Take it!

GANDALF: No, Frodo.

FRODO: You must take it!

GANDALF: You cannot offer me this Ring!

FRODO: I'm giving it to you!

GANDALF: Don't tempt me Frodo! I dare not take it. Not even to keep it safe. Understand Frodo, I would use this Ring from a desire to do good. But through me, it would wield a power too great and terrible to imagine.

FRODO: But it cannot stay in the Shire!

GANDALF: No! No, it can't.

Frodo closes the Ring inside his palm and looks up at Gandalf.

FRODO: What must I do?

Scenario 2: *Frodo looks down into the cavern and sees a small figure leaping from stone to stone. Startled, he walks over to where Gandalf is sitting.*

FRODO: There's something down there!

GANDALF: *(without surprise)* It's Gollum.

FRODO: Gollum?

GANDALF: He's been following us for three days.

FRODO: He escaped the dungeons of Barad-Dûr!

GANDALF: Escaped? Or was set loose? And now the Ring had drawn him here. He will never be rid of his need for it. He hates and loves the Ring, as he hates and loves himself.

Dark and dirty fingers clasp a stone implement. From the distance below, Gollum looks up, his large eyes piercing the darkness.

GANDALF: Sméagol's life is a sad story. Yes, Sméagol he was once called. Before the Ring found him... before it drove him mad.

FRODO: It's a pity Bilbo didn't kill him when he had the chance!

GANDALF: *(glancing sharply at Frodo)* Pity? It was pity that stayed Bilbo's hand. Many that live deserve death, and some that die deserve life. Can you give it to them, Frodo?

Frodo looks down, silently.

GANDALF: Do not be too eager to deal out death in judgment. Even the very wise can not see all ends. My heart tells me that Gollum has some part to play yet, for good or ill...

Gollum pulls back into the darkness, wrinkling his nose.

GOLLUM: Gollum.

GANDALF: ...before this is over.

Gollum slinks off.

GANDALF: The pity of Bilbo may rule the fate of many.

Frodo sits down next to Gandalf.

FRODO: I wish the Ring had never come to me. I wish none of this had happened.

GANDALF: So do all who live to see such times, but that is not for them to decide. All we have to decide is what to do with the time that is given to us. There are other forces at work in this world, Frodo, besides the will of evil. Bilbo was meant to find the Ring, in which case you also were meant to have it. And that is an encouraging thought.

Unit 7 Fantasy Movies 奇幻影片

II. Fill the blanks with the missing words or phrases after listening to the lines taken from the film.

The light dims, and before the Fellowship the Lord and Lady, Galadriel and Celeborn, halt. The Lady's eyes focus on Frodo, but Celeborn speaks.

CELEBORN: The 1)_____ knows you have entered here. What hope you had 2)_____ is now gone. Eight there are here, yet nine there were, 3)_____ Rivendell. Tell me, where is Gandalf?

As he speaks, Galadriel's eyes flicker to Aragorn's, who looks up.

CELEBORN: For I much 4)_____ to speak with him... I can no longer see him from afar.

GALADRIEL: Gandalf the Grey did not pass the borders of this land. He has 5)_____ shadow.

Aragorn nods slightly. Celeborn turns to Galadriel.

LEGOLAS: He was 6)_____ both Shadow and Flame: a Balrog of Morgoth. For we went needlessly into the net of Moria.

Gimli bows his head, sadly.

GALADRIEL: Needless were none of the deeds of Gandalf in life. We do not yet know his whole purpose. Do not let the great emptiness of Khazad-dûm fill your heart, Gimli, son of Glóin.

The Dwarf looks up as her words.

GALADRIEL: For the world has grown full of 7)_____. And in all lands, love is now 8)_____ grief.

Boromir turns his pained face to the Lady, blinking and swallowing hard. The Lady stares back. Boromir looks away, weeping.

CELEBORN: What now becomes of this Fellowship? Without Gandalf, hope is lost.

GALADRIEL: The quest stands upon the edge of a knife. 9)_____ but a little and it will fail to the ruin of all.

Boromir looks back up at her, unsure.

GALADRIEL: Yet hope remains while the company is true.

Galadriel looks at Sam and smiles.

GALADRIEL: Do not let your hearts be troubled. Go now and rest for you are 10)_____. Tonight you will sleep in peace.

She whispers to Frodo in his mind, casting her eyes sideways at him.

GALADRIEL: Welcome, Frodo of the Shire... one who has seen the Eye!

Galadriel's eyes, the same ones that Frodo saw upon entering Lothlórien, flash through his mind again.

III. Complete the following memorable lines by translating the Chinese into English.

1. I have nothing greater to give, (胜于你已有的天赋)_____.

2. I know what you would say. And it would seem like wisdom (但只能打从心底警醒我)_____.

3. The Ring passed to Isildur, who had this one chance to destroy evil forever. But the hearts of Men are easily corrupted. And (戒指的力量有它自己的意志)_____.

4. I was expecting you sometime last week! Not that it matters, you come and go as you please. Always have done and always will. (你让我有些措手不及)_____, I'm afraid.

IV. Oral practices—answer the following questions.

1. What is the personality of Frodo, the hero of the film?

2. What should be owed to the final victory of the Fellowship?

Part 5 More Fantasy Movies

Plot Summary of *Pirates of the Caribbean*: *The Curse of the Black Pearl*

As Governor Weatherby Swann, his 12-year-old daughter, Elizabeth, and Lieutenant James Norrington sail to Port Royal, Jamaica, their vessel encounters a shipwreck with a sole survivor, the boy Will Turner. Elizabeth hides a gold medallion that the unconscious boy is wearing, fearing it will identify him as a pirate. She glimpses a ghostly pirate ship, later identified as the Black Pearl.

The notorious pirate Captain Jack Sparrow arrives in Port Royal to commandeer a ship. He rescues Elizabeth from sea, but Commodore Norrington recognizes Jack as a pirate and arrests him. Jack Sparrow briefly takes Elizabeth hostage in order to escape and ducks into a blacksmith's shop, encountering Will Turner, now a blacksmith's apprentice. That night Port Royal is besieged by the Pearl. Elizabeth is captured and invokes parley.

Will Turner, who loves Elizabeth, persuades Jack Sparrow to help him rescue her in exchange for Jack's freedom. Jack agrees after learning Will's surname is "Turner", believing he can use Will to reclaim the Pearl. Will and Jack commandeer the HMS Interceptor and recruit a crew in Tortuga with help from Jack's old friend, Joshamee Gibbs. They set sail for Isla de Muerta, as Jack knows the pirates will go there to break the curse, turning them into immortal skeletal beings whose true forms are revealed in moonlight. The curse can be lifted if the coins and each pirate's blood is returned to the chest. William "Bootstrap Bill" Turner, Jack's only supporter, sent a coin to his son, Will, believing the crew should remain cursed. Barbossa had Bootstrap Turner tied to cannon and thrown overboard, only later to learn his blood was needed to break the curse.

After reaching the island, Will suspects Jack Sparrow may betray him and knocks him out. He rescues Elizabeth and they escape to the Interceptor leaving Jack behind. Will reveals he is Bootstrap Bill Turner's son and demands that Elizabeth and the crew be freed, or he will shoot himself and fall overboard, foiling Captain Barbossa's plan to break the curse. Captain Barbossa agrees but applies another loophole, marooning Elizabeth and Jack on the island Jack was on ten years earlier.

Elizabeth burns the cache of rum to create a signal fire that Commodore Norrington's ship spots. She convinces Commodore Norrington to rescue Will by accepting his marriage proposal. Returning to Isla de Muerta, Commodore Norrington sets an ambush while Jack persuades Captain Barbossa to form an alliance. He tells him to delay breaking the curse until they have taken Commodore Norrington's ship, the Dauntless. Jack's plan goes awry when Barbossa orders his crew to infiltrate the Dauntless from underwater. It is then revealed that Jack had taken a medallion from the chest during the earlier negotiations to become immortal so that he could fight Barbosa without fear of death.

Norrington spots his ship under attack and orders his men to return. They make it to the ship and engage the cursed pirates. Meanwhile, when Barbossa attempts to kill Elizabeth, Jack shoots Barbossa as Will drops the last two medallions, stained with his and Jack's blood, into the chest. No longer immortal, Barbossa collapses and dies.

Will is pardoned and allowed to marry Elizabeth. The crew rescues Jack, appointing him captain. The film ends with Jack looking at his compass while singing "A Pirate's Life for Me".

Memorable lines in the film

Settings: Elizabeth and Jack Sparrow are marooned on an island which Jack was on ten years earlier. Elizabeth discovers how Jack escaped: the island was used as a cache by rum runners and Jack managed to barter passage off. So Elizabeth flatters Jack when they drink the left rum at night and he tells her his understanding of ships.

Jack Sparrow: Not just the Spanish Main, my love. The entire ocean. The entire world. Wherever we want to go, we'll go. That's what a ship is, you know. It's not just a keel and a hull and a deck and sails, that's what a ship needs but what a ship is... what the Black Pearl really is... is freedom

不只西班牙海域，亲爱的，是所有的海洋，全世界。我们想去哪就去哪。这就是船，你知道的。它不单是龙骨、船壳、甲板和帆，那些是船的配备，而船则是……"黑珍珠号"的真正意义是……自由。

Plot Summary *of Harry* Potter Film series

Harry Potter is an orphaned boy brought up by his unfriendly aunt and uncle. At the age of eleven, half-giant Rubeus Hagrid informs him that he is actually a wizard and that his parents were murdered by an evil wizard named Lord Voldemort. Surviving from the disaster, Harry became extremely famous in the Wizarding World. Harry begins his first year at Hogwarts School of Witchcraft and Wizardry and learns about magic. During the year, Harry and his friends Ron Weasley and Hermione Granger become entangled in the mystery of the Philosopher's Stone which is being kept within the school.

The trios return to Hogwarts for their second year, which proves to be more challenging than the last. The Chamber of Secrets has been opened, leaving students and ghosts petrified by an unleashed monster. Harry must face up to claims that he is the heir of Salazar Slytherin (founder of the Chamber), learns that he can speak Parseltongue, and also discovers the properties of a mysterious diary only to find himself trapped within the Chamber of Secrets itself.

In the third year, Professor R. J. Lupin joins the staff as Defence Against the Dark Arts teacher, while convicted murderer Sirius Black escapes from Azkaban Prison. The Ministry of Magic entrusts the Dementors of Azkaban to guard Hogwarts from Black. Harry learns more about his past and his connection with the escaped prisoner.

During Harry's fourth year, the Dark Mark appears in the sky after a Death Eater attack at the Quidditch World Cup, Hogwarts plays host to a legendary event: the Triwizard Tournament, there is a new Defence Against the Dark Arts professor Alastor Moody and frequent nightmares bother Harry all year. Harry's name is also produced from the Goblet making him a fourth champion, which results in a terrifying encounter with a re-born Lord Voldemort.

Harry's fifth year begins with him being attacked by Dementors in Little Whinging. Later, he finds out that the Ministry of Magic is in denial of Lord Voldemort's return. Harry is also beset by disturbing and realistic nightmares while Professor Umbridge, a representative of Minister for Magic Cornelius Fudge, is the new Defence Against the Dark Arts teacher.

In Harry's sixth year at Hogwarts School of Witchcraft and Wizardry, Lord Voldemort and his Death Eaters are increasing their terror upon the Wizarding and

Muggle worlds. Albus Dumbledore persuades his old friend and colleague Horace Slughorn to return to Hogwarts as a professor as there is a vacancy to fill. While in a Potions lesson, Harry takes possession of a strangely annotated school textbook, inscribed 'This is the property of the Half-Blood Prince', which contains astonishing information. Meanwhile, Dumbledore and Harry secretly work together to discover the method on how to destroy Voldemort once and for all.

After unexpected events at the end of the previous year, Harry, Ron, and Hermione are entrusted with a quest to find and destroy Lord Voldemort's secret to immortality – the Horcruxes. The trios undergo a long adventure with many obstacles in their path and Harry's connection with the Dark Lord's mind becoming ever stronger. However, now that the Dark Lord has obtained the yet unbeatable Elder Wand, he aims to complete his final stage to ultimate power and launches an attack on Hogwarts School, where the trio return for one last stand against the dark forces that threaten to take over the Wizarding and Muggle worlds.

Memorable lines in the film

Settings: Hogwarts School is holding an opening ceremony of a new semester. After a chorus of students, the principal Dumbledore gave a speech to all students.

Dumbledore: A word of caution: dementors are vicious creatures. They will not distinguish between the one they hunt and the one who gets in their way. Therefore I must warn each and every one of you to give them no reason to harm you. It's not in the nature of a dementor to be forgiving. But you know happiness can be found even in the darkest of times, when one only remembers to turn on the light

警告各位：摄魂怪是邪恶的怪物，它们不会区分猎物和阻碍者。因此，我必须提醒你们每一个人不要给它们任何理由来伤害你。慈悲并不是摄魂怪的天性，但你们知道，即使在最黑暗的时刻还是可以找到快乐，只要记住打开明灯。

UNIT 8

Social Dramas 社会问题影片

Part 1 Chinese Summary

社会问题影片

如果把电影按照题材划分类型，社会问题片就是反映某个严肃的社会主题的影片。托马斯·沙茨说过："由于类型片是仪式性的，他可以用独特的概念形式来表现一些深刻的文化矛盾和冲突，这种概念形式是广大观众所熟悉的，也是容易接受的。"按照他所说，那么社会问题片作为类型片的一种，是用人物的刻画或剧情的发展来表现一些深刻的社会矛盾和冲突。

社会问题片让电影提供一个平台，以讨论一些严峻的社会问题。一方面可以引起人们对这个问题的注意，提高认识；另一方面，可以让观众在想象的层面讨论这个问题——思考可能的原因、问题的后果、以及一些可能的解决方法。这就是社会问题片存在的意义。社会问题片的动机是很高尚的，旨在实现虚构的故事不仅要娱乐也要训诫的目的。它让我们意识到一些可能忽视的社会问题，戏剧化地向我们展现了问题可能带来的结果，以及可能的解决方法。

社会问题片虽然就题材来讲自成一类，但是因为社会问题要通过人物或剧情才能反映出来，所以社会问题片与相当一部分其他类型的影片关系密不可分。社会问题片通过其他类型影片的剧情或人物来反映其社会问题，而其他类型通过反映社会问题使其在原有宗旨上更具有一定的意义。但是这并不意味着社会问题片和其他类型影片没有区别，后者有着其自己的主题宗旨，对于后者，社会问题只是顺带表现出来；对于前者，他的主旨就是鲜明地反映社会问题。例如，影片《美国丽人》就是一部典型的社会问题片，他常常被人看作是经历中年危机的男性困惑坎坷的典型经历，不仅于此，也有人认为他是对过度的女权主义、消费主义和"以自我为中心"的生活哲学的控诉，可以说这部影片从头至尾讲述的都是反映社会问题的。相比而言，黑帮片中史诗级的作品《教父》，也揭示了美国当时社会的表层下最隐蔽的黑暗。可以这么说，《教父》所反映的社会问题只是这部影片的表层元素，除去揭露当时社会黑暗现象这一表层元素，《教父》的核心类型元素仍然是强调当时美国地下势力集团之间真刀真枪的黑帮争斗。所以黑帮类型更接近该片的内核，理应成为《教父》的类型。而《美国丽人》的核心类型元素就是反映一个又一个存在于美国中产阶级家庭中的社会问题，脱离了这些元素该片也就失去了意义。所以，从这两个例子可以看出，很多影片看似是社会问题片，实际上不是。

《美国丽人》American Beauty（1999）的一个主题："stay, look closer"。没有一个人看得清楚自己，每个人都在盲目地为人生价值寻找定位。生活自然有它所必然经历的美好，然而这些美好是转瞬即逝的，如果没有安静感恩的心灵，注定会错过它们。影片给了中年危机及中产阶级家庭危机这一老问题新的生命。它没有压得令人喘不过气来的沉重空气，而是将戏剧效果与黑色喜剧融合起来，形成了独特艺术风格。

《撞车》Crash（2004）由一场司空见惯交通事故引出了人与人之间错综复杂的矛盾纠葛。剧情以洛杉矶为背景，反映了美国社会中不同种族、文化、语言等带来的各种隔阂和冲突。可以说影片借助种族矛盾关注现代人自身的问题并提倡对自我进行反思。人性的善良与弱点也许只有一步之遥，一念之差。影片让撞车这一单个事件超越了种族、社会、国家而凸现出更为深刻的寓意。

《贫民窟的百万富翁》Slumdog Millionaire（2008）并没有被构想为一种固定的类型片。它是一个狄更斯式的传奇流浪冒险故事，以一个真实的印度为背景，涵盖了印度的阶级结构、伊斯兰教与印度教的教派冲突、犯罪集团以及大众传媒等方面。影片让更多的人了解到第三世界国家最底层人民的生活状况。美与丑的强烈对比，苦难与欢笑的平行存在，这样的文化让人迷惑、辛酸，又迷恋。

Social Dramas

Generic categories are generally defined on the basis of subject matter, formal properties, style or affective response. In terms of subject matter, social drama can be classified as a kind of film reflecting serious social topics. As Thomas Schatz[1] puts it, "In its ritualistic capacity, a film **genre** transforms certain fundamental cultural contradictions and conflicts into a unique conceptual structure that is familiar and accessible to a mass audience[2]." According to this opinion, social drama, as a kind of genre, is to reflect serious social contradictions and conflicts through the portrayal of characters and development of stories.

Social drama provides a **forum** in which certain pressing social problems can be presented. In one part it is a "consciousness-raising" activity that brings social problems to light. In another, it is a way for the audience to deal imaginatively with the problems——to consider possible causes, to imagine possible consequences, and to *hypothesize* possible solutions. This is the meaning of the existence of social dramas. Social dramas stem from the most noble and honorable motives. They attempt to fulfill the ancient dictum that fiction should instruct as well as entertain. They help us to recognize a social issue that we might otherwise overlook, and show us in dramatic form both its possible consequences and its possible solutions.

Social dramas have an inseparable relationship with quite a lot of other genres for

the reason that social problems should be reflected through characters or stories. Social dramas reflect social problems through the stories or characters of other genres, while other genres embody some extra meanings on the original purpose by reflecting social problems. However, it doesn't **denote** that there is no difference between social dramas and other genres. The latter has its themes and purposes. With regard to the latter, the social problems are just indicated incidentally, and as to the former, the vivid reflection of social problems is its core purpose. For instance, *American Beauty*, a typical social drama, is often considered to be depiction of one man's troubled experiences brought about by a stereotypical mid-life crisis. At the same time it is also a controversial indictment of the excesses of feminism. Compared with *American Beauty*, *God Father*, one of the most famous gangster films ever, unveils more than the deepest darkness of the American society back then. It highlights violent and cruel conflicts and clashes between various crime lords. So we can say that many films that seemingly belong to social dramas, as a matter of fact, are not social dramas.

The greatest difference between the social dramas of Britain and America and those of other countries is the different social problems they reflect. Every country has its specific social problems. For example, America, as a melting pot, has its distinct racial issues which are rare in China. Likewise, some Chinese social problems, such as the rural-urban **disparities**, are also rare in America. Of course, there are also some common social problems which exist in different countries like global social problems such as poverty, environmental protection. However, for British and American societies, the problems roughly centre on the aspects of racial discrimination, medical welfare reform, poverty, etc.

After-reading questions

1. Which of the following purposes of social dramas is WRONG ?
   A. To reveal some social problems.
   B. To show possible causes of some social problems.
   C. To arouse people's concerning on social problems.
   D. To show the characters and stories in certain social circumstances.
2. According to the context, what is the closest meaning of "**hypothesize**" (Line 4, Para 2)
   A. To make.
   B. To imagine.
   C. To come to a conclusion.
   D. To list.
3. According to the article, WHY is *American Beauty* classified as a social drama?
   A. Because its situation is in American society.

B. Because it embodies some social problems.

C. Because its core purpose is to reflect social problems.

D. Because it is concerned with some unique social problems in America.

4. Which of the following social problems are NOT mentioned in the article?

A. Racial issues.

B. Poverty.

C. Environmental protection.

D. Shortage of food.

Words and expressions

1. **genre** *n.* a kind of literary or artistic work.（文学、艺术等的）类型，体裁，风格
2. **ritualistic** *adj.* of or characterized by or adhering to ritualism. 仪式的
3. **forum** *n.* a public facility to meet for open discussion. 平台
4. **denote** *v.* have as a meaning 意指
5. **disparity** *n.* inequality or difference in some respect.（尤指因不公正对待引起的）不同，不等，差异，悬殊

Notes

1. **Thomas Schatz** is a professor of communications, the university of Texas, main research interests: Hollywood films and studio systems.

   托马斯·沙茨是美国得克萨斯大学传播学教授，主要研究领域为好莱坞电影和制片厂制度。

2. In its ritualistic capacity, a film genre transforms certain fundamental cultural contradictions and conflicts into a unique concecptual structure that is familiar and accessible to a mass audience.

   译文：由于类型片是仪式性的，他可以用独特的概念形式来表现一些深刻的文化矛盾和冲突，这种概念是广大观众所熟悉的，也是容易被接受的。

3. Social dramas stem from the most noble and honorable motives. They attempt to fulfill the ancient dictum that fiction should instruct as well as entertain.

   译文：社会问题片的动机是很高尚的，旨在实现虚构的故事不仅要娱乐也要训诫的目的。它让我们意识到一些可能忽视的社会问题。

American Beauty[1]

If one were to go by journalistic and media chatter alone, there would be little doubt that *American Beauty* was the best film of 1999. Usually, the film is described as an

assault (攻击) on the emotional sleepwalking (梦游) that passes for life in the American suburb; and something of the sort does appear to have been among the intentions of the director Sam Mendes[2], who makes prominent (突出的，显著的) use of aerial shots (高空镜头) floating over the anonymous, tree-lined streets where the characters live. The suburbs have been so frequently ridiculed on the score of crass (愚钝的) materialism and abject (可怜的) conformity over the past 50 years that it is a wonder their residents do not rise up to get revenge on their metropolitan tormentors (带来苦恼的人).

  My own view is that American Beauty is a vital but uneven film. Although it has little to say that is entirely new, it nevertheless manages to render certain experiences vividly, most memorably when it deals with the ways that teenagers and adults imagine each other's lives, as in the relationship between the protagonist, Lester Burnham, and his daughter's friend Angela. The spectacle of a middle-aged man genuinely (真实的), if absurdly, rejuvenated (焕发青春) by the illusions of freedom and fulfillment embodied by an underaged girl is not exactly unfamiliar; however, like the most enduring literary treatments of this theme (e.g., Lolita[3]), *American Beauty* succeeds as an exercise in romantic irony. In this regard, Kevin Spacey[4]'s ability to project an unflappable (镇定的) cool image, even after his character has crossed over into ludicrousness (滑稽), is a palpable (明显的，易察觉的) strength; and at the end of the film, after Lester declines to take advantage of the girl's vulnerability (易受攻击的), he comes to resemble the speaker in Keats' "Nightingale" ode[5], left bemused by the ability of his own fancy to create an unreachable paradise, but also brought to a greater humanity by the experience as a whole. For her part, the girl is the most believable teenager in the film. The energy she devotes to trying to live up to an unworthy image of herself is painfully familiar, and there is a nice symmetry in the fact that she is chasing empty images of adulthood at the same time that Lester is cultivating equally empty fantasies about youth.

  Unfortunately, the other adult characters are actually based on well-known stereotypes (刻板形象). For example, Annette Bening[4]'s character (Lester's wife) is a ferocious (惊人的) mockery (拙劣模仿) which seems to come straight form the yellowed pages of all-but-forgotten jeremiads (伤心故事) like Philip Wylie[6]'s *Generation of Vipers*[7], which ascribed (to 归因于) the most bland (冷漠的) and wasteful traits of suburban consumer culture to a phenomenon that the author called "momism" — essentially the claim that the backbone of the American family was being warped (使弯曲) by the voracious (贪婪的), manipulative (圆滑的), yet contemptibly anesthetic (麻醉的) tastes of a certain kind of mother, who was becoming more common and even getting the upper hand as a result of the American male's failure to be a man. Not only were such mothers trying to take the place of fathers, but they were also bound to raise troubled and rebellious children, since for them childrearing (抚养孩子) was accomplished largely by means of bribery (行贿) with the promise of access to consumer goods and pleasures.

The filmmakers correctly see that all art involves the risk of manipulation, and that pleasure, including the pleasure of looking at a woman's body, need not be simply equated with sadism (虐待狂) of fetishism (恋物癖). Rather, with the help of a video camera, Lester's self-denigrating (自我贬低的) daughter Jane learns to see herself through her lover's eyes, suggesting that such aesthetically informed ways of seeing are inseparable (不可分割的) from human relationships and the growth of a mature sense of self.

Ricky's video clip of a plastic bag blowing around tends toward an essentially religious conception of beauty, which distracts from what the filmmakers have to show us about its role in human relationships by locating the source of beauty outside of us in the world of things, or even somewhere beyond. The curious thing about the plastic sequence is that it really is the kind of thing that a teenage aesthete might consider "deep"; however, the filmmakers evidently mean for us to be as moved by it as the kids in the film are. Even allowing that the children of dysfunctional (功能紊乱的) families are often saner (心理健康的) and more mature that their parents, one nevertheless comes to suspect that this uncannily (神秘的，不寻常的) cool-headed and clear-sighted young man is something of a fantasy figure, a creation of the filmmakers' own narcissism (自恋).

Without question *American Beauty* is a bold, ambitious piece of filmmaking that showcases (展现) some fine acting and reveals the considerable talents of its director and screenwriter in a variety of ways; it fully deserves to be seen and discussed by anyone who cares about American cinema. When the discussion has ended, however, one hopes that the participants will have made a genuine effort to sort out the film's strengths and weaknesses, instead of merely repeating the handiest clichés (陈词滥调) about its setting.

After reading questions

1. In Paragraph 1 of the review, the author says that many discussions about *American Beauty* concentrate on its description of _____.
   A. the aerial shots of the movie
   B. the anonymous tree-lined streets in the movie
   C. the pathetic suburban lives in America
   D. the revenge of the suburban people against the metropolitan ones.

2. What's the author's view point on the performance of Kevin Spacey (the protagonist of the movie)?
   A. rejuvenated
   B. vulnerable

C. ludicrous

D. strong

3. Why does the author mention the work *Generation of Vipers* by Philip Wylie?

   A. Because it first terms "momism".

   B. Because it criticizes the mothers who warped their families.

   C. Because Lester's wife shares the same characters as those mothers mentioned in the work.

   D. Because it provides the first aware of the danger of momism in America.

4. In the movie, Rocky shows a video clip of a plastic bag blowing around. According to the author in Paragraph 5, which is most likely the function of this part in the movie?

   A. To show the essential religious conception of beauty.

   B. To show the admiration of a teenager.

   C. To showcase the filmmakers' own deep ideas.

   D. To move the audience.

5. In the last paragraph, the author hopes that the participants of discussing *American Beauty* should _____.

   A. watch the movie more carefully

   B. repeat the reviews in an creative way

   C. not use clichés to discuss it

   D. give genuine and original reviews on the film

Notes

1. ***American Beauty*** (1999): was released by Universal Picture and directed by Sam Mendes. It won five Oscar awards in the year of 1999, including Best Director and Best Picure. 由环球公司于1999年发行的影片，萨姆门德斯导演，荣获当年包括最佳导演、最佳影片在内的五项奥斯卡奖项。

2. **Sam Mendes**: (born August 1, 1965) was a British director. In 1999, he got the chance to direct his first feature film, *American Beauty* (1999). The movie earned 5 Academy Awards including Best Picture and Best Director for Mendes, which is a rare feat for a first-time film director. He married British actress Kate Winslet in May 2003。萨姆·门德斯首次导演电影就凭借《美国丽人》获得了奥斯卡最佳导演奖。2003年与电影*Titanic*女主角扮演者凯特·文斯莱特结为伉俪。

3. ***Lolita*** (1997)《洛丽塔》改编自弗拉基米尔·纳博科夫的同名小说，叙述了一个中年男子与一个未成年少女的恋爱故事。

4. **Kevin Spacey** an American actor, director, screenwriter, producer. Won a Best Actor Academy Award for American Beauty in 1999. 凯文·史派西, 美国电影演员，导演，编剧，制作人。于1999年凭借《美国丽人》荣获奥斯卡最佳男主角

奖。

5. **Keats' "Nightingale" ode**: *Ode to a Nightingale* describes a series of conflicts between reality and the Romantic ideal of uniting with nature. 济慈《夜莺颂》，描述了现实和浪漫的自然理想之间的矛盾。

6. **Annette Bening** is an American actress, a Oscar nominee for her roles in *American Beauty*. A four-time Oscar nominee and twice Golden Globe Awards winner. 安妮特·贝宁，凭借《美国丽人》荣获当年奥斯卡最佳女配角提名，并且曾四度被奥斯卡提名，获得两次金球奖。

7. **Philip Wylie** a prolific American author 飞利浦·维利，一位多产的美国作家。

8. *Generation of Vipers* 《一代毒蛇》飞利浦的作品，其中特别提到momism，母权至上主义。突出强调过度女权主义带来的危害。

9. For example, Annette Bening's character (Lester's wife) is a ferocious mockery which seems to come straight form the yellowed pages of all-but-forgotten jeremiads like Philip Wylie's *Generation of Vipers*, which ascribed the most bland and wasteful traits of suburban consumer culture to a phenomenon that the author called "momism" — essentially the claim that the backbone of the American family was being warped by the voracious, manipulative, yet contemptibly anesthetic tastes of a certain kind of mother, who was becoming more common and even getting the upper hand as a result of the American male's failure to be a man.

译文：比如，安妮特·贝宁所饰演的莱斯特妻子一角，就是对飞利浦·威利的《一代毒蛇》的极力戏仿。这部已淡出人们视野的作品描写了一种母权至上的现象，这种现象导致了的一种乏味的、浪费的郊区式消费模式。母权至上主义影响了美国的家庭，这些家庭中的母亲贪心世故，趣味索然，令人鄙夷。由她们主导的家庭越来越多，因为美国男性已枉为男人。

Part 4 Exercises

I. Answer questions after listening to the dialogues taken from the film.

1. Why does Ricky say that the white plastic bag is the most beautiful thing he has ever filmed?
2. According to Lester, what kind of girl Carolyn was?
3. Why did Lester quarrel with Carolyn about the couch?

Script

Scenario 1: *On VIDEO: were IN an empty parking lot on a cold, gray day. Something is floating across from us... it's an empty, wrinkled, white PLASTIC BAG. We follow it as the wind* carries it in a circle around us, sometimes whipping it about violently, or, without warning, sending it soaring skyward, then letting it float gracefully down to the ground...

RICKY: You want to see the most beautiful thing I've ever filmed?

RICKY: It was one of those days... When it's a minute away from snowing, and there's this electricity in the air, you can almost hear it, right? And this bag was like, dancing with me.

Like a little kid begging me to play with it. For fifteen minutes. And that's the day I knew there was this entire life behind things, and ... this incredibly benevolent force, that wanted me to know there was no reason to be afraid.

RICKY: Video's a poor excuse. I know, But it helps me remember ... and I need to remember...

(JANE is watching him.)

RICKY: Sometimes there's so much beauty in the world I feel like I can't take it, like my heart's going to cave in.

Scenario 2: (LESTER is sprawled on the couch in his underwear, drinking a beer and watching TV. His working out is beginning to produce results. Carolyn enters through the kitchen. She stands there, staring at Lester. After a moment, he looks up at her.)

LESTER: Christ, Carolyn. When did you become so ... joyless?

CAROLYN: Joyless? I am not joyless. There happens to be a lot about me ... that you don't know, Mr. Smarty Man.

LESTER: There's plenty of joy in my life. Whatever happened to that girl... Who used to fake seizures at frat parties when she got bored? Who used to run up to the roof of our first apartment building ... to flash the traffic helicopters? Have you totally forgotten about her? Because I haven't.

CAROLYN: LESTER, you're going to spill beer on the couch.

LESTER: So what? It's just a couch.

CAROLYN: This is a $4,000 sofa, upholstered in Italian silk. This is not just a couch.

LESTER: It's just ... a ... couch! This isn't life! This is just stuff, and it's become more important to you than living. Well, honey, that's just nuts. I'm only trying to help you!

CAROLYN: Don't.

II. Fill the blanks with the missing words or phrases after listening to the lines taken from the film.

LESTER: I had always heard your entire life 1)_____ in front of your eyes the second before you die. First of all, that one second... isn't a 2)_____ at all. It 3)_____ on forever, like an ocean of time. For me, it was 4)_____ at Boy Scout camp, watching falling stars. And yellow leaves from the maple trees that 5)_____ our street. Or my grandmother's hands and the way her skin seemed like paper. And the first time I saw my cousin Tony's brand-new Firebird. And Janie And Janie And... Carolyn. I guess I could be pretty 6)_____ about what happened to me, but it's hard to stay mad when there's so much beauty in the world. Sometimes I feel like I'm seeing it all at once and it's too much. My heart 7)_____ like a balloon that's about to 8)_____. And then I remember to relax and stop trying to 9)_____ it. And then it flows through me like rain, and I can't feel anything but 10)_____ for every single moment of my stupid little life. You have no idea what I'm talking about, I'm sure. But don't worry. You will someday.

III. Complete the following memorable lines by translating the Chinese into English.

1. **Lester**: It's a great thing when you realize you still _____ (拥有能让自己惊奇的能力). Makes you wonder what else you can do that you've forgotten about.

2. **Estate King**: ... but it is my philosophy that in order to be successful, one must _____(永远维持成功人士的形象)

3. **Lester**: Remember those posters that said... "_____(今天是你余生的第一天)?" Well, that's true. With every day except one... the day you die.

4. **Carolyn**: Because you're old enough now to learn the most important lesson in life: _____(除了自己，不可依靠任何人) You know, it's sad but true, and the sooner you learn it, the better.

5. **Colonel Fitts**: You have no respect for other people's things and for authority... _____(你不能事事为所欲为)；here are rules in life.

IV. Oral practices—answer the following questions.

1. In the final of the scene Lester was looking at his family photo, and in front of him there's a vase of "America Beauty", the roses. What do the roses stand for?
2. How do you understand "what is beauty"?

Part 5 More Social Dramas

Plot Summary of *Crash*

"Crash" is a complex movie with a simple premise: set in Los Angeles it follows 8 main characters (and many, many more supporting) from all walks of life and races whose lives intersect at some point during one 24 hour period. These people are all different yet all alienated, to the point of breaking, so much so that when they come together, things explode.

The complexity of the film comes from the encounters between characters and their

tangled lives and worlds. Haggis' screenplay is so intricate and delicately written I couldn't begin to try to summarize the actual plot line (which destines this article to be kind of vague), but everyone meets everyone else at some point in the film (and there are a whole lot of characters). Suffice it to say these meetings are variably intense, casual, fleeting, or dangerous, but they all effect the participants in profound and provocative ways, causing lives to find enlightenment or swerve violently, and watching it all unfold is mesmerizing because Paul Haggis (Oscar Nominated writer of Million Dollar Baby) made the film meaty with messy characters and topics and stories to chew and hurtle along with.

The all-encompassing theme of the film is racism, and it is dealt with bluntly, honestly, and without reservation. Every single character participates in the perpetuation of the ugly cycle but also suffers because of it. Where racism makes for an interesting enough subject for an already provoking and fairly experimental film, it's only the catalyst for a deeper, resounding story of redemption and the universality of our lonely situation which the movie becomes during its second hour (what you could call Act II). It switches from a somewhat depressing contemplative (思考的) amalgamation (合并) of moments about racism in everyday life and how destructive it is, to a throbbing (悸动的), intense web of choices and consequences — life and death, vivifying or soul killing — and the chance at redemption.

Following their actions in Act I, everyone meets a fork in the road or is given a second chance of some sort. Some take it, some don't, but regardless, by the end of the movie everyone has changed. This is what gives the movie wings during its second hour, makes it interesting, keeps you guessing and on knife's-edge. It also gives the characters depth and souls and shows that despite perceived and upheld differences, when it comes down to it we aren't different (which we see in a shattering scene between Ryan Philippe and Larenz Tate after Tate notices that he and Philippe have the same St. Christopher statue), in fact we desperately need each other. It's one of the few films I've seen where everyone is at fault somehow and yet there are no villains. It makes it hopeful, particularly with something as ugly as racism: everyone's fallible, but everyone has the capacity for good and nobility. That said, each of these character's inner struggles makes for all the conflict and resolution you need.

A talented ensemble drives the film, sharing almost equal amounts of screen time, but the folks who really stood out and had my full attention each time were Terrence Howard (plays a TV director), Matt Dillon (as a patrol cop), Sandra Bullock (a rich housewife), Don Cheadle (a detective), and Michael Peña (a locksmith). These five gave deeply, deeply felt performances portraying a wide range of emotions and personal situations, giving souls — alone, yearning, and searching in a world that doesn't seem to care — to shells of imperfect people. But the actors triumph in little moments of human contact: a glance, an embrace, a pause, a smile, a wince, things that breathe the film to life and with simple visuals give it profundity. This is beautifully illustrated in a small scene between the downward spiraling Jean (Sandra Bullock) and her maid after she's begun to realize all her problems may not be about the two black guys who car jacked her, but her own life.

Some closing notes: it's obvious it's a debut. At times the dialogue and acting can be stilted (呆板的) and unnatural; some of the initial "racial" situations seem forced; certain scenes could have used some editing or fine tuning, but by the end I didn't care. It also may be helpful to know that the first hour spends its time setting everything up for Act II, although it will seem more like a photo essay on racism than a setup. But by the time Act I ends you're ready for something substantial to happen, and at the perfect moment, stuff happens. With his debut (首演) Haggis made a film that magically maintains a storytelling balancing act about people's lives that almost seamlessly flows, takes an honest look at racism with an understanding of mankind, a belief in redemption, and even hope.

Memorable lines in the film

Settings: *At the beginning of this film, Graham and a female officer appear on the screen in a dark night. Graham seems to talk with himself when they rear-ended a traffic jam.*

Graham: It's the sense of touch. In any real city, you walk, you know? You brush past people, people bump into you. In L.A., nobody touches you. We're always behind this metal and glass. I think we miss that touch so much, that we crash into each other, just so we can feel something.

格拉汉姆：这就是接触的感觉。你知道吗？走在任何城市里，你都会和别人擦身而过，别人也会撞到你。但在洛杉矶，没有人会碰到你。我们总是像隔着层金属和玻璃。我想我们很怀念那种接触，我们只有互相撞击，才会感觉到什么。

Settings: *Anthony and Peter, two black man, are walking on a street which is full of white people. When a pair of white couples come, the woman, who feels nervous, hugs the man tightly.*

Anthony: Look around! You couldn't find a whiter, safer or better lit part of this city. But this white woman sees two black guys, who look like UCLA students, strolling down the sidewalk and her reaction is blind fear. I mean, look at us! Are we dressed like gangbangers? Do we look threatening?

安东尼：看看你的周围！你不可能找到更多白人，更安全，或者比这个城市更好的地方了。但是这个白女人看见两个黑人，两个就像加州大学洛杉矶分校的学生从便道走来，她的反应就只有恐惧？看看我们，哥们儿。我们的衣着像黑帮的吗？我们看起来很有威胁吗？

Plot Summary of *Slumdog Millionaire*

Danny Boyle's Slumdog Millionaire is a breathless, exciting story, heartbreaking and exhilarating (令人兴奋的) at the same time, about a Mumbai orphan who rises from rags to riches on the strength of his lively intelligence. The film's universal appeal will present the real India to millions of moviegoers for the first time.

Slumdog Millionaire bridges between a world of poverty and the Indian version of "Who Wants to be a Millionaire." It tells the story of an orphan from the slums of Mumbai who is born into a brutal existence. A petty thief, impostor (骗子) and survivor, mired (深陷) in dire poverty, he improvises (临时凑成) his way up through the world and remembers everything he has learned.

His name is Jamel (played as a teenager by Dev Patel). He is Oliver Twist. High-spirited and defiant (反抗的) in the worst of times, he survives. He scrapes out a living at the Taj Mahal, which he did not know about but discovers by being thrown off a train. He pretends to be a guide, invents "facts" out of thin air, advises tourists to remove their shoes and then steals them. He finds a bit part in the Mumbai underworld, and even falls in idealized romantic love, that most elusive (难以捉摸的) of conditions for a slumdog.

His life until he's 20 is told in flashbacks intercut with his appearance as a quiz show contestant. Pitched as a slumdog, he supplies the correct answer to question after question and becomes a national hero. The flashbacks show why he knows the answers. He doesn't volunteer this information. It is beaten out of him by the show's security staff. They are sure he must be cheating.

We will see that *Slumdog Millionaire* is one of those miraculous entertainments that achieves its immediate goals and keeps climbing toward a higher summit.

Memorable lines in the film

Setting: *When Jamal Malik fled to Taj Mahal, where he made a living by acting as a tour guide in cheating two visitors with his improvised guide introductions.*

Woman: Please, would it be possible to show us around now? Obviously we understand that it costs more for just the two of us.

Jamal Malik: But of course madam! Please follow me. The Taj Mahal was built by Emperor Khurrama for his wife Mumtaz, who was the maximum beautiful woman in the world. Then when she died, the emperor decided to build this five-star hotel, for everyone who would like to visit her tomb. But he died in 1587 before any of the rooms were built, or any of the lifts. But this swimming pool as you can see was completed on schedule in top class fashion.

Woman: It says nothing of this in the guide book.

Jamal Malik: The guide book was written by a bunch of lazy good-for-nothing Indian beggars. And this lady and gentlemen is the burial place of Mumtaz.

Woman: How did she die?

Jamal Malik: A road traffic accident

Woman: Really?

Jamal Malik: Maximum pile-up.

Man: I thought she died in childbirth

Jamal Malik: Exactly sir. She was on the way to hospital when it happened

游客女：拜托，可以现在带我们四处逛一下吗？我明白只为我们两个人服务价格会高一些。

贾穆尔：当然可以，夫人！请跟我来。泰姬陵是Khurrama皇帝为他的妻子Mumtaz建造的，她可是世界上最漂亮的女人。后来她死了，于是皇帝决定为所有前来参观他妻子的陵墓的人建造一座五星级的宾馆。但是皇帝也在1587年去世了，那时宾馆还没有一间房，没有楼梯。但是，这个游泳池就像您看到的一样已经按期高质量的完成了。

游客女：但是这在这本指南上一点都没有提到。

贾穆尔：那本指南是一群混饭吃的懒人写的。女士，先生，这就是Mumtaz埋葬的地方。

游客女：她是怎么死的？

贾穆尔：车祸。

游客女：真的？

贾穆尔：严重的连环撞车事故。

游客男：我以为她是难产死的。

贾穆尔：准确的讲是这样的。车祸就发生在她去医院的路上。

UNIT 9

Thrillers 悬疑影片

Part 1 Chinese Summary

悬疑片：意料之外，情理之中

悬疑片具备各种不同的形式：谋杀神秘剧、私人侦探故事、追逐惊悚片、法庭和司法惊悚片、超现实的灵异肥皂剧和阴郁复杂的心理剧等。比起犯罪片，悬疑片通常会淡化侦探与犯罪相关的情节，而将重心集中在因此而产生的悬疑和危险之上。这也是悬疑片始终追求的目标：提供惊悚悬疑的体验，更强调内在心理的紧张和参与，令观影成为一种更高级也更深层的观影审美体验。对不少悬疑片爱好者来说，恐怖大师希区柯克 Sir Alfred Hitchcock是最令人敬重的入门导师。他已经成为了悬疑惊悚的代名词。作为导演，希区柯克的目标是向观众提供有益的震颤。《惊魂记》Psycho（1960）作为20世纪60年代的黑白经典悬疑片，是精神分裂杀人狂悬疑片的开山之作，希区柯克充分运用自己的看家本领一次次地制造和设置悬念，全片的悬念，段落的悬念，细节悬念，又一个个地揭开其中的疑团。开头千头万绪，最后一目了然。悬疑片可大致分为以下几类：

宗教类：《七宗罪》Se7en（1995）；《人骨拼图》The Bone Collector（1999）；《万能钥匙》The Skeleton Key（2005）等。这类悬疑片往往与宗教教义相关联。用为人所熟悉的命题来制造悬疑。

心理类：《惊魂记》Psycho（1960）；《心理游戏》The Game（1997）；《记忆碎片》Memento（2000）；《穆赫兰道》Mulholland Dr.（2001）；《迷雾》The Mist（2007）；《闪灵》The Shining（1980）；《第六感》The Sixth Sense（1999）；《小岛惊魂》The Others（2001）；《幻影凶间》1408（2007）；电影大师斯坦利·库布里克Stanley Kubrick的恐怖名作《闪灵》The Shining（1980），是一部让观众灵魂受到惊吓的电影。斯坦利·库布里克用一种好莱坞导演所罕有的沉稳和冷静为观众编织噩梦，使人相信，天地间确实存在一种不可名状的邪恶力量，随时随地会突显狰狞。在这众多结局式影片中，《第六感》The Sixth Sense（1999）一面极力的打造各个细节以达到前后的完美结合，一方面又精彩的刻画着人物的微妙心理，毫不矫情的传达着浓浓的亲情。论情节设计的精妙程度和结局翻天覆地的震撼程度，还是对人性和感情的挖掘，都令人啧啧称奇。

犯罪类：《沉默的羔羊》The Silence of the Lambs（1991）；《非常嫌疑犯》The Usual Suspects（1995）；《十二宫》Zodiac（2007）；《电锯惊魂》Saw（2004）。

时空类：《死亡幻觉》Donnie Darko（2001）；《恐怖游轮》Triangle（2009）；

《关键下一秒》Next（2007）；《蝴蝶效应》The Butterfly Effect；《盗梦空间》Inception（2010）；当独特的拍摄手法与深刻的哲学命题相结合，悬疑片显示出别样的意义。《恐怖游轮》Triangle（2009）的主题探讨的是人生轮回和因果报应，对于一部低成本的电影而言，它的深刻哲学含义已经远远超过了剧情本身。而《盗梦空间》Inception（2010）作为"一部发生在意识结构内的当代科幻动作片"，故事设定在钢筋水泥浇铸成迷宫般的梦境中。当我们的时空观念被颠覆了无数次，诺兰Christopher Nolan所要传达的也渐渐明晰：总有一个信念，可以让你为之天涯奔走，甚至付出生命，而所处的世界是虚幻或真实，都已不再重要。

密室类：《立方体》Cube（1997）；《阻击电话亭》Phone Booth（2002）；《致命ID》Identity（2003）；《玩命记忆》Unknown（2006）；《迷雾》The Mist（2007）等。由于高度封闭，结构集中，这里的故事更具体验性和代入感，因此，同类型的密室推理电影自成一派发扬光大，经典佳作层出不穷。互有牵连关系的游戏者，精巧的整体布局，绝对意想不到的结局，这一切构成了《致命ID》Identity（2003）诡异而又丰富刺激的世界。而《异次元杀阵》Cube（1997）中令人深思的空间理论，《迷雾》The Mist（2007）中超现实的怪物，这些则是从科幻的角度解析人性。在这种密室电影中，导演把众多角色扔进一个狭小的'瓶子'里面，看他们如何互相作用。其中，《异次元杀阵》以其超乎寻常的想象力，大胆的讽刺暗喻，开创了一种新的密室系列，即以数学、物理学等高等技术理论为依托的推理模式。而面对生死存亡的挑战，在立方体逃生的过程中，也许真正恐怖的并不是凶手，而是丑态毕露的人性。

高度的关注、超常的期待感、不确定性、焦虑和绷断神经的紧张感，这是全身心投入悬疑片后最畅快淋漓的观影体验。前段的伏笔重重，中段的解谜阶段紧张而精彩，直至将剧情推向令人瞠目结舌高潮的最后结局！此时，我们松了一口气：最后谜底已揭开，高悬的期待被轻轻放下，紧张的情绪得到了释放，猎奇的心理得到了满足。而我们也不禁发出由心的感叹：看悬疑片，不到最后，不要觉得那就是结尾！

《致命ID》Identity（2003）一个典型而又引人入胜的悬疑故事：一个汽车旅馆里，住进了10个人，他们一个接一个的死去，并且按照顺序留下牌号。10个人存活下来的渐渐变少，他们开始恐慌，互相猜忌，却无意间发现了彼此间的联系。但是，大家怀疑的嫌疑人却纷纷死去，谜团笼罩在旅馆狭小的空间里，这样的凶杀案件却有着人们猜不到的真相……

《小岛惊魂》The Others（2001）这是一部心理惊悚片，继承了《闪灵》的诡异和幽闭氛围，画面灰暗迷蒙，阴森的古堡似乎不用特意渲染，就已令人不寒而栗。这类恐怖片故事里面的悲伤、敏感、阴郁会给影迷深刻的感受，这往往得益于拍摄手法、演员的演绎、气氛的渲染和故事的逐渐深入发展以及结局的震慑力量。影片把闹鬼的古宅，梦境与现实的混淆，阴阳两界的明争暗斗诠释的淋漓尽致，同时也以悬疑电影的手法表达了战争对人性的摧残。

《沉默的羔羊》The Silence of the Lambs（1991）根据著名小说家哈里斯·托玛斯的同名小说改编而成，是20世纪90年代以来深刻反映美国社会犯罪问题的经典之作。这是一部令人毛骨悚然的心理悬念片。虽然影片的场景设置以封闭的室内环境为主，缺乏激烈火爆的动作性，但由于采用了希区柯克式的悬念手法和现代恐怖片的心理分析方法，使得整部影片的情节扑朔迷离，将观众引入了一个象征性的人类潜意识的世界。影片通过探索人物心理疾患，试图探寻当代美国社会恐怖的根源，这使得影片的主题得以深化。寓示了好莱坞文以载道的策略。

Part 2 Text 1

Highlight in Suspense, Can You Get It?

Walking the **tightrope** between the mainstream and the **avant-garde** with remarkable balance and skill, thrill films bring to the screen a **singularly** dark and disturbing view of reality, a nightmare world **punctuated** by defining moments of extreme violence, **bizarre** comedy, and strange beauty.

Thrillers are mostly characterized by an atmosphere of **menace**, violence, crime and murder by showing society as dark, **corrupt** and dangerous, though they often feature a happy ending in which the villains are killed or arrested. Thrillers rely heavily on literary devices such as plot twists, **red herrings** and **cliffhangers**. They also promote moods, such as a high level of anticipation, **adrenaline** rush, arousal, **ultra**-heightened expectation, uncertainty, anxiety and sometimes even terror. The tones in thrillers are usually **gritty**, slick and **lurid**.

A genuine, standalone thriller is a film that provides thrills and keeps the audience cliff-hanging at the 'edge of their seats' as the plot builds towards a climax. The tension usually arises when the character is placed in a **menacing** situation, mystery, or an escape from which escaping seems impossible. Life is threatened, usually because the principal character is unsuspecting or unknowingly involved in a dangerous or potentially deadly situation.

Traveling in time and dreams has always been an interest for everyone. The idea of combining parallel timelines with fascinating dreams is so clever and **intricately** structured that it may require repeat **retrospects**[2]. Such films as *Mulholland Dr*, *Memento* and *The Butterfly Effect*, are easier to admire than to fully grasp or be moved by.

In *Mulholland Dr.* (2001), *David Lynch* succeeds not only in picturing the surface of human behavior life but also in **grappling** with everything beneath that: human desires, dreams, obsessions and fears — all that remains unspoken, emotions that are often repressed[1].

The Butterfly Effect[3] is a terrific thriller that keeps you on the edge of your seat. The movie's caption shows "One little change will bring about tremendous changes". This theme shows in every alternate reality he tries to effect. As they say in the movie, You Can't Play God. Time will catch up to you no matter what you do to change it. The whole film is just like a long engaging thrill journey.

When it comes to such things as the **emasculation** of an entire generation of young men, the growing isolation we all feel from one another and the need to find something to draw us back together. *Fight Club*[4], is the film which you'll have to see more than once to truly understand. The story is like one big twisting, turning tunnel with barely a glimmer of a light at the end. The cast is great, the settings are appropriately scary with no short measure of red herrings to keep you guessing.

Thrillers provide such a rich film feast. What gives the variety of thrillers a common ground is the intensity of emotions they create, particularly those of **apprehension** and **exhilaration**, of excitement and breathlessness, all designed to generate that all-important thrill. By definition, if a thriller doesn't thrill, it's not doing its job.

The thriller that actually genuinely scares you does so because it messes with your mind. Most will "hate" this movie; they don't like their brains being tampered with. There are moments in these films of such mind-gnawing anxiety, such high-adrenaline terror that you have to tell yourself, "Calm down, it's just a movie."[5]

After-reading questions

1. When seeing thrillers, people will NOT feel _____.
   A. a high level of anticipation
   B. easy and pleasant
   C. at the 'edge of their seats'
   D. their brains are being tampered with
2. The "Mulholland Dr" (Paragraph 4) mentioned in the text is NOT to _____.
   A. pay tribute to the idea of combining parallel timelines with dreams in the movie
   B. give prominence to David Lynch's consummate mining of Human Nature
   C. give an obvious characteristic of chamber films
   D. give the hint that this film is easier to admire than to fully grasp.
3. From the text we learn that "Fight Club" is a film that _____.
   A. bridges the generation gap between growing young men and parents.
   B. keeps you pondering what result social segregation has and the need to find something to draw us back together
   C. depicts human natures and depth of mind, thus provoking us to do more thinking
   D. revealing the film topic through analysis of personality psychology
4. Which of the following is TRUE according to the text?
   A. The gritty and lurid tones in thrillers are just to reveal the dark side of society.
   B. David Lynch differs with Freud on the Interpretation of Dreams.

C. The sentence "You Can't Play God" (Paragraph 6) indicates that little changes may lead to great disasters.

D. The sentence "Calm down, it's just a movie" (the last Paragraph) indicates that one might be overwhelmed by thrillers' gripping plots.

Words and expressions

1. **tightrope** *n.* tightly stretched rope or wire on which acrobats perform high above the ground 钢丝 walk the tightrope 走钢丝
2. **avant-garde** *n.* any creative group active in the innovation and application of new concepts and techniques in a given field (especially in the arts) 先锋派，前卫派
3. **singularly** *adv.* in a noticeable way 异常，特别
4. **punctuate** *v.* emphasize 强调
5. **bizarre** *adj.* strange and difficult to explain 离奇的；奇特的
6. **menace** *v.* a possible source of danger or harm 胁迫，威吓；威胁
7. **corrupt** *adj.* immoral or dishonest, especially as shown by the exploitation of a position of power or trust for personal gain 腐败的，堕落的，品行坏的；贪污的（官吏等）
8. **red herrings** *n.* an idiomatic expression referring to a rhetorical tactic of diverting attention away from an item of significance 转移他人目标之物
9. **cliffhanger** *n.* an unresolved ending in a part of a serialized drama or book that leaves the audience or reader eager to know what will happen next 吊人胃口的东西
10. **adrenaline** *n.* a hormone secreted by the adrenal glands and by some nerve endings, that increases the speed and force of heart contraction 肾上腺素
11. **ultra** *adj.* exceeding or going beyond all other of the same kind 过度的，过激的，极端的
12. **gritty** *adj.* courageous, resolute, or persistent; having a stark realism 粗砂质的；勇敢的，坚韧不拔的
13. **lurid** *adj.* full of unpleasant things that are meant to shock or interest people 可怕的；悲惨；耸人听闻的
14. **menacing** *adj.* intended to threaten or frighten someone 威胁的，咄咄逼人，令人恐怖
15. **grapple** *v.* to struggle with somebody in a close hand-to-hand fight 与……格斗；抓住；努力解决
16. **intricately** *adv.* containing many details or small parts that are combined in a particularly complex or skillful way 复杂的，交错的，错综的，杂乱如麻，错综复杂；弯弯曲曲的
17. **retrospect** *n.* the remembering of past events 回顾；怀旧，追忆；对证，参照

18. **emasculation** *n.* deprive somebody or something of effectiveness, spirit, or force 柔弱；去势；阉割；（植）去雄

19. **apprehension** *n.* a feeling of anxiety or fear that something bad or unpleasant will happen 恐惧；不安，忧虑；疑惧，恐慌，畏惧心理

20. **exhilaration** *n.* Something make somebody feel happy, excited, and more than usually vigorous and alive 高兴，兴奋

21. **villain** *n.* the main bad character in a story, play, movie, etc. The main good character is the hero or heroine 反派人物，反面人物

22. **sadistic** *adj.* getting pleasure from hurting or being cruel to someone else 虐待症的

Notes

1. *In Mulholland Dr.* (2001), *David Lynch* succeeds not only in picturing the surface of human behavior life but also in grappling with everything beneath that: human desires, dreams, obsessions and fears——all that remains unspoken; emotions that are often repressed.
   译文：大卫·林奇在《穆赫兰道》中的成功之处，不仅在于成功地刻画了人类所生存的客观世界，更能深入挖掘其中的深层隐喻：人的欲望、梦想、执着和恐惧，以及常被压抑着的情感。
   注：穆赫兰道（Mulholland Drive），由Universal Focus公司2001年出品。是大卫·林奇（David Lynch）又一部鲜明、尖刻、歇斯底里又令人难以忘怀的影片。影片主要探讨我们所生存的客观世界与我们的认知之间的哲学关系：质疑影像的真实与认知的真实，对认知的可能性说"不"。

2. Travelling in time and dreams has always been an interest for everyone. The idea of combining parallel timelines with fascinating dreams is so clever and intricately structured that it may require repeat retrospects.
   译文：（导演们知道）穿梭于时空和梦境中的旅行，必能点燃人们兴趣。而华丽梦境与平行时间相结合的叙事手法，如此精巧又复杂的电影结构，值得（人们）的重复回想。
   注：此类型影片的代表作是《记忆碎片》。在这部关于失忆的电影中，导演克里斯托夫·诺兰通过彩色和黑白两种画面的交替、顺叙和倒叙两种叙事手法的穿插演绎出具有悬念的故事情节。两条故事线泾渭分明，一条以彩色画面倒叙，另一条以黑白画面顺叙，每隔几分钟穿插一次，直至片尾将所有片断天衣无缝地连接起来推出真相。

3. *The Butterfly Effect* a 2004 American science fiction psychological thriller film. The title refers to the butterfly effect, a popular hypothetical example of chaos theory which illustrates how small initial differences may lead to large unforeseen consequences over time. 美国科幻心理悬疑片《蝴蝶效应》。蝴蝶效应是混沌学理论中的一个概念。它是指对初始输入端微小的差别会迅速放大到输

出端。

4. ***Fight Club***（1999）《搏击俱乐部》

5. Most will "hate" this movie, they don't like their brains being tampered with. There are moments in these films of such mind-gnawing anxiety, such high-adrenaline suspenses that we had to tell ourselves, "Calm down, it's just a movie."

译文：大部分人会"讨厌"这些电影，他们不喜欢自己的大脑被"烧糊"。当投入于这些令人心跳加速，肾上腺激素上升的这些悬疑片时，我们不得不说服自己，"冷静下来，它只是一部电影"。

Part 3 Text 2

Identity[1]

Malcolm Rivers (Pruitt Taylor Vince) is a murderer who has a multiple personality syndrome （人格分裂症）. In this film, he only shows up a few times but the story is actually caused by his imagination in which many personalities are created. Malcolm's illusion used to drive him to kill people in reality and now he's faced with the death sentence. When his kind-hearted psychiatrist （精神科医生） wants to help him conquer the disorder by analyzing this special mental illness to the law officers, he has another imagination. This is how the story happens. For Malcolm, the feasible way to get rid of the death sentence is that he has to reduce the personalities until the evil identity vanishes and make sure the only identity of him is clean （清白的，无罪的）. In the murder of Malcolm's hallucination （幻觉）, the disappearance （消失） of those dead bodies means the identities die out （消亡）. Unluckily, the evil part is still in Malcolm's mind and leads to a bad result, of course. The key word "identity" is mysterious for the imaginary world, but it's pretty （相当） clear if we see it in the real world. So are you ready to find out which world is real or invented （捏造的）?

Just like other typical whodunit （侦探片）[2] and thriller movies, the atmosphere is gloomy and intense. In the middle of a rainstorm, the judge and lawyers involved in the case of murderer Malcolm Rivers (due for execution the next morning) are called together to discuss evidence that the defense （辩护律师） believe had been illegally suppressed （压制）. Meanwhile a series of car accidents, damaged phone lines and flooded roads means that a group of strangers end up stranded in a desolate （荒凉的） Nevada （内华达州） motel. These eleven strangers include a policeman (Ray Liotta)

with a prisoner who both are actually prisoners, a driver named Ed (John Cucask), a little boy called Timothy (Bret Loehr), a motel manager (John Hawkes) who is actually a desperate gambler who once found the owner of this motel dead and then took charge of it, and a prostitute (妓女) called Paris (Amanda Peet). When the prisoner of the cop escapes and a murder occurs, they group together to try and capture him. However, the deaths continue each with a room key[3] forming a morbid (病态的) countdown as the remainder try to survive the night.

As the clues show and in the light of the usual storyline (故事情节) in a thriller, the murderer must be one of the survivors. But what happens afterwards totally astonishes them, because the dead bodies are all gone. This seems not usual at all. They are confused for a while but then they come to realize that the only thing they have in common is their birthday— May 10th. How can this one in a trillion (万亿) thing happen and who is the invisible ghost? Bad things occur hour after hour and there are only four people left. Ed, however, suddenly figures something out.

Flashback (回顾), what is the Malcolm Rivers-thing about? The connection between Malcolm and the motel murder doesn't become clarified until Ed turns into Malcolm, mentally. From the psychiatrist's description, Malcolm develops these 11 characters and there's an evil one who tries to kill others. This explains why he is sentenced to death, he (or the evil side of him) took those victims for his split personalities and committed the crimes four years ago. At the moment, the evil is in one of the survivors and Malcolm has to control his mind as a good one to erase the killer. In Malcolm's imagination again, after Ed and the policeman (at least he seems bad) kill each other, Paris thinks she is just out of woods (脱离危险).

But the real murderer finally goes for (攻击) her when she finds the key numbered 10 which is buried underground. Before she dies with a horrible look in her eyes, the boy Timothy says, "Whores don't get a second chance." The evil part exists in the boy identity because Malcolm hates prostitutes just like he hates his whore mother who left him in the motel and got him abused when he was young, as the beginning of the movie. The psychiatrist who accompanies Malcolm and has always helped him, unfortunately, is the sacrificial lamb (牺牲品) this time. What's ironic is that the psychiatrist never thought his patient would do this as he is confident in his diagnosis and treatment. In addition, the judge who is persuaded to lift (撤销) the death sentence finally has the trouble of doing a retrial (重审) of this case and the case might be uncertain again. No one can tell what range the crimes committed by psychiatric patients are within.

"When I was going up the stairs, I met a man who wasn't there. He wasn't there again today. I wish, I wish he'd go away." Malcolm says that again and again, and it traps him into even deeper mind disassociation (分离) and he has to live with it. It reflects that the wound he got in his childhood will never go away even though his body has grown to an adult. His personality is still a child who madly resents (憎恨) prostitutes. So his insanity creates all these incidents and a series of murders in the motel on a stormy night.

In terms of overall situation, there's nobody from the beginning to the ending of the murder existing except Malcolm. It's hard to believe that no one in the motel is real but it's the unique idea that makes this thriller outstanding. The whole story is not only a mixture of several genres, from thriller, to mystery, to whodunit with gore (血块), but it also shows a twist throughout which different relationships continually shift. Yet slowly killing each person off as they're stuck in an isolated setting is a traditional 10 Little Indians[4] horror film motif (主题) that writer Michael Cooney employs. As for the audience, it's impossible to deconstruct (解构) the rest of the movie beforehand and the ingenious (新颖的) multilayered (多层的) approach leave them pondering (深思) the notions of identity and reality for days. Maybe the only way to understand the whole story is to think what the leading character thinks because Descartes[5] once said, "I think, therefore I am." (我思故我在)

After reading questions

1. Which word is inappropriate to describe a thriller?
    A. Sentimental.
    B. Dread.
    C. Depressing.
    D. Creepy.
2. Compared with the usual thriller, what is the unique element in this movie?
    A. The killer and the victims are actually the same person.
    B. The murderer kills people in a certain order.
    C. The clue is not shown clearly.
    D. The depressed surrounding of a stormy night.
3. Which one is true about the psychiatrist, mainly according to Paragraph 4?
    A. He shows no care about Malcolm.
    B. He is the only one who stands up for Malcolm through the case.
    C. He is killed by Malcolm in the end.
    D. He knows which personality is the killer inside Malcolm's mind.
4. In these eleven personalities, who reflects the final identity of Malcolm?
    A. The driver Ed.
    B. The Timothy boy.
    C. The prostitute.
    D. The policeman.
5. From the last paragraph, we can infer the similarity between *10 little Indians*

(details are in notes) and *Identity* is almost the same in _____.

A. theme of the movie

B. scene where the murder happens

C. director

D. mode of killing people

Notes

1. ***Identity*** — was released by Columbia Pictures Industries and directed by James Mangold. 致命身份（2003）

2. **Whodunit**: is a complex, plot-driven variety of the detective story in which the puzzle is the main feature of interest. The reader is provided with clues from which the identity of the perpetrator of the crime may be deduced before the solution is revealed in the final pages of the book. The investigation is usually conducted by an eccentric amateur or semi-professional detective. The locked-room mystery is a specialized kind of a whodunit. Representative movie *Sherlock Holmes*. 侦探片是一种复杂的，靠情节推动的侦探故事类型。这类故事中，案情成为主要关注点。在故事最终揭示真相之前读者或许能够通过所提供的蛛丝马迹推断罪犯的身份。这类小说中，通常是一个古怪的业余或半职业侦探展开调查。密室杀人就属于一类侦探片。代表影片是《福尔摩斯》。

3. **Room key**: Once a person is killed, there will be a hotel room key around the body and it implies that the numbers of Malcolm's personalities are being cut down (减少). The last key "10" is found by the prostitute and brings death to her. So it's easy to tell the eleventh person is exactly the murderer.

4. **10 Little Indians** is a nursery rhyme (童谣). When it comes to movie, it's a thriller released in 1965 UK. There are eight guests and two servants for the weekend, but one by one, they are being knocked off (谋杀) as in the poem of "Ten Little Indians". As the number of survivors decreases, they begin to believe that the killer is one of the group, but are unable to decide on which one he or she may be.

5. **René Descartes** (1596—1650, French) is one of the most important Western philosophers of the past few centuries. During his lifetime, Descartes was just as famous as an original physicist, physiologist and mathematician. But it is as a highly original philosopher that he is most frequently read today. He is titled as "the Father of Modern Philosophy" by Hegel.

勒奈·笛卡尔（1596—1650，法国人）是近几个世纪来最重要的西方哲学家之一。生前，笛卡尔只是作为物理学家、生理学家和数学家而出名。但是，如今他的哲学思想也是一直为人拜读。他被黑格尔称作"现代哲学之父"。

Part 4 Exercises

I. Answer questions after listening to the dialogues taken from the film.

1. Did Malcolm commit murders in 1998?
2. What does "10 identities" mean?

● Script

Scenario 1: *At the beginning of the movies, the psychiatrist Dr. Mallick was listening to the tape on his patient Malcolm's medical history.*

MALCOLM: As I was going up the stairs, I met a man who wasn't there. I met a man who wasn't there. He wasn't there again today. I wish, I wish he'd go away.

DR. MALLICK: Where did you learn that? Where did you learn that poem?

MALCOLM: I made it up. When I was a kid, I made it up.

DR. MALLICK: What else do you remember from back then?

MALCOLM: Don't beat around the bush. Don't beat around the bush, doc!

DR. MALLICK: Tell me what you remember about your mother.

MALCOLM: I remember my mom. I remember my mom. I remember my mom was a whore.

DR. MALLICK: How long would she keep you there?

MALCOLM: As long as she was busy.

DR. MALLICK: Do you understand why you're talking with me now?

MALCOLM: You're supposed to be good with...I need something more than aspirin. Know what I mean?

DR. MALLICK: Do you remember the murders?

MALCOLM: I remember...that Columbia is the capital of South Carolina.

DR. MALLICK: I remember that—Are you the person who murdered six residents...of the Lakeworth Apartments on May 10,1998?

MALCOLM: That's my birthday.

DR. MALLICK: Who am I speaking to right now? What should I call you?

MALCOLM: Call me whatever you want.

Scenario 2: *Dr. Mallick, the prosecutor, the defense and Judge Taylor were discussing whether Malcolm was guilty and how to deal with the murders he committed.*

MALCOLM: Why won't you let me help you? Where did you go? Where did you see? I saw you...in an orange grove.

DR. MALLICK: The question, Your Honor, is whether to convict the body or the mind. His body committed these murders, that is true.

Unit 9 Thrillers 悬疑影片

	The person who remains inside did not.
THE PROSECUTOR:	Judge Taylor, that may not be true...
THE DEFENSE:	We witnessed the destruction of 10 identities tonight. Nine were innocent and one was guilty.
JUDGE TAYLOR:	They're not real.
PROSECUTOR:	The violence that existed in him has been executed.
DR. MALLICK:	Your Honor, Malcolm belongs in a state hospital.
JUDGE TAYLOR:	In the matter of Rivers Nevada, it is the recommendation of this court...that Mr. Rivers' execution be stayed. I am transferring Mr. Rivers to state psychiatric services...under the care of Dr. Mallick.

II. Fill the blanks with the missing words or phrases after listening to the lines taken from the film.

DR. MALLICK:	Where have you been?
MALCOLM:	All right, I was driving this actress...and we got 1)_____ at the hotel. There was a storm. We couldn't get out because of the storm.
DR. MALLICK:	What happened at the motel?
MALCOLM:	People started dying. And then their bodies...It didn't 2)_____. They disappeared.
DR. MALLICK:	Edward, I'd like to show something to you, if I may... Do you 3)_____ this man?
MALCOLM:	No.
DR. MALLICK:	That man, Edward, is Malcolm Rivers. He's had a very troubled life. He was 4)_____ four years ago...and 5)_____ the murder of six people in 6)_____.
THE DETECTIVE:	He did this.
DR. MALLICK:	Detective, please. Edward, listen to me. When faced with an 7)_____, a child's mind may fracture... 8)_____. That's exactly what happened to Malcolm Rivers. He developed a condition that is commonly known as 9)_____ Personality Syndrome.
MALCOLM:	Why are you telling me this?
DR. MALLICK:	Because you, Edward, are one of his 10)_____.

III. Complete the following memorable lines by translating the Chinese into English.

1. (我们被困在这里了)_____, George. I don't think we can get out tonight.

2. Judge Taylor, sir, _____(请恕我冒犯，我们应该等被告来了才开始，他有出席的权利)

3. An insanity plea was refused by the court...despite the fact that my client is a certifiable Axis IV dissociative. (他到现在对他所犯的罪都毫不知情)_____ _____. As you know, in 1986, the Supreme Court ruled decisively that states cannot execute a person who does not understand why he's being put to death.

4. This notebook contains entries just before the murders twelve years ago. (重点是他的笔迹、语调和观点都有很大的改变。)_____ _____. What you are looking at are the private thoughts of several different people.

IV. Oral practices — answer the following questions

1. What is the plot-driven role of the explosion of the car with Timmy?
2. How do you explain the all the disappearance of all the bodies?

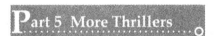

Part 5 More Thrillers

Plot Summary of *The Others*

Grace Stewart (Nicole Kidman) is a Catholic mother who lives with her two small children in a remote country house in the immediate aftermath of World War II. The children, Anne (Alakina Mann) and Nicholas (James Bentley), have an uncommon disease, xeroderma pigmentosa, characterized by photosensitivity, so their lives are structured around a series of complex rules designed to protect them from inadvertent exposure to sunlight.

The new arrival of three servants at the house — an aging nanny and servant named Mrs. Bertha Mills (Fionnula Flanagan), an elderly gardener named Mr. Edmund Tuttle (Eric Sykes), and a young mute girl named Lydia (Elaine Cassidy) — coincides with a number of odd events, and Grace begins to fear that they are not alone. Anne draws pictures of four people: a man, a woman, a boy called Victor, and an old woman, all of whom she says she has seen in the house. A piano is heard from inside a locked room when no one is inside. Grace finds and examines a "book of the dead," which shows mourning portraits taken in the 19th century of recently deceased corpses. Doors which Grace believes to have been closed are found mysteriously ajar. Grace tries hunting down the "intruders" with a shotgun but cannot find them. She scolds her daughter for believing in ghosts — until she hears them herself. Eventually, convincing herself that something unholy is in the house, she runs out in the fog to get the local priest to bless the house. Meanwhile, the servants, led by Mrs. Mills, are clearly up to something of their own. The gardener buries a headstone under autumn leaves, and Mrs. Mills listens faithfully to Anne's allegations against her mother.

Outside, Grace loses herself in the heavy fog, but she miraculously discovers her husband Charles (Christopher Eccleston), who she thought had been killed in the war, and brings him back to the house. Charles is distant during the one day he spends in the house, and Mrs. Mills is heard telling Mr. Tuttle, "I do not think he knows where he is." Grace later sees an old woman dressed up like her daughter. Grace says, "You are not my daughter!" and attacks her. However, she finds that she has actually attacked her daughter instead. Anne refuses to be near her mother afterward, while Grace swears she saw the old woman. Mrs. Mills tells Anne that she too has seen the people, but they cannot yet tell the mother because Grace will not accept what she is not ready for. Charles is stunned when Anne tells him the things her mother did to her. He says he must leave for the front and disappears again. After Charles leaves, Anne continues to see things, including Victor's whole family and the old woman. Grace breaks down to Mrs. Mills, who claims that "sometimes the world of the dead gets mixed up with the world of the living."

One morning, Grace wakes to the children's screams: all of the curtains in the house have disappeared, as Anne had said they might. When the servants refuse to help look for them, Grace realizes that they are somehow involved. Hiding the children from the light, she banishes the servants from the house. A series of loud noises from the upper storey of the house follows this event.

That night, Anne and Nicholas sneak out of the house to find their father and stumble across the hidden graves. They find that the graves belong to the servants. At the same time, Grace goes to the servants' quarters and finds a photograph from the book of the dead and is horrified to see that it is of the three servants. The servants appear and follow after the children, who make it back into the house just as Grace emerges to hold off the servants with a shotgun. They then say that they had died of tuberculosis more than 50 years before. The children run upstairs and hide, but are found by the strange old woman. Downstairs, the servants continue talking to Grace, telling her that the living and the dead have to learn to live together. Upstairs, Anne and Nicholas discover the old woman is acting as a medium in a séance with Victor's parents. It is then that they learn the truth: the real ghosts are none other than Anne, Nicholas, and their mother, who is believed to have killed them in a fit of psychosis before committing suicide. Grace loses her temper and supernaturally attacks the visitors by ripping and throwing pieces of paper that lay on the table. However, the visitors are only able to see the paper ripping of its own accord, further confirming Grace and her children are indeed the ghosts. The truth finally clear to Grace, she breaks down with the children and remembers what happened just before the arrival of their new servants. Stricken with grief for her missing husband and increasingly frustrated by living in isolation, she went insane, smothered her children with a pillow, and then, in shock after realizing what she had done, put a rifle to her forehead and pulled the trigger. When nothing happened and upon hearing the laughter of Nicholas and Anne, Grace assumed that God had granted her family a miracle by offering them a second chance at life. Grace and the children realize that Charles is also dead, but he is not aware of it. Mrs. Mills appears and informs Grace that they will learn to get along, and sometimes won't even notice the living people who inhabit their house. She also informs them that since the children no longer have their mortal bodies, they are no longer sensitive to light, and for the first time the children freely enjoy the sunlight coming through the windows. From the window, Grace and her children look out as Victor's family moves out.

Memorable lines in the film

Settings: *Grace was knocked down by the suddenly closed door and scared by the re-opened piano. Ms. Mills was trying to calm her down.*

Milles: I do believe it, ma'am. I've always believed in those things. They're not easy to explain. but they do happen. We've all heard stories of the beyond...now and then, And I think that, sometimes...the world of the dead gets mixed up with the world of the living.

迈尔斯：我相信，太太。我一直都相信那种东西。这很难解释，但确实存在。我们都听说过有关前世今生的故事。我想，有些时候，阴阳两地交织在一起。

Settings: *Grace loses herself in the heavy fog, but she miraculously discovers her husband Charles who she thought had been killed in the war, and brings him back to the house. Charles knew the truth and wants to leave.*

Grace: What are you talking about? You're not going. Do you hear me? You left us once already. YOU CAN'T GO. Why? Why did you go and fight that stupid war that had NOTHING TO DO WITH US. Why didn't you stay like the others did?

格蕾丝：你说什么？你不能走，你听到吗？你已经离开过我们一次了。不准走。为什么？为什么你要去那个和我们无关的鬼战场？为什么不和别人一样留下来？

Plot Summary of *The Silence of the Lambs*

In *The Silence of the Lambs*, Starling is a student at the FBI Academy. She hopes to work at the Behavioral Science Unit, tracking down serial killers and ultimately apprehending them. Her mentor, FBI director Jack Crawford, sends her to interview Dr.Hannibal Lecter, a brilliant psychiatrist and cannibalistic serial killer. He is housed in a Baltimore mental institution. Upon arriving at the asylum for her first interview with Lecter, the asylum manager Frederick Chilton makes a crude pass at her, which she rebuffs; this helps her bond with Lecter, who also despises Chilton. As time passes, Lecter gives Starling information about Buffalo Bill, a currently active serial killer being hunted by the FBI, but only in exchange for personal information, which Crawford has specifically warned her to keep secret from Lecter.

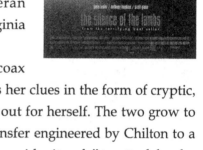

She tells Lecter that she was raised in a small town in West Virginia with her father, a police officer. When she was about 10 years old, her father was shot when responding to a robbery; he died a month after the incident. Starling was sent to live with her uncle on a Montana sheep and horse farm, from which she briefly ran away in horror when she witnessed the lambs being slaughtered (the title of the book refers to her being haunted by the screaming she heard from the lambs).

She spent the rest of her childhood in a Lutheran orphanage. She graduated from the University of Virginia and applied to the FBI's training school.

During the investigation, Starling is assigned to coax Lecter into revealing Buffalo Bill's identity; Lecter gives her clues in the form of cryptic, riddling information designed to help Starling figure it out for herself. The two grow to respect each other, so when Lecter escapes during a transfer engineered by Chilton to a state prison in Tennessee, Starling feels that he "would consider it rude" to attack her by surprise and kill her without talking to her first.

Starling deduces from Lecter's hints that Buffalo Bill's first victim had a personal relationship with him, and so goes to the victim's home in Belvedere, Ohio, to interview people who knew her. She unknowingly stumbles onto the killer himself, Jame Gumb (he is living under the alias "Jack Gordon" when they meet). When she sees a Death's Head moth, the same rare kind that Bill stuffs in the throats of each of his victims, flutter through the house, she knows that she has found her man and tries to arrest him. Gumb flees, and Starling follows him into his basement, where his latest victim is alive and screaming for help. Gumb turns off the electricity in the basement, and stalks Starling through the rooms wearing night vision goggles. He is about to shoot her when she hears him behind her and opens fire into the darkness, killing him. The victim is rescued.

Weeks later, Lecter writes Starling a letter from a hotel room somewhere in Detroit asking her if the lambs have stopped screaming.

The final scene of the novel has Starling sleeping peacefully at a friend's vacation house at the Maryland seashore.

Memorable lines in the film

Setting: Agent Clarice Starling came to the prison and meet with Hannibal Lecter for the first time.

Hannibal: You know what you look like to me, with your good bag and your cheap shoes? You look like a rube. A well-scrubbed, hustling rube with a little taste. Good nutrition's given you some length of bone, but you're not more than one generation from poor white trash, are you, Agent Starling? And that accent you've tried so desperately to shed: pure West Virginia. What is your father, dear? Is he a coal miner? Does he stink of the lamp? You know how quickly the boys found you... all those tedious sticky fumblings in the back seats of cars... while you could only dream of getting out... getting anywhere... getting all the way to the FBI.

汉尼拔：你知道我是怎么看你的？你拿着不错的包却穿着廉价的鞋，看上去像个乡巴佬。一个整洁干净而强加进一点品味的乡巴佬。良好的营养让你的骨骼生长，可你还是贫穷白人的后代，是吧，斯塔琳特工？你拼命想摆脱你的口音，纯正的西弗吉尼亚口音。亲爱的，你的父亲是做什么的？他是矿工？他带着羔羊的臭味？你知道男孩们多快就找到了你……所有那些在汽车后座上令人乏味的笨手笨脚……你梦想逃离，去投奔联邦调查局。

Setting: Clarice met with Hannibal for the fourth time. Hannibal was leading Clarice to open her mind and to tell him the worst memory of her childhood.

Clarice Starling: I went downstairs, outside. I crept up into the barn. I was so scared to look inside, but I had to. (I saw) lambs. The lambs were screaming. First I tried to free them. I... I opened the gate to their pen, but they wouldn't run. They just stood there, confused. They wouldn't run. ...I didn't have any food, any water and it was very cold, very cold. I thought, I thought if I could save just one, but... he was so heavy. So heavy. I didn't get more than a few miles when the sheriff's car picked me up. The rancher was so angry he sent me to live at the Lutheran orphanage in Bozeman. I never saw the ranch again.

克拉丽斯：我下了楼梯走到外面，蹑手蹑脚的来到牲口棚。里面的场景太吓人了。羔羊们在号叫。起初我想放掉它们。我打开了门，可它们却不动，只是困惑的站在那，它们不想跑。……我没有食物和水，天气很冷，我想如果我可以哪怕只救出来一只，可是……他太重了。我还没跑出几英里就被抓到了治安官的车上。农场主很生气，他把我送进波兹曼的路德教会孤儿院，我再没看到过那家农场。

UNIT 10

Teen Movies 青春影片

Part 1 Chinese Summary

青春影片

  青春电影(也被称为青少年电影、校园电影或者成长型电影)，顾名思义，主要是指以青少年生活为题材的电影，一直备受美国乃至世界各地青少年观众的喜爱。这些主要以青少年生活为题材的电影，尽管故事风格不同，表现手法多样，却都不同程度地反映出了美国青少年的心理特征及生活状态。而当代的美国年轻人，作为多元化的一代，在美国青少年电影中也折射出了不同类型、风格迥异的青少年形象。

  最容易为观众拍手称赞的青春电影为青春励志型电影，它给我们塑造了一系列积极向上、不断进取、不怕挫折，并充满热情的青少年形象。在这种类型中，青春成为主题，青春片是一种并不纯粹的电影类型。如果把它放到一个世界性的类型参照系中，它既不像西部片那样有着明显的视觉符码，也不像歌舞片那样有着固定的外部表演模式，甚至也不像喜剧电影那样谈得上有稳定的风格效果。在青春片那里，只有一些通常的母体式的主题类型或某些常见的环境标志，如家庭、校园。确切地说，青春片更接近于一种题材，而励志则成为叙事的主线，成为主体的行为动机。这类电影多以喜剧为主，尽管剧情有时落入俗套，却丝毫影响不了人们对于此类电影的热衷。作为涉及机能与情感的作品，好莱坞青春电影尊奉着一条体现在所有幽默中的心理规律，即它们令观众身心放松。这也成为青春电影经久不衰的原因之一。

  以爱情为主线的美国青少年电影也是深受年轻人喜爱的校园电影。这类电影给我们塑造了充满活力并纯情浪漫的青少年形象。而好莱坞的一些青春片中青少年的浪漫形象则由于好莱坞的商业机制而表现为另外一种特点。

  美国的青春类型影片非常注意将校园文化和青少年流行文化的元素融合在一起，因此在这些影片中，我们可以看到年轻人健康美丽的形体和优美动感的舞姿；可以欣赏到在年轻人中受欢迎的流行音乐和摇滚乐；可以听到高中生流行口头语；而生日派对、毕业舞会这些高中生活必不可少的场景也频频出现。

  在近些年出现的美国青春电影中，青少年的形象大体可以概括为积极的、浪漫的、堕落的以及颠覆性的青少年形象等几种。这些形象的出现和青少年的生活状态与心理特征等方面的因素紧密相连。无论积极向上，活力浪漫，还是堕落颓废，美国青春电影中所塑造的各种青少年形象都不同程度地给我们展示了青少年的生活方式和精神面貌。这让我们更

好地了解当代青少年的喜、怒、哀、乐和他们当中所存在的问题。跃动的青春,教会了美国青年们坚持自己的梦想,也教会了美国家长们尊重孩子的梦想。

由于好莱坞成熟的商业体制以及美国文化的影响力,好莱坞青春片这一美国类型的电影越来越频繁的进入普通观众的视野。实际上,除了好莱坞之外,在世界范围内都曾出现过一些引起人们关注的青春电影,而20世纪90年代以来,美国青春电影更是进入了一个高产期。

《朱诺》*Juno*(2007)是美国青春题材电影的一个典型代表。该片讲述的是一个年仅16岁的中学生朱诺·麦加夫,她是个倔强有个性的女孩儿,做事从不考虑后果。在与同班的男同学保利·布里克初尝禁果之后,便发现自己已经怀孕了。朱诺在经过了反复的思考之后,决心要把孩子生下来。在好友和家人的支持和帮助下,朱诺平安的孕育着新生命,最终,还找到了一对家境富裕但无法生育的罗林夫妇来收养这个孩子。这部影片获得了第80届奥斯卡最佳原创剧本奖。

《重返十七岁》*17 Again*(2009)是一部爱情喜剧类型的青春影片。影片中的男主角迈克是学校里的风云人物,身为篮球运动员的他本可以拿到奖学金并直接保送进大学的,但是,为了和女友在一起,他放弃了这一机会。20年后,人到中年的迈克事业上一事无成,与孩子们之间缺少共同语言,甚至和相爱的妻子离了婚。然而,一次偶然的机会让他重新回到了17岁那年,并引发了一系列的搞笑事件。

《贱女孩》*Mean Girls*(2004)是一部青春校园影片。影片的女主角凯蒂是一个在非洲长大的15岁青春少女,她本以为自己已经学会了适者生存这个道理,但是,当她重回到美国伊利诺斯州开始新生活时,她才发现有很多的不同。而且,当她爱上亚伦时,由此又给她带来了新的麻烦。被人排斥的凯蒂总算是明白了弱肉强食这个道理,但同时,她也深深的认识到自己对亚伦的爱。

Part 2 Text 1

Teen Movies in America

Hollywood has always made films about young people. It has also made films designed or presumed to cater for what it called 'the juve trade'—**juvenile** spectators. However, the teenpic itself is normally held to have emerged, like modern teenage culture, during the course of the 1950s.

One of the conditions underlying its **emergence** was a growing awareness on Hollywood's part of the importance of the teenage audience. Audience research conducted in the late 1940s indicated that 'age was the most important personal factor by which the movie audience is characterized' and that 'the decline of movie attendance with increasing age is very sharp'. Coming at a time when the industry faced **unprecedented** challenges and changes such as, competition from television and other leisure pursuits, suburbanization and a shift in audience demographics, and a **precipitous** decline in ticket sales and audience attendance, these findings reinforced the growing importance of the teenage market for films and of targeting this market by drawing on aspects of teenage culture and by catering for teenage interests, tastes and concerns[1].

The industry's uncertainties were reflected at first. The teenpic was at this early period **heterogeneous**, multi-dimensional, and often **contradictory** in its forms, concerns and modes of address. A number of genres, traditions and production trends, some of them quite distinct, contributed to its initial development.

The clean teens films of the late 1950s and early 1960s are particularly **exemplary** of the problems and issues at stake here, especially in so far as they tend to centre on female characters, and especially in so far as they share a number of the features and concerns of contemporary woman's films[2]. But **subsequent** teenagers have since then comprised "the primary battleground for commercial motion picture patronage in America," not least because 'Since 1960, teenpics have been an industry staple, if not the dominant production strategy for theatrical movies', and therefore not least because the relationship between what is marginal and what is central, what is minor and what is mainstream, has shifted and changed[3].

There have been important variations in the nature and volume of teenpics since the early 1960s. In the late 1960s and early 1970s, 'youth movies' drew much more on an image of **counter-cultural rebellion** than on an image of irresponsible juvenile **delinquency**. And as the boundaries between counter-culture and mainstream culture are **evaporated**, films mounted serious critiques of the parent culture. Following a crisis **wrought** by overproduction in the late 1960s and early 1970s, and **in the wake of** a counter-culture in general decline, the industry resumed production of teenpics in regular numbers in the late 1970s and 1980s.

As teen-oriented movies have become the industry's representative product, the throwaway, unconscious artistry of the 1950s has been **supplanted** by a new kind of calculated and consciously reflexive teenpic. Thus films aimed at teenagers are more carefully marketed. Along with developments like the **advent** of black teenage films, the trend towards pre-teens films in the early 1990s, and a recent decline in the proportion of teenagers in America's population, in the proportion of teenagers attending Hollywood's films, and therefore in the volume of teenoriented films, questions like these **testify to** the complexity and interest of a genre which has for years been important to Hollywood.

After reading questions

1. What promotes the development of Hollywood's teen movie?
   A. The new film's technology.
   B. A growing awareness on Hollywood's part of the importance of the teenage audience.

C. The directors' efforts.

2. What is the most important personal factor by which the movie audience is characterized?

A. Age.

B. Appearance.

C. Feeling.

3. What has been supplanted by a new kind of calculated and consciously reflexive teenpic?

A. The throwaway, unconscious artistry of the 1950s.

B. The pre-teens films in the early 1990s.

C. Youth movies in the late 1960s and early 1970s.

Words and expressions

1. **juvenile** *adj.* especially related to law connected with young people who are not yet adults 少年的，未成年的

2. **emergence** *n.* an unexpected and dangerous situation that must be dealt with immediately 紧急情况，不测事件

3. **presumption** *n.* an act of thinking that something is true because it is very likely 假定，推测，设想

4. **unprecedented** *adj.* never having happened before, or never having happened so much 空前的，前所未有的

5. **precipitous** *adj.* dangerously high or steep 险峻的，陡峭的

6. **heterogeneous** *adj.* consisting of parts or members that are very different from each other 混杂的

7. **contradictory** *adj.* two statements, beliefs, etc. that are different and therefore cannot both be true 矛盾的，抵触的

8. **exemplary** *adj.* excellent and providing a good example for people to follow 模范的，可作楷模的

9. **subsequent** *adj.* coming after or following something else 随后的，继……之后的

10. **counter-culture** *n.* a culture with lifestyles and values opposed to those of the established culture 反主流文化（20世纪60和70年代美国青少年中盛行的一种思想）

11. **rebellion** *n.* an organized attempt to change the government, or other authority, using violence 造反，叛乱，起义

12. **evaporate** *v.* lose or cause to lose liquid by vaporization 蒸发，消失

13. **delinquency** *n.* an action that is illegal or immoral 违法的行为，不道德的行为

14. **wrought** *adj.* shaped to fit by or as if by altering the contours of a pliable mass 锻造的，加工的

15. **in the wake of** 紧随而来

Unit 10 Teen Movies 青春影片

16. **supplant** *v.* take the place or move into the position of 代替，排挤掉
17. **advent** *n.* arrival that has been awaited (especially of something momentous)（重大事件）的到来，出现
18. **testify to** indicate, prove 证明，表明

Notes

1. Coming at a time when the industry faced unprecedented challenges and changes such as, competition from television and other leisure pursuits, suburbanization and a shift in audience demographics, and a precipitous decline in ticket sales and audience attendance, these findings reinforced the growing importance of the teenage market for films and of targeting this market by drawing on aspects of teenage culture and by catering for teenage interests, tastes and concerns.

   译文：在新的时期电影事业面临着前所未有的挑战和变化,诸如电视和其他休闲方式带来的竞争，更多人搬到市郊居住，观众群体的变化，票房数量和观众参与度的急剧下滑等因素，使得青少年电影市场日趋重要，而同时需要更关注青少年文化，去迎合他们的兴趣、口味和关切点。

2. The clean teens films of the late 1950s and early 1960s are particularly exemplary of the problems and issues at stake here, especially in so far as they tend to centre on female characters, and especially in so far as they share a number of the features and concerns of contemporary woman's films.

   译文：(关于影片类型)问题的重点在于20世纪50年代末60年代初的纯粹的青春影片，特别是当时的青春影片中的主要角色是女性，并且这些影片与当时女性影片的特点和关注点相似。

3. But subsequent (随后的) teenagers have since then comprised 'the primary battleground for commercial motion picture patronage in America', not least because 'Since 1960, teenpics have been an industry staple, if not the dominant production strategy for theatrical movies', and therefore not least because the relationship between what is marginal and what is central, what is minor and what is mainstream, has shifted and changed.

   译文：然而，在此以后青少年构成了（电影）赞助商主要争夺的对象。这一现象不仅因为20世纪60年代以来青春影片成为面向影院策略的一种商业产品，也是因为一些观念发生了变化：比如边缘与核心的区分，小众与主流的区分。

Juno[1]

Juno is what most teen movies are not: non-commercial, with an agenda between its screenplay (电影剧本) pages. This isn't a film promoting a soundtrack (电影配乐) and because it's a low budget movie, it can take risks without worrying about its bottom-line and risk it does, much like 2003's *Thirteen*[2]. The story of Juno revolves around teen pregnancy but its more about the girl who gets pregnant, her quirky (古怪的) personality and what she decides to do about her bun in the oven.

Juno is set in a high school where a girl, Juno MacGuff (Ellen Page[3]) likes a boy; Paulie Bleeker (Michael Cera), whom she thinks is "boss", and she decides to have sex with him. The result of that sexual encounter is Juno's pregnancy. As a film, Juno has some of the freshest, quirkiest and most unique dialogue I've heard in a teen drama / comedy since 1995's *Clueless*[4] (though Clueless seemed to create new slang: as if, coastal, etc.), far funnier than the prose (散文) found in *Superbad*[5]. Many of the phrases, slangs and references in Juno I've heard before but it's mixed together, packed and packaged in a way that makes you take notice, smile on a regular basis and sometimes laugh.

The pregnancy, its effect on Juno, her relationship with her would-be boyfriend, parents, her school, are all handled with a surreal (超现实的) lightness not very well rooted in reality. Juno's character is well established early in the film so you see why she is able to deal with the tough situation she finds herself in with the bravado (逞能) and in the manner that she does. In effect, the film's main fault turns into its greatest strength. It's refreshing (有新鲜感的) to see a movie about teens that does not have to do with cars, bikes, dancing or fights while simultaneously (同步地) marketing a soundtrack (超现实的) and other affiliated（相关的） products. None of the films I just alluded (略微提及) to deal with any real issues facing contemporary (当代的，同龄的) teenagers; not like Juno. How the issue is handled in the film is a topic of debate but at least the issue is brought up and is sparking (触发) new discussion. With Jamie-Lynn Spears[6] now pregnant at sixteen (an ordinary occurrence in the 1300 to late 1700s), a more prevalent (流行的) and open forum (论坛) on the subject might have created a different outcome for her and many other sexually active teens.

The supporting cast in Juno is very effective, including Vanessa Loring (Jennifer Garner) and Mark Loring (Jason Bateman), the would-be adoptive parents of Juno's unborn child. Juno's father, Mac MacGuff (J.K. Simmons), and Juno's step-mother, Brenda MacGuff (Allison Janney), are also very good in this film and serve as a stable and knowledgeable element in Juno's life. These characters are for all intents and purposes the realistic elements in Juno. If it were not for these characters and a handful of dramatic moments, Juno might be seen only as a comedy like *Knocked Up*[7] instead of a drama with comedic elements.

The range of emotions Juno goes through throughout the course of the film speaks very highly of Ellen Page as an actress. Jennifer Garner and the way her character is acted is also a welcome surprise. Vanessa is basically the opposite of Juno's character: Vanessa wants a child, Juno does not. Vanessa is ready for a child in her life, Juno is not. Vanessa is fully capable of supporting the new born; Juno is still a child herself, has not even graduated high school yet and is unemployed. Vanessa is willing to re-arrange her life to welcome the new born into her home, Juno is willing to give her child away to ensure it has a good home and everything else it could possibly need in the future.

Because of the quick decisions Vanessa and Juno make, Vanessa's husband finds himself at a crossroads in his life as well, just in a different form. Mark's crossroad involves his life of "contributing" with Vanessa, the death of his ambitions and being thrust (插入，挤入) head first into fatherhood. The careful viewer soon realizes that in *Juno*, not one but three people are at an important crossroads in their lives: a pregnant teen and the two adoptive parents of her unborn child.

For all intents and purposes, Juno is a funny entertainment movie that involves teenagers, teen romance and teen pregnancy. The way this film handles the latter issue is sure to spark controversy but at least *Juno* does not take the road well traveled; it is original and is well written.

After-reading questions

1. What's the meaning of the underlined sentence in Paragraph 1?
   A. A small round bread.
   B. Her pregnancy.
   C. Something burned in the oven.
   D. A tragedy.
2. Which of the following in *Juno* impressed the writer of the review most as a movie? (Paragraph 3)
   A. The attractive story.
   B. The low cost of the movie.
   C. Freshest, special dialogue.
   D. The natural performance of Ellen Page.
3. How did Juno deal with her baby?
   A. She sent it to a orphanage.
   B. She had an abortion.
   C. She found a pair of adoptive parents for her baby.
   D. She took care of the baby by herself.
4. The careful viewer of Juno will realize that, besides Juno, whose life(lives) is(are)

influenced by the unborn child?

A. Juno's parents.

B. Vanessa.

C. Mark.

D. Both Vanessa and Mark.

Notes

1. ***Juno*** (2007) won the original screenplay Oscar in 2008 partly because of its fresh and unique dialogues. 电影《朱诺》于2008年获得奥斯卡最佳原创剧本奖。其获奖部分得益于影片生动而又贴近美国青少年的语言风格。

2. ***Thirteen*** (2003) The film caused controversy upon its release, because it dealt with topics such as drug and alcohol abuse, underage sexual behavior and self-mutilation. 电影《十三岁》, 这部电影放映后引发了一些争论。因为影片涉及滥用毒品和酒精、未成年性行为以及自残等话题。

3. **Ellen Philpotts-Page** was born on February 21, 1987, in Halifax, Nova Scotia. She wanted to start acting at an early age and attended the Neptune Theater School. Her first appearance was in the TV show "Pit Pony," for which she received a Young Artist and Gemini nomination for Best Performance. Ellen won the Outstanding Performance by a Female Actor Award (from the Atlantic Film Festival) and another nomination for Wilby Wonderful.
主演Ellen Philpotts-Page很早就想要从事表演行业, 于是她就参加了海王星戏剧学院。她第一次上镜是在电视剧"Pit pony"中, 并且获得了青年艺术家和双子座的最佳表演奖。Ellen凭借《精彩威尔比岛》中的表演获得最佳女演员（在大西洋电影节上）以及另一个双子座奖项。

4. ***Clueless*** (1995) is an American comedy film loosely based on Jane Austen's 1815 novel Emma. It is set in the town of Beverly Hills. 《一枝独秀》, 现代版《爱玛》, 故事背景是比弗利山庄的贵族中学。

5. ***Superbad*** (2007) American comedy film with an authentic take on the awkwardness of the high school experience. 《非常坏》, 一部真实反映高中生尴尬经历的美国喜剧片。

6. **Jamie-Lynn Spears,** The younger sister of pop star Britney Spears, was just 16 when she had one of the most high-profile teen pregnancies in Hollywood history. 杰米·林恩·斯皮尔斯, 小甜甜布莱尼的妹妹。16岁怀孕产女, 成为好莱坞备受瞩目的未成年妈妈。

7. ***Knocked Up*** (2007) a comedy about an unintended pregnancy 《一夜大肚》关于意外怀孕的一部喜剧影片。

8. **Jason Reitman** (born October 19, 1977) is a Canadian-American film director, screenwriter, producer, and actor, best known for directing the films *Thank You*

for *Smoking* (2006), *Juno* (2007), and *Up in the Air* (2009). 贾森·雷特曼出生于加拿大的好莱坞电影导演、编剧演员。曾导演《感谢你抽烟》，《在云端》和《朱诺》。

Part 4 Exercises

I. Answer questions after listening to the dialogues taken from the film.

1. What did MAC think about the person who is worth sticking with?
2. What makes Juno feel upset?

Script

Scenario 1: *After Juno found that the marriage of Mark and Venessa is not as perfect as the photo shows, Juno came home with mixed emotions. While Juno was entering her father was sitting at the table.*

JUNO: Hi Dad.

MAC: Hey, big puffy version of Junebug. Where have you been?

JUNO: Dealing with stuff way beyond my maturity level. Where is everyone?

MAC: Bren took Liberty Bell to her tot ice skating class.

JUNO: Tot ice skating? Tots can't ice skate. Liberty Bell's still getting the hang of stairs.

MAC: No, but you know Bren. She dreams big.

JUNO: Yeah, she does.

MAC: You look a little morose, honey. What's eating you?

JUNO: I'm losing my faith in humanity.

MAC: Think you can narrow it down for me?

JUNO: I guess I wonder sometimes if people ever stay together for good.

MAC: You mean like couples?

JUNO: Yeah, like people in love.

MAC: Are you having boy trouble? I gotta be honest; I don't much approve of you dating in our condition, 'cause... well, that's kind of messed up.

JUNO: Dad, no!

MAC: Well, it's kind of skanky. Isn't that what you girls call it? Skanky? Skeevy?

JUNO: Please stop now.

MAC: (persisting) Tore up from the floor up?

JUNO: Dad, it's not about that. I just need to know that it's possible for two people to stay happy together forever. Or at least for a few years.

MAC: It's not easy, that's for sure. Now, I may not have the best track record in the world, but I have been with your stepmother for ten years now, and I'm proud to say that we're very happy.

MAC: In my opinion, the best thing you can do is to find a person who loves you for exactly what you are. Good mood, bad mood, ugly, pretty, handsome, what have you, the right person will still think that the sun shines out your ass. That's the kind of person that's worth sticking with.

JUNO: I sort of already have.

MAC: Well, of course. Your old D-A-D! You know I'll always be there to love and support you, no matter what kind of pickle you're in.

MAC: Obviously.

II. Fill the blanks with the missing words or phrases after listening to the lines taken from the film.

JUNO: It is really 1)_____ looking. It's like it's not even real. I can't believe there are saps who actually cry at these things.

BREN: What? I'm not made of stone.

ULTRASOUND TECH: Well, there we have it. Would you like to know the sex?

LEAH: Aw, please Junebug?

JUNO: No way. No, I definitely don't want to know.

ULTRASOUND TECH: Planning to be surprised when you 2)_____?

JUNO: I want Mark and Vanessa to be surprised, and if I know, I won't be able to keep myself from telling them and 3)_____ the whole thing.

ULTRASOUND TECH: Are Mark and Vanessa your friends at school?

JUNO: No, they're the people who are 4)_____ the baby.

ULTRASOUND TECH: Oh. Well, thank goodness for that.

BREN: Wait, what's that supposed to mean?

ULTRASOUND TECH: I just see a lot of teenage mothers come through here. It's obviously a 5)_____ environment for a baby to be raised in.

JUNO: How do you know I'm so poisonous? Like, what if the adoptive parents turn out to be evil 6)_____?

LEAH: Or 7)_____ parents!

BREN: They could be utterly 8)_____. Maybe they'll do a far shittier job of raising a kid than my dumb-ass 9)_____ ever would. Have you considered that?

ULTRASOUND TECH: No... I guess not.

BREN: What is your job title, exactly?

ULTRASOUND TECH: Excuse me?

BREN: I said, what-is-your-job-title, Missy?

ULTRASOUND TECH: I'm an ultrasound technician, ma'am.

BREN: Well I'm a 10)_____ technician, and I think we both ought to stick to what we know.

ULTRASOUND TECH: What are you talking about?

BREN: You think you're special because you get to play Picture Pages up there?

BREN: My five year-old daughter could do that, and let me tell you, she is not the brightest bulb in the tanning bed. So why don't you go back to night school in Manteno and learn a real trade!

JUNO: Bren, you're a dick! I love it.

III. Complete the following memorable lines by translating the Chinese into English.

1. Juno: My step-mom is forcing me to eat really healthy. She (甚至不准我站在微波炉前) _____ or eat red M&Ms.

2. It's just that, we went through a situation before where (什么都落空了) _____.

3. They can apparently hear speech in there, even though it (听起来像是一万米深海传来的) _____.

4. (另一些人将会找到基督所赐的珍贵祝福)_____ in this garbage dump of a situation.

IV. Oral practices—answer the following questions.

1. Why did Juno give up the idea of abortion?
2. What profound significance does *Juno* give you?

Part 5 More Teen Movies

Plot summary of *Mean Girls*

The 16-year-old home-schooled daughter of zoologist parents living somewhere in East Africa, Cady Heron, is unprepared for her first day of public high school at fictional North Shore High School in Evanston, Illinois. With the help of social outcast Janis, Cady learns about the various cliques. She is warned to avoid the school's most exclusive clique, the Plastics, the reigning trio of girls led by the acid-tongued queen bee Regina George. Regina was once Janis's best friend but they have grown to despise each other since Regina started a rumor about Janis's sexuality in 8th grade. However, the Plastics take a shine to Cady and invite her to sit with them at lunch and go shopping with them after school.

After realizing that Cady has been accepted into the Plastics, Janis hatches a plan to get revenge on Regina for what she did to her, using Cady as a pawn in order to infiltrate the Plastics. Cady supports her after Regina mistreats her at a Halloween party. Janis's plan involves cutting off Regina's "resources", which include separating her from her boyfriend Aaron Samuels, destroying her beauty, and turning Regina's fellow Plastics against her: insecure rich girl Gretchen Wieners and sweet but dimwitted Karen Smith.

Having ingratiated herself with the Plastics per Janis's plan, Cady learns about the "Burn Book," a top secret notebook of Regina's filled with slandering rumors, secrets, and gossip about all the other girls in their class. Cady soon falls in love with Aaron, whom Regina successfully steals back from Cady in a fit of jealousy. In her efforts to get revenge on Regina, Cady gradually loses her individual personality and remakes herself in the image of Regina. Her act soon becomes reality, and she becomes as spiteful as Regina, abandoning Janis and Damien in the process and focusing more on her image. Regina, now slightly overweight due to Cady's diet sabotage, is excluded from the Plastics and Cady becomes the new Queen Bee. In celebration of her newfound status, Cady throws a party with the Plastics and does not invite Janis or Damien. Janis and Damien then renounce Cady as a friend. During the party, she also alienates Aaron with her unsavory new personality.

Now that she is without friends, shunned by Aaron, and distrusted by everyone at school, Cady decides to make amends by taking full blame for the Burn Book. Though severely punished by her confession, her guilt dissolves and she returns to her old personality. As punishment for her part, Ms. Norbury has Cady join the Mathletes—which Damien & Regina both described earlier as "social suicide"—in their competition. There, Cady has an epiphany competing against a very unattractive girl, realizing that even if she made fun of the girl's appearance, it would not stop the girl from beating her. Cady wins the tournament and returns to school for the Spring Fling.

At the Spring Fling dance, Cady is elected Spring Fling Queen and gives a speech to her class that her victory is meaningless; they are all wonderful in their own way and thus the victory belongs to everyone.

Memorable lines in the film

Settings: The film ends with the Plastics disbanding by the start of the new school year: Regina joins the lacrosse team as a way to channel her anger positively, Karen becomes the school weather girl. Gretchen joins the "Cool Asians" clique and is their biggest follower, and Cady dates Aaron as well as hanging out with Janis and Damien. Now reasonably well-liked, Cady reflects that the "Girl World" she lives in is at peace.

Cady: Calling somebody fat won't make you any thinner, calling somebody stupid doesn't make you any smarter and ruining Riginer's life doesn't make me any happier.

嘲笑别人胖并不能使你变瘦，嘲笑别人笨并不能使你变聪明，背后恶意中伤对方并不能使你获得快乐。

Plot Summary of *17 Again*

In 1989, Mike O'Donnell (Zac Efron) was a big success in high school: he was the star of his high school basketball team, a student for a college scholarship and dating his soul mate, Scarlett. He seemingly had it all, but, right before the championship basketball game, his girlfriend Scarlet Porter (Allison Miller) informed him she was pregnant. In that moment, he made the decision to throw everything away (including basketball and a chance at a scholarship) and proposed to her.

About twenty years later, Mike's (Matthew Perry) life has come to a standstill. Scarlet (Leslie Mann) has separated from him. His job is going nowhere, and his kids Maggie (Michelle Trachtenberg) and Alex (Sterling Knight) want nothing to do with him. While visiting Hayden High School to reminisce about the life he threw away, he encounters a mysterious janitor (Brian Doyle-Murray). On the way home, he sees the janitor standing on the edge of a bridge— apparently about to commit suicide, Mike runs towards him, but his path is blocked momentarily by a passing truck. When he reaches the edge, the janitor is gone, and there is a strange vortex (漩涡) below the bridge. Mike slips and falls into the vortex. Later, he discovers that he has been magically transformed into his 17-year-old self.

With Ned posing as his father, Mike enrolls at Hayden High as "Mark Gold". He believes he has been given the chance to live his life over again, "but to do it right". With "Mark"'s help, Alex gets a place on the basketball team and the girlfriend he desires. "Mark" comforts Maggie when she is dumped by Stan, who was pressuring her for making love. "Mark" also meets Scarlet. He helps her decorate her garden, gaining a new appreciation for her, and dances with her before she goes on a date to the song that he and Scarlet danced to at their wedding. "Mark" and Scarlet clearly felt a connection as they danced, and might have been about to kiss, right when "Mark" lifts Scarlet into his arms and spins her around, until Alex walks in on them. At first Scarlet seemed uncaring that her son is right there, but then all of a sudden she feels embarrassed and tells "Mark" that she is Alex's mother and that this is inappropriate.

Meanwhile, Ned is attracted to the principal of Hayden High, Jane Masterson (Melora Hardin). Although his initial attempts to 'peacock' her fail, they soon bond over a love of The Lord of the Rings. However, when he takes her back to his house, they discover an out-of-control party raging there. To celebrate Alex scoring the winning basket in a game, "Mark" is throwing a victory party. Scarlet appears, looking for Alex, and Mike's tells her that Alex could be having a girlfriend by the end of the party and brings her up to the balcony to show her. As they are talking, Mike's feelings for her are reawakened, (especially after she tells him "he's really become a part of the family). But when he kisses her, she is appalled, and slaps him and calls him a "weirdo little man child" even though he chases after her and tries to tell her that he is Mike. This exchange is witnessed by Maggie and her friends, who are all disgusted, especially since Maggie has become smitten with "Mark".

The next morning, Ned reminds Mike that it is the date of his divorce hearing with Scarlet. "Mark" appears in court to read a letter from Mike O'Donnell. Scarlet is touched by the letter. But then she sees that the "letter" is really just a piece of paper with directions on it, and realizes that "Mark" spoke extemporaneously. Later, at the championship game, Mike makes a gesture which she recognizes as his. Realizing that she is in the same situation as twenty years ago, she flees the scene. Mike follows, handing the ball to Alex, who goes on to make the winning shot. The janitor catches sight of Mike and changes him back into his adult self. Mike promises Scarlet to spend the rest of his life making it up to her. Scarlet and Mike kiss and reunite.

In the end, Mike happily reconciles with his family, and becomes the coach of the Hayden High basketball team, while Ned and Ms. Masterson seem to have a "relationship".

Memorable lines in the film

Setting: *"Mark" saw Maggie his loving daughter who was dumped by Stan crying sadly.*

Mark: When you're young, everything feels like the end of the world. Its not, it's just the beginning. I mean you might have to meet a few more jerks. One day, you're going to meet a boy who treats you the way you deserve to be treated. Like the sun rises and sets with you.

在你年轻的时候，任何伤心事都感觉像是世界末日。其实不是末日，一切才刚刚开始。我的意思是，你可能会再遇到几个这样的混蛋。但是，总有一天，你会遇到一个男孩，一个认真对待你的男孩，如同太阳日升日落般，永远伴随着你。

Setting: *The classes are giving a discussion on human sexuality. The official school position is that we protect the high students for safe sex now. So the teacher are giving contraceptives* *away to the students.*

Mark: You know when you're ready to make that love and turn into a baby. That is what love is. It's that first moment when you hold your baby girl and you didn't think that anything could be so small or so delicate. And you feel that tiny beat...and you know that you couldn't love anything more in the whole world and you hope that you could do right by that little girl...and always be there to catch her when she falls, and nothing ever hurts her. not a broken arm or a bad dream or a broken heart.

你知道，当你准备好让爱情结晶为一个婴儿，那正是爱情所在。就在你抱着心爱女孩的那一霎那，你从不知道刚出生新生的婴儿会如此小或者如此娇弱，你感受到她小小的心脏在跳动，你就会明白到世界上不会有你再爱的东西了。你希望你能正确养育这个小女孩儿，随时准备在她跌倒的时候扶起她，不让她受一点伤害，希望她不要骨折，从不作噩梦，从不伤心。

Bibliography 主要参考文献

1. **Annette Insdorf**, 3rd. Indelible Shadows: Film and the Holocaust[M]. Cambridge, 2002.
2. **Annette Kuhn**, Women's Pictures: Feminism and Cinema[M]. the 2nd edition, Verso, 1992.
3. **Andrew Lynn**著, 霍斯亮译.《英语电影赏析》[M]. 外语教学与研究出版社, 2005.
4. **Douglas V. Porpora** Personal Heroes, Religion, and Transcendental Sociological Forum[J], Vol. 11, No. 2, 1996, Personal Meta narratives.
5. **Gary Hentzi**, Reviewed work(s): American Beauty by Sam Mendes[J], Film Quarterly. Vol No. 54. 2001, 43—50.
6. **Harvey Greenberg**, Spielberg's Holocaust Critical Perspectives on Schindler's List[J], Film Quarterly, vol. 51, 1998, 58—60.
7. **James Walters**, Fantasy Film, a critical introduction[M]. 2011, Berg, UK, 132.
8. **Janet Mccabe**, Feminist film studies: writing the woman into cinema[M]. Wallflower Press, 2004.
9. **J.M. Tyree**, on Frivolity and Horror in 2008's Summer Superhero Movies: the Dark Knight, the Incredible Hulk, and Iron Man[J]. Film Quarterly, spring 2009, 28—34.
10. **John Belton**著, 米静等译.《美国电影美国文化》[M]. 世纪出版社, 上海人民出版社, 2009.
11. **Louis Giannetti**, Understanding Movies, 9th edition[M]. Prentice Hall, 2001, 437—442.
12. **Marjorie Rosen**, Popcorn Venus: Women, Movies and the American Dream[M]. Coward, McCann and Geoghegan, 1973: 31—42.
13. **Paul Wells**, Understanding Animations[M]. Routledge, 1998.
14. **Paula Cantor**, The Simpsons: Atomistic Politics and the Nuclear Family, Political theory[J]. Vol. 27 No.6, December 1999, 734—749.
15. **Patricia White**, Feminism and film, the Oxford Guide to Film Studies[M]. Oxford University Press, 1998, 117—134.
16. **Simone De Beauvori**, The Second Sex[M]. London: Penguin., 1984.
17. **Steve Neale**, Genre and Hollywood[M]. Routledge, 1998, 112—125.
18. **Steven J. Ross**, Movies and American Society[M]. Blackwell Publishers, 2002, 313—

343.

19. **Thompson Kirsten Moana**, Animation and America book reviews[J]. Film Quarterly, Winter 2004/2005; 58,2.

20. **Yvonne Tasker**, Fantasizing Gender and Race: Women in Contemporary US Action cinema, Contemporary American Cinema[M]. open University Press, 2006.

21. 陈芳庆. 论"奇幻电影"的文化渊源、类型特征与价值意义, 华中师范大学硕士学位论文.

22. 段波. 魔幻与现实交相辉映传统与现代水乳交融——试析《哈利·波特》系列小说创作渊源[J]. 《西安外国语大学学报》, 2007年6月.

23. 郭蕾. 从电影《朱诺》看美国青少年的语言风格[J]. 《电影评介》, 2010年1月.

24. 巩杰. 美国魔幻片现象初探, 电影文学[J]. 2007, 19—20.

25. 郝建. 《影视类型学》[M]. 北京大学出版社, 2002.

26. 凌海衡. 历史创伤的再现———大屠杀电影叙事的两种方法[J]. 《文艺研究》, 2010年第1期.

27. 李洋. 大屠杀的目光伦理——西方电影的大屠杀话语及其困境[J]. 《电影艺术》, 第327期.

28. 马菡. 科幻英雄片中超级英雄隐喻的美国社会文化[J]. 《电影文学》, 2009年第16期.

29. 彭俊. 从乐观主义到黑色幽默基于《辛普森一家大电影》的文化考察[J]. 《北京电影学院学报》, 2009.3.

30. 孙慰川, 丁磊. 论美国皮克斯动画电影的现代化叙事策略[J]. 《北京电影学院学报》, 2009.3.

31. 汤定九. 托尔金《魔戒》的文化解读[J], 《江西社会科学》, No.10.2003.

32. 吴越. 好莱坞科幻片类型研究. http://www.docin.com/p-226999.html#documentinfo.

33. 王爽. 青少年在美国青春电影中的形象分析, [J], 《电影文学》, 2009年第15期.

34. 王炎. 成长的终结?—解析福兰克·墨罗蒂的《世界的存在方式》[J]. 《外国文学》. 2006年3月.

35. 杨晓林主编. 《世界动画电影》[M]. 中国传媒大学出版社, 2009年8月.

36. 战晓微. 《哈利波特》中英雄成长主题的探讨[J]. 《长春师范学院学报》(人文社会科学版), 2010年3月.

37. 周小玲. 试论美国电影中的英雄情结[J]. 《渝西学院学报》(社会科学版), 2002年6月.

《英文类型影片赏析》

尊敬的老师：

　　您好！

　　为了方便您更好地使用《英文类型影片赏析》，我们特向使用该书作为教材的教师赠送本书配套参考资料。如有需要，请完整填写"教师联系表"并加盖所在单位系（院）或培训中心公章，免费向出版社索取。

北京大学出版社

教 师 联 系 表

教材名称	《英文类型影片赏析》			
姓名：	姓别：		职务：	职称：
E-mail：	联系电话：		邮政编码：	
供职学校：		所在院系：		（章）
学校地址：				
教学科目与年级：		班级人数：		
通信地址：				

　　填写完毕后，请将此表邮寄给我们，我们将为您免费寄送本教材配套资料，谢谢！

北京市海淀区成府路205号
北京大学出版社外语编辑部　李颖　　　邮 购 部 电 话：010-62534449
邮政编码：100871　　　　　　　　　　市场营销部电话：010-62750672
电子邮箱：evalee1770@sina.com　　　　外语编辑部电话：010-62754382